SPEAKING of GOD

Reading and Preaching the Word of God

JERRY CAMERY-HOGGATT

HENDRICKSON
PUBLISHERS

FOR ROGER JOHNSON
Patron. Saint.

© 1995 by Hendrickson Publishers, Inc.
P. O. Box 3473
Peabody, Massachusetts 01961–3473
All rights reserved
Printed in the United States of America

ISBN 1–56563–172–2

First Printing — November 1995

Library of Congress Cataloging-in-Publication Data

Camery-Hoggatt, Jerry.
   Speaking of God: reading and preaching the word of God   /
Jerry Camery-Hoggatt.
   Includes bibliographical references and index.
   ISBN 1–56563–172–2
   1. Preaching.   2. Rhetoric.   3. Reader-response criticism.
4. Bible—Hermeneutics.   I. Title.
BV4211.2.C25   1995
251—dc20   95–42127
                                                      CIP

TABLE OF CONTENTS

PART 3: TRYING ON THE LENSES

ACKNOWLEDGEMENTS

A number of people have read this piece and offered good advice—Kirsten Bailey, Doug Degelman, Peter St. Don, Jeff Gibbs, Roger Johnson, Grace Lange, Tim Moyers, Shirley Albertson Owens, Mikael Parsons, and my secretary Kim Kenney. I'm grateful also to the religion students of Southern California College, many of whom both encouraged me and corrected my work. Finally, a word of thanks to the staff at Hendrickson Publishers, especially the offices of my old sidekick and now editor Patrick Alexander. This is a better book because of their input.

LIST OF FIGURES

INTRODUCTION

I never was much of a juggler. I could usually manage two balls, sometimes three, but that was my limit. Somehow it always seemed that when I got more than three balls in the air, someone would toss in another, make a face to distract me, or whistle just out of pure spite, and then everything would go tumbling down in a heap. I would lose everything. Three balls was a lot; four was nothing at all. I suppose that I learned thus in a practical way that sometimes less is more and that when you try to accomplish too much, you end up accomplishing nothing

at all. In this book I've pushed my juggling skills to the limit—
three balls.

BALL ONE

First, I've tried to make some sense out of the chaos of
critical theories in biblical scholarship. Recently we have begun
to realize that where one comes out is often determined by
where one starts. We have Thomas Kuhn to thank for that
realization. Kuhn's theory of paradigms has recently caught the
ear of the academy as a whole. If one went to almost any
professional society conference these days and eavesdropped on
coffee shop conversations between theoreticians, it's a fair bet
that somewhere along the way one would hear Kuhn's name,
uttered in hushed and reverent tones. This is as it should be. By
pointing out the role of our interpretive paradigms, Kuhn has
provided us with a great service. Yet knowing about paradigms
is not the same thing as knowing how to use them responsibly. I
have addressed this first concern in Part 1. There I argue, first,
that one ought to recognize the strengths and limitations of the
paradigm one is using and, second, that there is a clear and
direct connection between a reader-oriented paradigm and the
preacher's concern for the rhetorical structure of the sermon.

BALL TWO

Every beginning preacher has heard that he or she must
learn how to do something called exegesis. But this is not at all
a straightforward process. Exegesis does not involve a single
paradigm but, rather, several paradigms in some sort of dynamic relationship with each other and the text. The beginning
exegete has to learn *which* paradigms to use *when,* a daunting
task in any interpretive climate, a nearly impossible one given
the present chaos of critical theories. Exegesis calls for discern-
ment, some basis for making judgments about what is important
and why. The working exegete needs a framework of integration
and a set of criteria by which to make those important decisions.
This is the question I take up in Part 2. There I have tried
to develop a working paradigm of exegesis that respects and
replicates the readerly activities that the writer assumed his

readers would use. Simply put, reader-oriented interpretation asks three basic questions: (a) Who is the reader for whom the text was prepared? (b) What is that reader expected to know as background to the reading process? (c) If the reader knows those things, how is he or she expected to respond to the text?

In short, what exactly do we do when we read? I am not the first to ask such questions. Thus far in the study of Scripture, interpretation that marches under the banner of reader-response criticism has taken two different paths. The most widely known approach travels also under the banner of postmodernism, and it takes its cues from the work of philosophers of language, such as Paul Ricoeur. According to this approach, when a text is written down, it is freed from the constraints of context in such a way that it becomes open to new dimensions of meaning. Those dimensions of meaning are open to the discretion of the reader, who is not so much *specified* by the text as *prompted* by it. The reader is treated as a creative partner with the author in the production of the text's meaning, a partner with full rights over his or her role in the reading process, who can legitimately read the text from the standpoint of his or her personal or cultural experience. This approach collapses the historical and cultural distance that separates us from the Bible, and the modern reader is set free to hear the text as though it addresses modern issues directly. The attractiveness here is that this fully enfranchises the reader—including the *modern* reader—regardless of skill or background in reading the material for a different culture.

The second approach to reader-oriented interpretation takes its underpinnings from contemporary literary scholarship, especially the work of Wolfgang Iser and Stanley Fish. This approach defines the term "reader" specifically in terms of skills and interpretive conventions that are assumed in the text itself. Thus, reading is a managed activity, and the reader's latitude is strictly governed by the interpretive conventions operative for the text itself. The attractiveness of this program is that it recognizes and respects the "particular kind of event which is intended to take place between text and reader."[1] The stress here is on the word "intended": this is reader-response criticism

---

[1] Robert Tannehill, *The Sword of His Mouth* (Philadelphia: Fortress, 1975) 7.

that is governed by the text itself. The modern reader is enfranchised, but not entirely.

In this book I have proposed a third approach to reader-oriented interpretation, based on information the cognitive and social sciences are developing about language. The point where these concerns meet is the discipline of psycholinguistics, which focuses its attention on the psychological processes entailed when we interact with language. Thus, while the first two approaches to reading are based on philosophical or literary concerns, the approach worked out here is based on psychological ones.

BALL THREE

Finally, in Part 3 I've tried to demonstrate that this approach to biblical interpretation is eminently practical, with direct and clear implications for the construction of sermons. Every preacher faces a moment of truth along the path from exegesis to sermon: How am I to present this material to my congregation? Sometimes this challenge adds an element of the gymnastic to the difficult task of sermon construction. In the third section of this book, I have argued that the rhetorical structure of the text can help the preacher create the bridge to the sermon; the rhetoric of the first may become the rhetoric of the second.

BALL FOUR

Three balls was all I could juggle. There was one ball I wanted very much to pick up, but did not—the question of canon. Simply put, the question is this: What difference does it make that these texts come to us as part of a canon of sacred Scripture? Does that fact widen or narrow or modify in some way the readerly strategies by which we interact with the biblical texts? The question of canon is very much debated these days, and I look forward to seeing how those who are discussing this important question will respond to what I have written here. Was I wrong not to drop the exegesis ball in order to pick up the canon ball? Well, I suppose that's a toss-up.

OF GRACE, GRATITUDE, AND GRANDIOSITY

A Sermon

As a theologian I just can't help but be angry sometimes. I've taken comfort from the example of the Old Testament prophets, especially Jeremiah, whose name has given us the English word "jeremiad," which means a "doleful and thundering denunciation." Jesus sometimes got angry, too, and as I prepared my sermon this week, I was tempted to call attention to the fact that nothing angered Jesus more than the hypocrisy of the Pharisees. Just listen to the way he rails at them in his famous Olivet discourse in Matthew 23:

Woe to you, scribes and Pharisees, hypocrites! For you cross sea
and land to make a single convert, and you make the new convert
twice as much a child of hell as yourselves (Matt 23:15).

Woe to you, scribes and Pharisees, hypocrites! For you tithe mint,
dill, and cummin, and have neglected the weightier matters of the
law: justice and mercy and faith . . . (Matt 23:23).

Woe to you, scribes and Pharisees, hypocrites! For you clean the
outside of the cup and of the plate, but inside they are full of greed
and self-indulgence (Matt 23:25).

Woe to you, scribes and Pharisees, hypocrites! For you are like
whitewashed tombs, which on the outside look beautiful, but
inside they are full of the bones of the dead and of all kinds of
filth. So you also on the outside look righteous to others, but
inside you are full of hypocrisy and lawlessness (Matt 23:27–28).

Jesus could be royally angry!

And in his name, I can be, too. This week, yet another
televangelist was caught in the arms of a prostitute. Talk about
hypocrites! For months and months we watched this man rail
against the sins of the flesh on TV, literally pointing his self-
righteous finger at the world, all the while nursing his own dirty
little secret on the side.

Part of what makes me angry is that I, too, am a minister of
the gospel, and I'm angry because the overwhelming tendency
in the media will be to paint us all with the same brush.

I suppose I should not have been surprised. Traveling
evangelists have been getting involved with prostitutes for a
long time. This seems to be an occupational hazard. I guess that
one could make a pretty interesting study of the ways in which
these people were caught.

In 1899 Benjamin Hardin Irwin—founder of the Fire Bap-
tized Holiness Church—was on an evangelistic tour of the
so-called burned-over district of upstate New York when he was
caught coming out of a bawdy house with a cigar in his mouth.

In 1937 Finis Jennings Dake, editor of *Dake's Annotated
Reference Bible,* was convicted of violating the Mann Act by
transporting a sixteen-year-old girl across state lines for "illicit
purposes." Twice en route they registered in hotels as "Mr. and
Mrs. C. Anderson." That little lapse of wisdom—which Dake's
lawyer referred to as an "unfortunate mistake"—resulted in a
six-month jail sentence and the end of Dake's association with
the Assemblies of God.

One evangelist—who is so famous that you would all know him if I told you his name—actually showed up at a religious banquet with a call girl! During the dinner she got real close to him and just sort of hung there on his arm, like a red flag. It doesn't take much imagination to guess what the others in the room were thinking: "What sort of evangelist mixes it up in public with a call girl? Doesn't he have any sense of right and wrong? What if the media gets hold of the pictures? They'll paint us all with the same brush." The tension got very thick. It was the girl who finally broke the silence: "Is there something wrong, Jesus? Haven't they ever seen a sinner before?"

Does this anger you? It angered me, too, when I first read it. It's found in the Gospel of Luke. Turn with me now to the seventh chapter, and let's read this passage together. The story begins in verse 36:

> One of the Pharisees asked Jesus to eat with him, and he went into the Pharisee's house and took his place at the table. And a woman in the city, who was a sinner, having learned that he was eating in the Pharisee's house, brought an alabaster jar of ointment. She stood behind him at his feet, weeping, and began to bathe his feet with her tears and to dry them with her hair. Then she continued kissing his feet and anointing them with the ointment.

> Now when the Pharisee who had invited him saw it, he said to himself, "If this man were a prophet, he would have known who and what kind of woman this is who is touching him—that she is a sinner."

> Jesus spoke up and said to him, "Simon, I have something to say to you."

> "Teacher," he replied, "Speak."

> "A certain creditor had two debtors; one owed five hundred denarii, and the other fifty. When they could not pay, he canceled the debts for both of them. Now which of them will love him more?"

> Simon answered, "I suppose the one for whom he canceled the greater debt."

> And Jesus said to him, "You have judged rightly." Then turning toward the woman, he said to Simon, "Do you see this woman? I entered your house; you gave me no water for my feet, but she has bathed my feet with her tears and dried them with her hair. You gave me no kiss, but from the time I came in she has not

stopped kissing my feet. You did not anoint my head with oil, but she has anointed my feet with ointment. Therefore, I tell you, her sins, which were many, have been forgiven; hence she has shown great love. But the one to whom little is forgiven, loves little." Then he said to her, "Your sins are forgiven."

But those who were at the table with him began to say among themselves, "Who is this who even forgives sins?"

And he said to the woman, "Your faith has saved you; go in peace" (Luke 7:36–50).

Now, this story has some rather odd details about it, and I'd like to look at them one at a time. First, you should know that according to first-century sensibilities, what the woman did to Jesus was outrageous. In fact, it was downright sexy. I don't just mean that she rubbed Jesus' feet—which is pretty sensual even in our culture. What really makes this sexy is that the woman let down her hair in public. In Jesus' day, she might just as well have exposed her breasts. And Jesus didn't stop her. If we can judge by the Pharisee's private thoughts in verse 39, rendered in a more contemporary fashion, Jesus just let her do it, without objecting at all: "If this man were a prophet, he would have known who and what sort of woman this is who keeps on fondling him, for she is a whore" (author's trans.). Jesus suggests something of the same thing in verse 45: "From the time I came in she has not ceased to kiss my feet." Jesus just let her, knowing full well that the host would get all the wrong ideas.

It is not at all clear that the woman is intending something sexual. Apparently she had something else in view. It is her tears that give away that little detail. Why was she crying?

One explanation may have to do with the way the host has treated Jesus. Luke gives us that information in verses 44–46:

Then turning toward the woman, he said to Simon, "Do you see this woman? I entered your house; *you gave me no water for my feet,* but she has bathed my feet with her tears and dried them with her hair. *You gave me no kiss,* but from the time I came in she has not stopped kissing my feet. *You did not anoint my head with oil,* but she has anointed my feet with ointment" (Luke 7:44–46).

That is, the host has insulted his guest. These courtesies are an important part of social life in the ancient Middle East: The kiss—or perhaps an embrace—is a way of showing the status of the guest. The water is an important gesture in a culture where everyone wore sandals and trudged along dirt roads. A thoughtful host was expected to offer his guest a little oil for his skin, to counter the effects of the blistering sun. It was only common courtesy.

Jesus' host has not done any of that. This is a little like inviting you to be a guest in my home and then neglecting to take your hat and coat at the door. Or mixing up our good china with the ordinary dishes and sitting you at a place with the ordinary dishes. In our home, we serve guests first, then let them pass the plate on to the rest of the family. Imagine that we all sit down at table but I serve you last. There would be something of an insult involved, would there not? I can well imagine the onlookers snickering in their glasses as the guest is made the brunt of a bad joke. It may be that something like this happened to Jesus. One commentator says it rather bluntly: Simon had "declared war" on Jesus.

And that is why the woman is crying. She was moved by compassion for Jesus. Maybe. We can't know for sure. If she was, though, it would explain why she did what she did. She did it to correct the insult. It was awkward and embarrassing, and it was misunderstood, but it was a gesture that came from good intentions.

I wonder why Simon would do what he did? Why would he invite someone to his home, then insult him? Again, we cannot know for sure. What I think, though, is that he was bothered by the fact that Jesus had brought along the riffraff. The unwashed. Jesus' disciples don't wash properly before they eat. One interpreter has even suggested that the prostitute had slipped in with the disciples. The man has invited Jesus to his home, and now Jesus brings along a prostitute. At least, that *may* be what Simon thought. If it is, you can imagine his confusion and embarrassment when the woman starts fondling Jesus' feet and Jesus doesn't seem to mind in the least. What kind of evangelist mixes it up with prostitutes, anyway?

That's my explanation for what actually happened. Luke sure made it hard to get there, though. For one thing, he held back the note about the insult until we are well along in the story. Look at the story again. Luke has completed almost the entire exchange before he gives us any hint that there may be more going on than a bit of ribald sensuality in the middle of a dinner party. By the time we get there, we have already experienced something of a shock: Jesus is being fondled by a prostitute, and he doesn't do anything to stop it. If Jesus really were religious, he would avoid such people like the plague. Isn't religion about keeping one's self unsullied, untouched by the seductions of the world? And if not one's self, then surely one's reputation. What if the media got hold of the photograph?

For a moment, I want to focus on the shock here. There's a sense in which the shock in the reader's mind is exactly the same as the shock in Simon's mind. And very much like the shock I tried to administer to you when this sermon began. I think this shock comes from two sources:

> First, there is the perception that there is a difference of some sort between "us" and "them," between people like prostitutes, who need to repent, and people like us, who do not.

> Second, there is the perception that good people like us— and like evangelists—shouldn't have anything to do with bad people like "them."

There seems to be something grandiose about these paltry attempts at self-righteousness. For one thing, they require that we minimize our own need for grace. For another, they require that we maximize the differences between "people like us" and "people like them."

These two false perceptions are the circles around the bull's-eye center of the story, which is found in verses 41 and 42. Jesus has taken aim at Simon's religious grandiosity. I suspect that Jesus is also taking aim at Luke's reader, who is just as shocked as Simon, and—if we need to hear it—he may be taking aim at us as well:

> A certain creditor had two debtors; one owed five hundred denarii, and the other fifty. When they could not pay, he canceled the debts for both of them. Now which of them will love him more? (Luke 7:41–42).

Notice what Jesus does with this little parable. He aims for the truth Simon has been unwilling or unable to see: Simon, too, is a "debtor." Here the emphasis *may* be upon the fact that he was a debtor who "owed little." But I don't think so. The repetition of Simon's failures as a host places the emphasis rather clearly on the fact that he "*loved* little." Notice the way verse 47 ends:

Her sins, which were many, have been forgiven; hence she has shown great love. But the one to whom little is forgiven, loves little.

Jesus is being delicate here. He leaves it to Simon to figure out how far his religion has taken him from God, how much his self-righteousness has come to stand in the way of redemption. How about us? How about you? How about me? What would I do if I saw Jesus on the street with a whore? Would it offend my religious sensitivities?

Am I willing, when I am called upon, to be seen on the street with a prostitute if that's the price of her redemption? What if the media got hold of the photograph? Would I be willing to be seen with a drug addict? A pusher? Someone who had abused his children? Would I, if that were the path of his salvation?

I suspect that I would not. About ten years ago, a friend of mine, a coworker, a brother in Christ, was arrested for sexually molesting his stepchildren. To this day, I can hardly mention his name without seething inside. I did not visit him in prison, even though he was fully penitent. Perhaps there is room in the world for anger of that sort. Perhaps my friend needs to hear the clear message that what he did was intolerable. Perhaps he even needs to feel rejection on one level or another. But I suspect that mixed in with my indignation there is a bit of my own secret grandiosity. In looking down his nose at the prostitute, somehow Simon was also looking down his nose at her companion. I do that, too. In looking down my nose at my friend, I think I found myself looking down my nose at Jesus, too, who—I suspect—was there in his jail cell with him. In my heart of hearts, I tend to believe that I am above reproach while my friend the child molester is not. Or I am redeemable and worthy of redemption while my friend the child molester is not.

If this is the case, then I need to hear the message of this story: All of us have sinned and come short of the glory of God. This is the secret message of the parable at the story's center: A certain man had two debtors; both were liable, both in the wrong. With that secret message there is another: The creditor forgave them both.

The woman's sin was her prostitution, the Pharisee's was his self-righteousness. The woman's sin lay in her lack of scruples, the Pharisee's in his religious grandiosity. What is

religious grandiosity? It is scruples run amok, righteousness that
has room for repentance but not for redemption.

Notice something else, though. Jesus didn't simply dismiss
Simon's self-righteousness. He dealt with it. He called for Simon
to repent, though admittedly he did so with a deft hand. And his
intent is not to make the woman more like the Pharisee. It is,
instead, to make the Pharisee more like the woman!

We do not know how Simon responded to this indictment.
There are hints, though. The story closes with a general remark
from the onlookers:

Who is this who even forgives sins? (Luke 7:49).

Who indeed? What we can know here is that the same invitation
that was extended to the woman was extended as well to the
host. Forgiveness. A new beginning. All that was required was
that the Pharisee recognize he and the prostitute had more in
common than they had differences. He was in the same boat.
The Pharisee must paint himself with the same brush.

I can't tell you how that bothers me. My self-righteousness
is one of my most hard-won prizes. This is something I've
worked hard at, something I will only give up kicking and
screaming. I do not want to be painted with the same brush as
the sinners of the world. It makes me angry.

This is what I thought about this week, as I watched the
news slowly expose the human failures of another TV evangelist.
Even evangelists, of all people, stand in need of redemption.
And if they do, so too must I. I need redemption for my own
reasons, but I need redemption nonetheless.

And evangelists are redeemable, infinitely precious in the
sight of God. And if they are, so am I. And so are you. So,
indeed, are we all.

Shall we pray?

SHATTERED
SPECTACLES?

Critics are not simply well-informed general readers (though they like to cast themselves as such) but creative re-readers whose many selections specify and delimit what is to be perceived and how "best" it is to be understood by others. . . .

(We) might say that the critic grinds and assembles a series of lenses through which others are to read; and then the critic directs the sequence in which these lenses are to be utilized.

— John Darr

Through a Glass Brightly?

Kaleidoscoping Perspectives on the Anointing of Jesus in Luke 7:36–50

In this book we want to trace out the complex and subtle interpretive tasks of preaching. We are interested in the whole process, from the moment the preacher decides on a text to the moment the sermon is concluded and the preacher is leaving the pulpit. How does the preacher make the journey from one to the other, from the text to the proclamation?

Contrary to popular impressions, this is not always an easy journey. It can demand a large number of coordinated and difficult skills, but congregations are not always aware of those skills because successful preachers work hard at simplifying. Generally preachers know more than they can say. One is reminded of the axiom of the ballerina: The art of ballet is to make the difficult look effortless. Hidden behind—and revealed in—the successful dance performance may be countless hours of disciplined practice. More is going on than meets the eye. So it is with preaching. Hidden behind—and revealed in—the effective sermon may be hours and hours of disciplined work. More is going on than ever meets the congregation's ear.

But what? There are very many steps, but these can be sorted into two large movements—exegesis and exposition. *Exegesis* is the systematic recovery of the meaning of the text in its original context, the "there and then." (Someone who engages in exegesis is called an exegete.) *Exposition* is the appropriation of that meaning for an entirely different context, the "here and now." In actual practice, these two "stages" of sermon preparation are often intertwined, but it is clear that exegesis is the logically prior step. For this reason it is helpful to diagram this relationship as a sequence of movements (Figure 2.1).

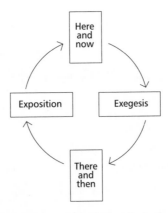

FIGURE 2.1: THE RELATIONSHIP BETWEEN EXEGESIS AND EXPOSITION

Of these two steps the first is more difficult, is less visible to the congregation, and is also less well understood: How do we come to understand what the text meant to its author and original readers? The second step builds upon the first: How do we organize the sermon so that it speaks that meaning afresh in a different cultural context?

The history of biblical interpretation is a fascinating kaleidoscope of perspectives on just how we accomplish these movements. In this chapter we will explore that kaleidoscope by looking at the ways other interpreters have approached the interpretive task. We shall take as our point of focus the story of the anointing, which was the basis of the sermon in chapter 1.

HOMILETICAL APPROACHES

Right from the start, the church has had difficulty knowing how to limit the imaginative uses to which this story could be put. Most of the difficulties are sparked by connections between this story and a similar story of an anointing at Bethany in Mark 14, Matthew 26, and John 12. Matthew, Mark, and John clearly describe the same event. All three place it in Bethany. All three place the anointing at the end of Jesus' life, and all tie it closely to the arrest of Jesus. John names the woman: This is Mary of Bethany, sister of Lazarus and Martha. Luke does not have an anointing at Bethany, but he has our story of an anointing in Galilee, placed much earlier in the sequence. Only Luke identifies the woman as a "sinner"—most likely as a prostitute. Thus, there are striking differences between the two traditions.

The problem is that there are also striking similarities. Luke agrees with Matthew and Mark in naming the host Simon. All four Gospels mention myrrh, and all the Synoptics mention the alabaster flask. Luke agrees with John in having Jesus anointed on the feet and in having the woman let down her hair to wipe up the excess ointment.

The Magdalen Legend

Because of the similarities, the two traditions of anointings were thought to describe the same event. Luke's "sinful woman" must have been John's Mary of Bethany. Early preachers guessed that "Mary of Bethany" was the preconversion name of Mary Magdalene. Thus they combined three women—Mary of Bethany, Mary Magdalene, and Luke's prostitute. This connection between the three women is the basis of an early tradition called the Magdalen legend. According to the Magdalen legend, Mary of Bethany—sister of Lazarus and Martha—left home at an early

age to become a prostitute on the streets of Magdala. Thus the
name change—Mary of Bethany becomes Mary Magdalene. Her
first encounter with Jesus came here, at the anointing in Galilee.
After her formal repentance, Mary joined the disciple band,
sometimes traveling with Jesus, sometimes providing hospital-
ity. In the light of Jesus' words in Luke 10 ("Mary has chosen the
better part," that is, sitting at Jesus' feet in study), she even
takes on the role of scholar and contemplative.[1] Eventually early
preachers represented Mary as the idealized penitent woman,
who leaves behind once for all the dissolute life of sexual
license. By making this movement, early preachers and moral
teachers could weave together a tale of conversion that moves
from the sordid to the sublime.[2]

This is a difficult reconstruction because it appears that
forces were at work on the text that could simply set aside
historical controls. Yet it may be precisely those forces which
enabled the interpreter to lift the details of the story out of one
historical context and make them serve the needs of a later
period of church life. For this reason it is not difficult to see why
the identification of the three women served as the opening
exegetical strategy that predetermined the interpretation of the
story itself. The conversion of Mary Magdalene is made into an
example to be followed. This is one way that early preachers got
from the "there and then" to the "here and now." The need for
historical accuracy came up against the need for homiletical
power, and homiletical power won hands down.

Chrysostom's Interpretation

Another way to make the movement from there and then
to here and now was to allegorize the story. Allegorical interpre-

---

[1]See Leonard Swidler, *Biblical Affirmations of Women* (Philadelphia: Westminster, 1979) 209f.; and Raymond Brown, "Women in the
Fourth Gospel," *Theological Studies* 36 (1975) 693 n. 14.

[2]M. J. Lagrange, "Jesus a-t-il été oint plusiers et par plusiers
femmes?" *Revue Biblique* n.s. 9 (1912) 504–32. For an extended discussion of the Magdalen legend, see "Mary" in John McLintock and James
Strong, *Cyclopedia of Biblical, Theological, and Ecclesiastical Literature*
(New York: Harper and Row, 1873) 5:843. Mary Magdalene is also
occasionally identified with the—again unnamed—woman taken in
adultery in the story preserved in some manuscripts of John 7:53–8:11.
This is, however, beside the point for our purposes.

tation resolves the problem of historical distance by diminishing the concern for history and resting the significance of the story on its purely theological meaning. According to the allegorists, every story has several levels of meaning. The historical level is only one. A deeper level, and one with greater latitude, is the spiritual meaning that shines *through* the history. To interpret the story for a different age, one needed to penetrate the historical level to the underlying spiritual meaning. This required a special way of correlating the details of the story with one's prior theological understanding. Each historical element (A, B, C, etc.) correlated to one theological reality (1, 2, 3, etc.), like this:

A = 1

B = 2

C = 3

An excellent example is the allegorical interpretation offered by St. John Chrysostom (345–407 CE). Chrysostom simply assumed that the two anointing stories described a single event. He focused on the detail that the stories shared, the woman's act itself. The anointing, says Chrysostom, represents Christ's teaching and his suffering. The feet of the Lord represent the apostles, who "have received the fragrant unction of the holy Ghost. . . . The tears are repentance; and the loosened hair deliverance from the love of finery" (*Paedagogus* viii).

It is easy to see why Chrysostom might have interpreted the story in this way. In his day, allegory was both a good apologetic tool and a resource for pastoral care. It allowed the interpreter to overcome the historical distance that separated him from the text. It also allowed the interpreter to spiritualize or personalize away any difficult or embarrassing details. In this way the story could be brought into conformity with the doctrine, the values, or the science of the day. Indeed, the notion that the loosening of the hair represented "deliverance from the love of finery" is exactly what we should expect from ascetic Christianity.

Even so, a number of difficulties here have left later interpreters uneasy. Perhaps most pointedly, it seems clear that neither Jesus, nor Luke, nor Simon the Pharisee would have understood the story the way Chrysostom did. At bottom, this sort of reading is not without controls, but the sort of controls it has are exactly those which would prevent us understanding what the story would have meant for Jesus and his listener, or for Luke and his reader.

Martin Luther's Interpretation

This response undergirds the position taken by Martin Luther. Luther rejected allegorical interpretation across the board, dismissing its extravagant conclusions as "monkey tricks." Instead, the meaning of Scripture must be restricted to its *sensus litteralis,* its "literal sense." But Luther took liberties of his own, turning this story into a lavish metaphor for sinful man in his relationship with a righteous God.[3] He achieved this metaphor by adding in language from the famous *kenosis,* or "emptying," passage in Philippians 2:5–9:

> Christ . . . did not regard equality with God as something to be exploited, but emptied himself, taking the form of a slave. . . . Therefore God also highly exalted him and gave him the name that is above every name.

With Paul's example of Christ "taking the form of a servant," Luther contrasted the attitude of the Pharisee toward the sinner (who Luther believed was Mary Magdalene). The Pharisee had thought that equality with God was a thing to be grasped, had even "taken the form of God" as the frame of reference for his arrogant condemnation of Mary! He was, however, "nothing but a sinner." Christ, the true servant, had in a master stroke of redemption divested the Pharisee of his righteousness and bestowed righteousness on Mary: He "ignored the form of servitude in her whom he has exalted with the form of sovereignty." Mary, the sinner, "is nothing but righteous, elevated to the form of God." Thus, with the self-emptying of Christ as its center, Luther turned the story into a kind of spiritualized reversal of fortunes, which illustrated not only that the "first will be last and the last first" but also that justification occurs by faith alone! The rhetorical force of this transformation is dazzling, but it, too, seems to have been worked out with theological mirrors rather than with a sensitive reading of the text itself.

---

[3]See *Luther's Works,* ed. Harold Grimm (Philadelphia: Muhlenberg Press, 1957) 31:303f.

Henry Mitchell's Interpretation

Perhaps what is needed is something that attends to the story in its own right. Sensitivity to the story in its own right was attempted by Henry Mitchell in a book about the twentieth-century crisis of preaching.[4] Mitchell's strategy was to embroider the details of the sermon with a specific listener in mind.

The venue was a summer camp held for a group of inner-city youths—adolescents and preadolescents. Attendance at morning worship was compulsory, and Mitchell tells us that the camp chaplain had taken to telling stories from the Bible as a way of keeping attention. During the week a particularly painful event had disrupted the life of the group. One of the girls, whom Mitchell calls Angela, had made the mistake of committing too many indiscretions with too many talkative boys. The rumors had begun to run rampant, and as Mitchell tells it, had "hung like a dark cloud over Angela." It is on this occasion that the chaplain elected to tell our story of the anointing of Jesus. I regret that I can only summarize:[5]

> There once was a really fine lookin' girl, but who was raggedy and poor. Wasn't no good jobs, and she and her family had run out of luck. Took to cleanin' houses to make a livin'; you know she was strong and she needed the money real bad.

> One day this dude comes along and offers her some long green for easy work. He said, "You know baby your pretty arms and sweet face ain't meant for work like this. You gotta think of your family." So before long, she was workin' for the dude, sellin' herself on the street. And the dude was right. There was big money in it for a girl with a pretty face. Trouble was, the more she did it, the uglier she felt. And dirty, too. Dirtier than anyone ever felt after cleanin' some bigshot's house. And all those men were dirtier than she was. Got to be so she hated to see a man on the street, 'cause they didn't even look at her, just her body—right through her clothes and all.

> Until one day she met this prophet-type man named Jesus, and he was real different. His look didn't stop where the other guys did.

---

[4]Henry Mitchell, *The Recovery of Preaching* (San Francisco: Harper and Row, 1977) 79–81.

[5]I have borrowed heavily and liberally from the original here.

When he smiled at her he wasn't hittin' on her or nothing; he just liked her.

One day there was a party in the house of some bigshot from the church, and she followed Jesus in. In those days, houses were more open, and people was always crashing parties. The girl looked at Jesus, all stretched out there on the sofa, and she finally couldn't take it no more. She started crying hard, and she used her tears to wash Jesus' feet.

Well, the host, this bigshot from the church, was takin' it all in. He was thinkin' "I thought this guy was supposed to be a great prophet; he doesn't even know that this is a prostitute who's gettin' familiar with him." Seemed like the host couldn't see nothin' but her body neither. But Jesus saw the look in his eye and said, "I got something to tell you," and the host said, "Go right ahead."

Then Jesus laid a story on him about this money lender who had two debtors, one who owed him a little bit of money, and one who owed him a lot. He forgave them both. "Now, which one do you think liked the money lender most?" he asked. And the host said, "The one who he forgave the most."

Then Jesus said to the host, "Well, it's like that with you and this girl here. She's been forgiven a whole lot, and so she's just pourin' out her gratitude. But you . . . Apparently, you ain't been forgiven very much because you're bein' real stingy with yours. Who are you to be badmouthin' her?"

Let us pause for a moment and examine this brief homily. What interpretive principles are evidenced in its construction? For one thing, the diction has been shifted dramatically to make it more understandable to its listener. Explanatory comments have been added to cover culturally specific information. The camp chaplain placed Jesus on a sofa with his feet sticking out to the side and in that way prevented the confusion that would naturally occur if Jesus were depicted sitting up at table. The note about "crashing parties" is colorful and exegetically on the money. An opening has been invented and tacked onto the story with the specific intent of fleshing out the character of the woman and bringing her into the center of the action. The listener is asked to sympathize, and in this way Angela, who is the chaplain's designated listener, is given a richer ground of identification with the woman. It is out of this sympathy that she is also invited to share in the woman's sense of forgiveness.

The story hit its mark apparently. Mitchell tells us by way of conclusion:

> The most important change in the audience was the tears that met under the chin of Angela. This message in folk story had given her the authority of God for forgiveness of her own sins, and her burden was lifted and she finished up the camp period with a heart perhaps lighter than she had had for many months or years.[6]

The interpretive movements are clear. By elaborating the details of the story in just this way, the preacher has lifted it out of its historical context and transformed it into a metaphor for the problems the girl Angela is now facing. There is a sense in which this rendering of the story is deeply poignant and moving. In its own way it extended to Angela something that Jesus had extended to the sinful woman who had come to him at a moment of decision. At the same time, it takes liberties with the historical details. The camp chaplain had invented traits and imposed these on real historical people, had elaborated dimensions of the woman's relationship with Jesus that are simply not found in the biblical story.

The problem here is representative of a problem preachers have always faced. In the attempt to make the story speak to the present time, we sometimes play fast and loose with history. If Christianity were merely a religion of "principles to live by" or "timeless truths," the temptation to abandon history would mean very little. The problem is, Christian faith is historical at its core. If God is revealed in historical events, then what actually happened really does matter. It appears that the solution to the problem must lie in historical study that is governed by strict boundaries of evidence and logic.

FORM-CRITICAL APPROACHES

Just as with the homiletical approaches, the historical research into this story is complicated by the similarities and differences among the various Gospel accounts—Matthew 26:6–13; Mark 14:3–9; John 12:1–8; and Luke 7:36–50. The similarities are odd, are restricted to the opening events, and for the most

---

[6]Mitchell, *Recovery of Preaching,* 81.

part do not seem to serve any theological or sociological agendas. What makes everything difficult is the fact that such an event is so very strange. Too many details violate social and religious norms. As odd as such a thing may be, the evangelists seem to report that it happened twice.

But is this likely? Could this strange event have happened twice? If so, how do we account for the similarities of language by which the openings are described? Could the traditions have somehow become confused with one another? On the other hand, if the event had happened only once, how do we account for the differences between the two anointing traditions? Could the story have been modified in different directions by the "needs of the moment"? This is the question posed by the form critics. On the surface of it, there seem to be only two options: Either there was one anointing and the traditions diverged, or there were two anointings and the traditions merged.

According to the form critics, the Gospels were cooked up in a sociological and theological pressure cooker. Traditions about Jesus had been preserved basically as small units, and as these had been taken up into the Gospels, they were made to serve the apologetic and homiletical needs of the moment. This is exactly what the allegorists and Luther and the camp chaplain had done with the story of the anointing of Jesus, but the form critics thought that the same thing took place before the Gospels were written down. Each of the Gospels has its own distinctive flavor because the evangelists had seasoned the stories to the spiritual diet and tastes of their audiences. The challenge is to boil everything down to what actually happened. One can only do this, said the form critics, if one can identify the modifications to the tradition. The historical trick is to reverse the process, working backward to ever earlier levels of tradition. This is rather like beginning with a stew and working backward to reconstruct the recipe, a difficult task but not impossible. Someone with a sensitive palate and a little experience in the kitchen just might be able to do it.

Andre Legault's Interpretation

In 1954 Legault employed the story as a refracting lens through which to explore the workings of form critical method generally.[7] Legault argued that there were two separate events. Two different traditions grew together. According to Legault, something like what Luke describes actually occurred early in Jesus' ministry. The pre-Lucan story was simpler and less encumbered with difficulty. In particular, it lacked those elements which are shared with the later event—the name of Simon, the perfume, and the anointing. Luke naturally imported these elements from the other event because of the similarities between the two. The placement of Simon's name in the middle of the story (Luke 7:40) led Legault to suspect "an involuntary, spontaneous, unconscious insertion, on the part of the narrator in his vivid dialogue. The narrator gets his story mixed up and inserts here the name of the host at Bethany."[8] Having made that association, asserted Legault, Luke then dropped the latter story because of his own distaste for repetition.

Robert Holst's Interpretation

In 1976 Robert Holst published a study that defended exactly the opposite conclusion.[9] According to Holst, there was a single anointing. The traditions grew apart. Holst reconstructed a primitive version of the story as follows:

> Jesus came to Bethany to the house of Simon the leper. And a woman bringing an alabaster jar of myrrh, valuable nard *pistikes,* anointed the feet of Jesus with the myrrh and with her tears and wiped them with her hair. Certain men reclining there said, "Why was this myrrh not sold for three hundred denarii and (the money) given to the poor?" But Jesus said, "Leave (plural) her alone. The poor you always have with you; (love?) you do not always have."[10]

If this is right, Luke must have made the following changes to the tradition: He removed the reference to the ointment and to Jesus' words about the poor because of his own concern for

---

[7]Andre Legault, "An Application of the Form-Critical Method to the Anointings in Galilee (Lk 7,36–50) and Bethany (Mt 26,6–13; Mk 14,3–9; Jn 12,1–8)," *Catholic Biblical Quarterly* 16 (1954) 131–45.

[8]Ibid., 144.

[9]Robert Holst, "The One Anointing of Jesus: Another Application of the Form-Critical Method," *Journal of Biblical Literature* 95 (1976) 435–46.

[10]Ibid., 446.

the social outcast. (Most of all, Luke did not wish to excuse waste, even here.) He added tears to increase the impression of contrition. He added the description of Simon as a Pharisee to heighten the religious significance of the story and to support a contrast with the woman. He added the identification of the woman as a sinner to establish the contrast with Simon. These two characters now stand as literary foils: "The public sinner acts in a manner more God-pleasing than the recognized religious leader."[11] Although Holst believed that the location of the story in Bethany was part of the original story, he argued that Luke simply removed the place-name and moved the story to Galilee as part of his wider program of adjustments to the tradition.

Here we encounter yet another interpretive problem. Legault and Holst had argued from the same premises, employed similar methods, and reached diametrically opposite conclusions. A rapid survey of the other form critics fails to break the deadlock:

- Martin Dibelius argued that there was one event and that Mark's version was most primitive.[12]

- Rudolf Bultmann thought there was one.[13]

- David Daube argued that there was one and that Luke's version was most primitive.[14]

- F. W. Beare thought there were two events, though only one anointing. The details of the anointing were combined with fragments of other controversy traditions.[15]

---

[11] Ibid., 438. One notes the parallel with Jesus' parable of the Publican and the Sinner in Luke 18:9–14.

[12] Martin Dibelius, *From Tradition to Gospel*, trans. Bertram Woolf (New York: Charles Scribner's Sons, 1919; reissue, 1934) 114f.

[13] Rudolf Bultmann, *The History of the Synoptic Tradition*, trans. John Marsh (1963, reprint; Peabody, Mass.: Hendrickson Publishers, 1993) 20f.

[14] David Daube, "The Anointing at Bethany and Jesus' Burial," *Anglican Theological Review* 32 (1950) 186–99. See also *The New Testament and Rabbinic Judaism* (1956, reprint; Peabody, Mass.: Hendrickson Publishers, 1994) 321–23. The earlier reference is largely taken up into the latter.

[15] F. W. Beare, *The Earliest Records of Jesus* (New York: Abingdon, 1962) 99f.

READER-ORIENTED INTERPRETATIONS

Beyond the obvious difficulty that the form critics have failed to come to consensus, there is another problem here. In their attempt to "get behind the story" to the underlying tradition, they ended up dismantling and basically discarding the story itself. This, of course, is not what the author intended that we do, and for this reason it yields interpretations that the author would have found puzzling. A case could be made that if we are to understand the story the way in which it was intended, we must do what readers are expected to do.

Charles Talbert's Interpretation

An attempt by Charles Talbert to read the story in a reader-oriented way was published in 1982.[16] Talbert argued that the primary emphasis of the story lies in the judgment that it wields against the attitude of the Pharisee. This attitude is embodied in Simon's unspoken remark in v. 39: "If this man were a prophet, he would know what sort of woman this is who is touching him, for she is a sinner." This posture, said Talbert, is the direct antithesis of a theological nuance that has been developed in the immediately preceding verse: "Wisdom is justified by her children" (v. 35). According to Talbert, what it means to be "justified by one's children" is difficult to understand in English. It "does not refer to a human's justification, but to God's. God's people justify him."[17] But this is exactly what the Pharisee has failed to do toward Jesus. His unexpressed but very real hostility brings him under the implied condemnation of the story. In a collateral theme that buttresses and develops this primary theme, Luke demonstrates that Jesus does, in fact, perform the work of a prophet—by reading Simon's unspoken thoughts (v. 40) and by speaking the mind of God in forgiving the woman's sins (v. 49).

Talbert observed that the exchange establishing these two themes is essentially Socratic: It takes the form of question, counter-question, forced answer, and refutation. According to

---

[16] Charles Talbert, *Reading Luke: A Literary and Theological Commentary on the Third Gospel* (New York: Crossroad, 1982) 84–89.
[17] Ibid., 84.

Talbert, this is a Hellenistic strategy that was taken over and
employed by both Jews and Christians in structuring and developing their traditions.[18]

Thomas Brodie's Interpretation

In 1983 Thomas Brodie approached the story from an
entirely different tack.[19] Brodie began with the observation
that the comparison with the anointing at Bethany has yielded
unreliable results. Perhaps the question had been posed pre-
maturely, he suggested. Brodie's evaluation therefore focused
exclusively on Luke's account, and it did not attempt to discover the connection between that account and the parallels in
the other Gospels. Like Talbert, Brodie found his organizing
strategy in a common Hellenistic rhetorical practice—*rhetorical
imitation.* This is a style of composition that aims at fidelity
not to historical facts but to a previous literary or oral tradition. According to Brodie, rhetorical imitation was a practice
widely endorsed among the Greeks, and it would have been
especially attractive in a context that revered a collection of
sacred texts. Brodie argued that Luke has shaped his telling of
the anointing at Galilee under the literary influence of the two
stories about Elisha in 2 Kings 4—the story of the woman
in debt (vv. 1–7), and the story of the Shunammite woman
(vv. 8–37). Overall structure, rhetorical emphasis, and pecu-
liar details of omission and inclusion all are marshalled as
evidence in support of this position.

Burton Mack's Interpretation

In 1988 Burton Mack provided yet another angle on the
story.[20] This appeared as part of an extended discussion of the
influence of Hellenistic chreias in shaping the gospel tradition. A
chreia is a form of story that focuses on some pointed action or

---

[18] Ibid., 86.

[19] Thomas Brodie, "Luke 7,36–50 as an Internalization of 2 Kings
4,1–37: A Study in Luke's Use of Rhetorical Imitation," *Biblica* 64 (1983)
457–85.

[20] In Burton Mack and Vernon Robbins, *Patterns of Persuasion in
the Gospels* (Sonoma, Calif.: Polebridge Press, 1989) 85–106.

saying.[21] According to Mack, this is a specialized form of chreia—Cynic chreia. The earliest tradition must have been composed of an objection and a rejoinder, though both are now lost or are incorporated into an elaborated version of the story. The development of the story itself is made along lines suggested by the classical rhetoricians for elaborated chreias. In particular, four central movements can be discerned:

- the *narratio,* which sets the scene, in vv. 36–38

- the *quaestio,* which poses the challenge, in v. 39

- the *argumentatio,* which records Jesus' response to the challenge, in vv. 40–48

- the restatement of the *quaestio,* which establishes the potency of the *argumentatio* and draws the story to its close, in vv. 49f.

Mack's argument differed from Talbert's in that it emphasized Jesus' own skill as crafter of the *argumentatio,* Jesus' ability to convince. By contrast, Talbert had emphasized the fiat of the thing: What counts is not Jesus' cogency but his authority, the way in which—without requiring logic—he simply reads the mind of the host, discerns the inner character of the woman, and pronounces forgiveness in the name of God.

John Darr's Interpretation

In 1992, John Darr explored the story from yet another angle: This is a "hellenistic symposium."[22] The genre signals unfold gradually, but soon enough it is clear to the reader that Jesus is caught up into a kind of formal dialogue in which the wise man is engaged in debate with "worthy opponents." The opponents here are the Pharisees, and to a lesser extent, others of their kind who are present at the table. What makes this

---

[21] For a brief discussion of chreias, see George Wesley Buchanan, *Jesus: The King and His Kingdom* (Macon, Ga.: Mercer University Press, 1984), esp. ch. 2, "Rhetoricians, Historians, and Literary Forms," 43–74.

[22] John Darr, On *Character Building: The Reader and The Rhetoric of Characterization in Luke–Acts* (Louisville: Westminster John Knox, 1992) 23, 35f. In this essay Darr develops and elaborates a thesis set forth by E. Springs Steele, "Luke 11:37–54—A Modified Hellenistic Symposium?" *Journal of Biblical Literature* 103: 379–94.

strikingly like other such symposia is the signal role of the *fait divers*—a kind of crisis of moment which prompts the discussion in the first place. According to Darr this is not a pure example of the type. The opponents are dumbfounded. In this way, they are shown to be less than worthy opponents after all:

> Luke modifies . . . this convention in such a way that the Pharisees are denied even the secondary status of the sage's "worthy opponents." Neither Simon nor the other Pharisees who dine with Jesus are allowed to dialogue with him or to rebut the serious charges he brings against them. The obvious implication is that they are unable to do so. Thus, the reader has nothing to place on the positive side of the Pharisees' ledger. Here and elsewhere in Luke symposia are used only as stages for Jesus to criticize severely his Pharisaic hosts and fellow guests; in no way do they paint the Pharisees as either colleagues or benefactors of Jesus. Indeed, as utilized in this story, their effect is quite the opposite. (p. 35)

The literature that was published after 1980 had a distinctively different air about it. For one thing, the reader-oriented interpreters appear to have stopped trying to recover the prehistory of the story and instead focused on the story itself. They show a decided tendency to read the story along lines dictated by Hellenistic rhetoric. Concern for literary context has also become more central. Even so, these commentators have continued to be divided on fundamental questions, and puzzlements remain. We may wonder if we are looking at Socratic dialogue, as Talbert argued, at rhetorical imitation of an Old Testament passage, as Brodie argued, at an elaborated chreia, as Mack argued. Is the emphasis on Jesus' skill in argumentation, as Mack and Darr envisioned it? Or is it upon the prophetic authority by which he reads the mind of the host and pronounces forgiveness in the name of God, as Talbert had it?

IMPLICATIONS

Let us pause now and review briefly. Throughout its long history, interpreters have read the story against a kaleidoscoping backdrop of historical and theological scenarios. Each change of backdrop or theological intention leads to a different conclusion:

- The story illustrates the cryptic meaning of v. 35: "Wisdom is justified by all her children" (Talbert).

- The story is a legend that contains important information about one of the saints. The story satisfies curiosity about the woman (Dibelius).

- The story is a controversy story organized around the parable of the two debtors in vv. 41f.; thus the parable is central, and the woman is secondary (Bultmann).

- The story is a way of emphasizing Jesus' care for the outcast, as is evidenced in Luke's redactional changes from his source (Holst).

- The story is about a simple act of devotion, developed under the literary influence of 2 Kings 4 (Brodie).

- The story is about Jesus' skill in argumentation, especially as he locks horns with the Pharisees (Mack, Darr).

It seems that the problem we have discovered in this chapter is more fundamental than a matter of differences of opinion about the meaning of the Bible. When the needs of a working pastor are taken into account, the diversity of interpretive options reflects an antecedent problem of greater magnitude: How is the preacher to deal with the fact that competent interpreters working in good faith with identical texts can reach radically different, and sometimes mutually incompatible, conclusions? Why does it seem so clear to Robert Holst that there was one anointing of Jesus, and equally clear to Andre Legault that there were two? Why do the Methodists disagree so violently with the Baptists? Why did Bultmann's program never occur to Chrysostom? For that matter, why did allegorizing seem so correct to Chrysostom but completely illegitimate to Luther?

A vantage point is needed from which to make critical decisions about the results of scholarship, a vantage point that rises above the mass of options. We turn to that question in chapter 3.

INTERPRETIVE LENSES

The Concept of Paradigms

I n chapter 2 we surveyed some of the options interpreters
have taken over the years in their attempts to extract fresh
meaning from Luke's account of the anointing of Jesus. What
we discovered is that instead of making the preacher's job easier,
the range of options makes it more difficult. Chapter 2 poses the
question rather sharply: Why in fact do competent interpreters
working with identical texts reach different, sometimes incompatible, conclusions?

It is clear that the problem of diverse and competing interpretations plagues areas of research other than theology. For

example, historian Thomas Kuhn has explored a nearly identical problem in the history of science: Competent scientists working with identical evidence sometimes reach incompatible conclusions.[1] In this chapter we tap briefly into Kuhn's analysis because it explains how the processes of research influence conclusions.

THE CONCEPT OF PARADIGMS

Kuhn began by observing that science does not develop smoothly through the gradual accumulation of data but, rather, with fits and starts and through dramatic revolutions of thought. This is very different from the commonsense idea that scientists simply collect more and more information and add it to the store of information that already exists. According to Kuhn, the historical facts are indisputable. Science advances by revolution, not evolution. The fact that we no longer believe that the world is flat is the result of a major revolution in scientific thought. The problem is not whether scientific revolutions take place but how they are to be explained. Kuhn's explanation is that they occur because of an aspect of scientific observation itself: The scientific mind is trained to observe in a certain way. The collection of data is guided by the scientist's training, his or her skills of observation, intentions, habits of mind, tools, methods of collecting data and keeping records, and the range of available contextual information. In practice this means that the scientist comes to the data with a model already in hand. The model limits what the scientist is likely to see in the first place.

Kuhn called these interpretive models paradigms, and he pointed out their central role in enabling scientific observation from its beginning. The term "paradigm" is much bandied about these days but also a bit difficult to unpack. Kuhn himself used it somewhat loosely,[2] but Walter Wink has provided an adequate shorthand definition. According to Wink, a paradigm is:

---

[1]Thomas Kuhn, *The Structure of Scientific Revolutions* (2d ed.; Chicago: University of Chicago Press, 1970).

[2]Kuhn puts forth one characteristic definition in the opening of *The Structure of Scientific Revolutions:* Paradigms are "accepted examples of actual scientific practice—examples which include law, theory, application, and instrumentation together. . . . [They are] models from

a constellation of presuppositions, beliefs, values and techniques
to manipulate data. Paradigms reduce the chaos of data to a
selective pattern which enables specialized research on small
pieces of the puzzle. Apart from the paradigm, fact-gathering and
observation would be random and diffuse.[3]

This, then, is roughly what paradigms do: They enable interpretation to take place, but they do so only by imposing structure
and pattern on the observation of facts. This can be demonstrated quite graphically. Scientists have long used visual tools
to illustrate the role of the mind in discovering patterns that
connect. One such image is the photograph in Figure 3.1.

FIGURE 3.1: DALMATIAN

The image is a high-contrast photograph of a dalmatian.
The dog is facing away from the camera, nose to the ground in
the dead center of the photograph. Many observers have difficulty seeing the image at first, but once they have seen it, they
can recall it or dismiss it at will. The eye can bring it in and out
of focus. The capacity for bringing the image into focus depends

which spring particular coherent traditions of scientific research" (p. 10).
But this is extraordinarily broad and, in the view of some interpreters,
entirely too flaccid. Margaret Masterman has found more than thirty-
two variations on the term in Kuhn's writings ("The Nature of a Paradigm," in *Criticism and the Growth of Knowledge,* ed. Imre Lakatos and
Alan Musgrave [Cambridge: Cambridge University Press, 1970] 59–89).

[3]Walter Wink, *The Bible in Human Transformation: Toward a New
Paradigm for Biblical Study* (Philadelphia: Fortress, 1986) 16f.

upon the mind's activity of organizing the details on the image in a particular kind of relationship to one another. To do this, the mind must heighten some elements of the image and suppress other elements. But on what basis? The mind can only make those decisions by bringing in outside information—what it knows about dalmatians.

A different image, but to similar effect, is noted in Figure 3.2. This image is a drawing of a woman. Some observers will see a young woman, wearing a choker about her neck. She is facing away from the observer, and the line of her jaw can be easily traced along the center of the picture. Other observers will more naturally see an older woman, facing forward and gazing slightly to the left of the picture. The line that was the young woman's jaw here becomes the shadow line of the old woman's nose. The choker becomes her mouth. Everything depends upon how one organizes the parts, on one's paradigm. Once the observer has seen both women, it is quite easy to toggle back and forth between them. The interpretive possibilities lie not only in the lines on the page but also in the way the mind chooses to organize the lines into meaningful patterns. This is what happens whenever we interpret anything. Paradigms enable interpretation to take place, but they do so by imposing structure and pattern on the observation and collection of data.

FIGURE 3.2: YOUNG/OLD WOMAN

For the paradigm to be viable, it must enable the interpreter to manage the data responsibly and sensibly. This means that in scientific research the value of a paradigm can be judged according to its ability to explain observable evidence and to enable reliable predictions about the results of experimentation. Thus, as a general rule, the more adequate the paradigm, the more it is able to account for reality with precision and scope. Where two paradigms can explain the same phenomena with equal precision and equal scope, the simpler of the two is to be preferred. This is called the rule of parsimony, or Occam's razor.

Difficulties, however, can occur. Kuhn pointed out that scientists sometimes uncover hard facts that are simply incompatible with the commonly accepted scientific paradigm. Then what? When that happens, the researcher is confronted not only with a new piece to the puzzle but also, and more importantly, with a challenge to the adequacy of the puzzle itself: The paradigm is itself called into question. A new paradigm is proposed, and if it succeeds in offering a simpler or more reliable explanation, it will eventually displace the older paradigm completely, though often not without a fight. After the smoke and dust settle, the theoretical battleground of one generation is plowed under and made into a new field of research for the next. The stuff of controversy becomes common knowledge.

An excellent illustration is the Copernican Revolution. By the sixteenth century, technical advances in the field of astronomy had made available a rapidly burgeoning field of data. Because of its very volume, the data about the universe had become increasingly difficult to explain with the older Ptolemaic model. Ptolemy, you will recall, had developed a model of the universe with the earth at its center and with the sun, moon, and stars rotating around the earth on a series of concentric spheres. With the introduction of the telescope, Galileo had made observations that could not be reconciled with the prevailing Ptolemaic paradigm. The world was knocked off center. Enter Copernicus. Copernicus demonstrated that the data could be more simply explained if we returned to the thinking of the pre-Ptolemaic Greek philosophers who had posited a solar system with the sun at its center. Thus, while the Copernican Revolution was forced by an increase in data, what gave it its coherence was a change in the way the data were organized and understood. As an alternative model of the universe, it called for a reformulation of the ways in which the data were construed, and that in turn called for changes in the ways data were collected.

In a rather interesting appropriation of Kuhn's paradigm theory, Stephen Covey describes what was for him a small but infinitely significant "paradigm shift" that took place one Sunday morning on the New York subway:

> People were sitting quietly—some reading newspapers, some lost in thought, some resting with their eyes closed. It was a calm, peaceful scene.
>
> Then suddenly, a man and his children entered the subway car. The children were so loud and rambunctious that instantly the whole climate changed.
>
> The man sat down next to me and closed his eyes, apparently oblivious to the situation. The children were yelling back and forth, throwing things, even grabbing people's papers. It was very disturbing. And yet, the man sitting next to me did nothing.
>
> It was difficult not to feel irritated. I could not believe that he could be so insensitive as to let his children run wild like that and do nothing about it, taking no responsibility at all. It was easy to see that everyone else on the subway felt irritated, too. So finally, with what I felt was unusual patience and restraint, I turned to him and said, "Sir, your children are really disturbing a lot of people. I wonder if you couldn't control them a little more?"
>
> The man lifted his gaze as if to come to a consciousness of the situation for the first time and said softly, "Oh, you're right. I guess I should do something about it. We just came from the hospital where their mother died about an hour ago. I don't know what to think, and I guess they don't know how to handle it either."[4]

The shift of information called for a completely different paradigm. As Covey tells us, "Everything changed in an instant."

In exactly the same way but on a larger scale, shifts of information or perspective have called for the radical transformations that have occurred in a variety of disciplines,[5] including theological study.[6] Sometimes human understanding changes by

---

[4]Stephen Covey, *The Seven Habits of Highly Effective People: Restoring the Character Ethic* (New York: Simon and Schuster, 1989) 30f.

[5]For a collection of essays evaluating the significance of Kuhn's theory for a variety of academic disciplines, see Gary Gattung, ed., *Paradigms and Revolutions: Appraisals and Applications of Thomas Kuhn's Philosophy of Science* (Notre Dame: University of Notre Dame Press, 1980).

[6]See Gordon Hall, "An Integration of Science and Theology in a Piagetian Epistemology," *Journal of Psychology and Theology* 8 (1980) 293–302; Cordell Strug, "Kuhn's Paradigm Thesis: A Two-Edged Sword

revolution—even by violent revolution—rather than by gradual adaptation of a working model.

THE STRUCTURE OF PARADIGMS

We can see how this theory might apply to the history of biblical scholarship by taking the model of a paradigm apart and looking at its pieces. In my view there are four basic parts, or dimensions, of a paradigm—presuppositions, predispositions, prior information, and protocols (Figure 3.3). Let us look at these elements one at a time. What we shall see is that a significant change in any part leads to significant changes in the conclusions the researcher will reach.

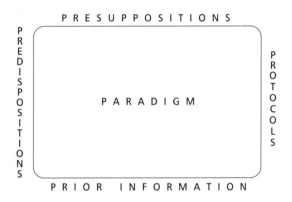

FIGURE 3.3: THE BASIC PARTS OF A PARADIGM

for the Philosophy of Religion," *Religious Studies* 20 (1984) 269–79; David Thompson, "Kuhn, Kohlberg, and Kinlaw: Reflections for Overserious Theologians," *Wesley Theological Journal* 19 (1984) 7–22; Paul Weibe, "Search for a Paradigm," *Journal of Religion* 64 (1984) 348–62; Robert Crotty, "Changing Fashions in Biblical Interpretation," *Australian Biblical Review* 33 (1985) 15–30; Richard Rhem, "Theological Method: The Search for a New Paradigm in a Pluralistic Age," *Reformation Review* 39 (1986) 242–54; James Martin, "Toward a Post-Critical Paradigm," *New Testament Studies* 33 (1987) 370–85. Further researches toward a postcritical paradigm are found in Hans Küng and David Tracy, eds., *Paradigm Change and Theology* (New York: Crossroad, 1991).

Presuppositions

By "presuppositions" we mean the a priori assumptions that are required if the interpretation is to be logical. These concern the limits of what is and is not thought to be possible. Because they are a priori, such assumptions are not demonstrable by logic or experiment. They are instead necessary components of logical thought itself. They must be in place beforehand if logic is to function as a way of demonstrating something else.

The acceptance or rejection of miracles is an example of an a priori presupposition of study. Many historians who work with the biblical material do so from the presupposition that miracles are impossible. Those who hold this view do so because of the nature of the historical record itself. By "historical record" we mean the evidence that has been left behind as the result of historical events. This includes both written records and physical remains. It is the nature of things that the historical record is incomplete because people do not systematically preserve everything and because, even when we do preserve things, we seldom do so because we are interested in providing a resource for later historians. This means that historians must do a fair amount of reconstructing. Wherever the evidence in the historical record is incomplete, it must be filled in by logical inference. Thus this problem: Inference is impossible to draw with certainty when reality is not consistent. If miracles happen, then reality is inconsistent and historical research is reduced to mere speculation.

On the other hand, other interpreters affirm the possibility of miracles as a matter of theological presupposition: The God who made the world out of nothing ought to be pretty good on spare parts. According to this view, the denial of miracles is a peculiarly modern conceit. If the Bible says that miracles happened and the God of the Bible is a faithful God, then miracles must have happened. This affirmation of miracles is sometimes extended to the accuracy of the text itself: By virtue of its character as the word of God, the biblical text is protected from error of any sort—scientific, historical, or theological.

Whether or not we intend it, the presupposition we adopt determines in advance the range of conclusions we will draw. In this regard it may be helpful to recall Robert Holst's interpretation of the anointing story.[7] According to Holst, Luke took over the story from Mark. When he did so, he deliberately made a series of changes to the tradition. Out of his own concern for the social outcast, he removed Mark's reference to the ointment and to Jesus' words about the poor. He added tears to increase the impression of contrition. He added the note that the woman was a "sinner" to support a contrast with Simon, and the note that the host was a Pharisee to develop that contrast into a theological theme. These two characters now stand as literary foils: "The public sinner acts in a manner more God-pleasing than the recognized religious leader."[8] Thus, Holst's position suggests that certain details of the story were invented for the sake of theological or homiletical interests.

But this sort of conclusion appears impossible for interpreters who begin with the presupposition that the Bible is ipso facto protected from error.

By "presuppositions" we also mean the interpreter's initial sense of where the meaning of the text resides. Is the meaning of the text resident in the historical events the text describes? In the author's intent? Can it be found in the insight the text provokes in the reader, insight that may lead the reader to a change in the way he or she thinks about the world? Is it somehow found in the text itself, without regard to historical accuracy or authorial intent? These are large questions, and the way in which we answer them can create enormous differences of opinion about the range and scope of responsible interpretation.

Predispositions

By "predispositions" we mean the interpreter's purposes in undertaking the investigation, and the results the interpreter comes expecting or intending or secretly hoping to find. These include both the interpreter's conscious intentions and his or her hidden agendas.

We can see this factor at work by contrasting Holst's interpretation with the one offered by Kenneth Bailey.[9] Holst

---

[7] Holst, "The One Anointing of Jesus," 435–46.
[8] Ibid., 438.
[9] Kenneth Bailey, *Through Peasant Eyes* (Grand Rapids: Eerdmans, 1980) 1–21.

dismantled the story, searching for clues about early Christianity. In the process he interpreted the details against a reconstructed background of early Christian theological and pastoral concerns. Bailey was quite content to take the story as it stands and to interpret it against a background of customs that would have been current for Jesus. According to Bailey, the host was obligated to provide Jesus with water for his feet, oil for his head, and a ritual greeting. The fact that he did not do so represented an insult of the first magnitude: "The insult to Jesus has to be intentional and electrifies the assembled guests. War has been declared and everyone waits to see Jesus' response."[10] In an undeniably dramatic gesture, the woman covers the faux pas out of her own resources, such as they were (vv. 44–46). This gesture inevitably sharpens Simon's hostility (v. 39). If Bailey is right, Jesus' response to Simon can only be understood as a counterattack. In Middle Eastern etiquette it is simply unheard of to correct one's host. The severity of Jesus' response is sharpened by the contrast between the behavior of the woman and the failures of the host (water/tears; head/feet; cheap olive oil/expensive ointment). The host is left to draw the unexpressed contrast between the woman's penitence and his own religious arrogance. In this context, says Bailey, Jesus' response to Simon is a "scathing rebuke."

This is a very different interpretation from the one Holst had reached. Why? While Holst was intending to reconstruct the early Christian influences that shaped the tradition, Bailey took the story at face value. The difference in predisposition produced a marked difference in conclusion.

Prior Information

By "prior information" we mean the outside repertoire of cultural information that is necessary if the interpreter is to fill in the gaps in the story and organize the parts into a coherent and meaningful whole. All interpretation requires that we bring outside information to bear.

We can see this factor at work quite easily by contrasting Bailey's interpretation with the one offered by J. Duncan M.

---

[10] Ibid., 8.

Derrett.[11] Bailey reached the conclusion that Jesus' response to Simon was a "scathing rebuke." In an article published just one year earlier, Derrett argued precisely the opposite position. According to Derrett, if there was embarrassment here, it lay with the prostitute. The host had been perfectly correct in his show of deference toward Jesus. To do more would have been excessive. When a whore appeared at his dinner party, Simon was understandably embarrassed. One of the town's more unsavory characters had invaded his home while he was entertaining a respected religious leader. Simon did not object at first because—apparently—the woman's presence raised no objection in Jesus. She began to fondle Jesus' feet and pour expensive perfume on them. Simon now found himself in a most indelicate position: She was insulting his guest directly.[12] Jesus was sure to be offended. What to do? Jesus' "extremely delicate" response salvaged the moment for everyone. It was, says Derrett, "the soul of tact."[13]

Bailey said this was a "scathing rebuke." Derrett thought it the "soul of tact." "Scathing rebuke"? "Soul of tact"? Which is it? It is difficult to imagine two more contrary interpretations of the same passage. What makes that contrast particularly interesting is the fact that both Derrett and Bailey employed basically the same method. Both sought an interpretation of the event itself, rather than a reconstruction of the ecclesiastical influences on the tradition. Both proceeded from the assumption that Luke's account is historically reliable, and both avoided importing details from the anointing at Bethany.[14] Both unpacked the story against an understanding of Palestinian culture. Yet starting from the same presuppositions and setting out in the same direction, they arrived at diametrically opposite destinations. Why? It is because, while both Derrett and Bailey read the story against a repertoire of Palestinian culture, they brought with

---

[11] J. Duncan M. Derrett, "The Anointing at Bethany and the Story of Zacchaeus," in *Law in the New Testament* (London: Darton, 1979) 266–78.

[12] Derrett did not raise this issue, but his interpretation also makes sense of the host's objection in v. 39: He was puzzled. Could Jesus not tell that he was being fondled by a prostitute?

[13] Derrett, "The Anointing at Bethany and the Story of Zacchaeus," 278.

[14] Bailey did intrude elements of this story into the latter story, however, though he did so without explanation.

them different understandings of what that repertoire must have been. The differences in their conclusions depend not upon what was said in the text but on prior information brought in from outside!

Protocols

By "protocols" we mean the ordered activities—the "interpretive conventions"—of research itself. These include analogies from similar examples, steps in the construction and testing of hypothetical models, and formulas for the resolution of difficulties. A good example is the use of "indicated procedures" in medical diagnosis. The appearance of symptoms in certain combinations "indicates" appropriate next steps in diagnosis. Those steps follow a rigidly prescribed sequence. Here, as elsewhere, the sequence of steps is an important factor in responsible research.

It is not difficult to demonstrate the effect of a change of protocols, again with reference to the anointing of Jesus. In 1954 Andre Legault argued that the anointing stories in Mark and Luke describe two very different events. In the course of transmission, the two stories grew together, with details from one being inserted into the other. This explains why both stories name the host Simon: "The narrator (Luke) gets his story mixed up and inserts the name of the host at Bethany."[15] In 1976 Robert Holst argued a diametrically opposite conclusion: There was only one event, and the traditions grew apart.[16] Holst's argument was designed specifically to refute Legault's. He did so with this explanation: "Legault's methodology and many of his presuppositions are out of date due to the scholarly advances in the disciplines of form and redaction criticism."[17] In other words, Legault had employed outdated protocols, and that is why his conclusions were wrong.

But Holst and Legault are more like each other than either is like Charles H. Talbert.[18] What distinguishes Talbert's interpretation is his refusal to dismantle the narrative into its component parts or to read it independently of its literary context in

---

[15] Legault, "The Anointings in Galilee," 144.
[16] Holst, "The One Anointing of Jesus."
[17] Ibid., 435.
[18] Talbert, *Reading Luke,* 84–89.

the Gospel of Luke. Instead, his protocols were designed to unpack the story as a *literary* whole. His declared context of interpretation is Luke's Gospel itself. Thus the story is understood as an elaboration of a comment found in v. 35: "Wisdom is justified by her children." Simon's hostility toward Jesus—epitomized by his silent remark in v. 39—is quite the point at issue. According to Talbert, Simon has failed to "justify God" and in that way has fallen under the implied judgment that the reader is asked to pass.

We can see a similar shift of interpretive protocols in the way in which John Kilgallen brought criticism against Joseph Fitzmyer's view that the woman in the story was a forgiven sinner. Fitzmyer's argument had depended upon a complex and subtle evaluation of the evidence. It is precisely for this reason that Kilgallen thought it unlikely:

> How can any reader be presumed to know, except by diligent reflection and study of the story, that one is to read the story with knowledge that the woman has already been forgiven? . . . Out of respect for good storytelling this key to understanding the story should have been made clear to the reader.[19]

What is important here is that Kilgallen's critique of Fitzmyer was based on a difference of method: Kilgallen questioned the adequacy of Fitzmyer's protocols.

When we change the protocols of research, the resulting change of conclusions is quite predictable. Holst and Legault were looking *through* the text at the underlying ecclesiastical environment that gave it its present form. Bailey was looking *through* the text at the historical Jesus, quite without regard to the ecclesiastical or literary environment in which Luke has couched the story. Talbert and Kilgallen were looking *at* the text in an effort to understand the effect it is expected to have on its reader. Different protocols, different conclusions.

These, then, are the basic building blocks from which paradigms are constructed: presuppositions, predispositions, prior information, and protocols. A major change in any component will lead to changes in the conclusions the paradigm is likely to yield. Because these are in place quite early in the interpretive process, they govern not only the interpreter's con-

---

[19] John Kilgallen, "John the Baptist, the Sinful Woman, and the Pharisee," *Journal of Biblical Literature* 104 (1985) 676f.

clusions but also the process of observation itself. In Kuhn's terms, "all interpretation is theory-laden."

IMPLICATIONS

Let us pause for a moment here and gather up the loose ends of this chapter. We began by posing the question raised in chapter 2: Why do competent interpreters working with identical texts sometimes reach conflicting or incompatible results? What we saw was that interpreters do not come neutral to the evidence but instead bring with them certain expectations, outside information, skills, strategies, and conventions, all of which influence interpretation in various ways. This investment of the interpreter into the interpretive process Thomas Kuhn called paradigms. All interpretation is theory-laden, even interpretation that does not perceive itself to be so.

For our purposes there are two basic implications of paradigm theory: First, *interpretation is not as neutral as it appears at first.* Whether we are aware of it or not, what we bring with us to the reading shapes what we ultimately will find. What we know or do not know, what we believe is or is not possible, the reasons we are undertaking the study, what we hope to find or we unconsciously avoid, our habits of research—everything is grist for the interpreter's mill. This is sometimes a disturbing implication for those who take the Bible as the word of God. It is disturbing because it suggests that even when we are trying very hard to get it right, we will sometimes get it wrong or misunderstand.

Yet no matter how hard we try, we cannot avoid taking up a position. It is quite possible and right to reject, say, John Chrysostom's allegorical interpretation of the story of the anointing of Jesus. Chrysostom ignored considerations that are central and controlling, he abandoned context, and he imposed meanings that neither Jesus' listener nor Luke's reader could possibly have understood. Yet we can only legitimately reject Chrysostom's stance by taking up some other particular stance—one that affirms what Chrysostom ignored (historical and literary context) and that ignores what Chrysostom affirmed (theological meaning supersedes historical facts). The decision to take up one paradigm rather than another can be made based on how well the paradigm fits the subject under study and on the uses to which the conclusions will be put.

This introduces a second implication of paradigm theory: *It is absolutely crucial that we recognize the strengths and limitations of our paradigms, that we create them thoughtfully and responsibly, and that we use them appropriately.* I am reminded of my father's anger when he found me pounding a nail into a board with his favorite socket wrench. His problem wasn't with the fact that I wanted to get the nail into the board, only that I was using the wrong tool to do so.

These two implications in turn raise other questions: How can we gain control over the range of paradigms available? Which is best for preaching? Which, indeed, is true to the truth of Scripture? We will turn to these questions in chapter 4.

Optometry!

The Science behind the Prescription

Chapter 3 closed with this question: Which paradigms are best for preaching? Are more than one? Which, if any, are true to both the character of the text and the context of the preaching event? Which shorten the journey from text to sermon?

Traditionally the dominant focus of exegesis for preaching has been on "authorial intent": The text means what the author meant. Yet as we saw in chapter 2, many of the paradigms which have been used in the study of the Bible have been designed to yield something other than this—historical information about "what actually happened," theological nuances that may have been only dimly visible to the writer and his reader, or perhaps just principles to live by. Yet these very intentions may mean that we treat the text in ways for which it was not intended. When we dismantle the story of the anointing of Jesus and look for earlier versions of the tradition, we are doing something that Luke would have found puzzling and probably even objectionable. By the same token, we may suppose that Luke would have been just as puzzled by the allegorical spin Chrysostom put on the story, and while he would have marveled at Luther's rhetorical twist, he would not have recognized his own hand in it. The thumbprint here is Luther's, not Luke's.

I am reminded here of a brief conversation I had with my daughter when she returned home from preschool. "Daddy," she said, "would you like to hear the story of Little Red Riding Hood?" I am always ready for a good story, so I sat down to listen. She began:

> Once upon a time there was a little girl named Red Riding Hood. Her grandma was sick, so her mother sent her off to grandma's house with a basket of goodies—biscuits and wine.

Now, mention of biscuits and wine caught my ear. We seldom have biscuits, and we do not keep wine in our house. I guessed that she was reciting to me a version of the story she had heard at school. Suddenly I found my interest shifting. Rather than listening to the story, I was listening for other clues about the version she had taken over. Had she heard it at school? Was its diction British? In a sense, I was listening *through* the story, rather than to it. My daughter was wise enough to stop me: "Daddy," she said. "You're not listening to my story! Now pay attention!" And she was right. By focusing on the matter of sources, I had permitted myself to lose track of the story itself. This may be exactly what happens when biblical scholars dismantle the text in search of underlying historical facts. We lose track of the story itself.

IN SEARCH OF A PARADIGM FOR PREACHING

In recent years an increasing number of interpreters have begun to attune their sensitivities to the effects the text is expected to have on the readers for whom it was written.[1] It is

---

[1]For discussions of reader-response criticism in the biblical literature, see especially Robert Fowler, "Reader-Response Criticism and the

the thesis of this book that this emerging paradigm is especially helpful for preachers because the rhetorical structure of the text can inform and sometimes directly shape the rhetorical structure of the sermon. In an important recent discussion, *Preaching and the Literary Forms of the Bible,* Thomas Long suggests exactly the same about the literary *form* of the text:

> The literary form and dynamics of a biblical text can and should be important factors in the preacher's navigation of the distance between text and sermon. . . . More and more, biblical scholars have augmented the methods of textual interpretation to include literary and rhetorical approaches, thereby expanding both the avenues of access to biblical texts and the range of possibilities for hearing the claims of those texts on contemporary life.[2]

When we make this affirmation, we need not abandon authorial intent as the primary control for interpretation. Indeed, authors intentionally design their texts to be read in particular ways. If we wish to understand the texts in the ways that authors intend them, we must design our paradigm to replicate what authors expected their readers to do. In practical terms this means reconstructing the presuppositions, predispositions, prior information, and protocols that the biblical authors assumed on the part of their readers.

This is something that the texts themselves ask of us. If we use the historical dimensions of a text for some other purpose—and surely this is legitimate—we nevertheless read against the grain. In the introduction to his superb "close reading" of the Jesus sayings, Robert Tannehill voices exactly this concern:

Gospel of Mark," in *Loaves and Fishes: The Function of the Feeding Stories in the Gospel of Mark* (Chico, Calif.: Scholars Press, 1981) 149–79; and James L. Resseguie, "Reader-Response Criticism and the Synoptic Gospels," *Journal of the American Academy of Religion* 52 (1984) 307–24. Fowler's book is now carried forward in *Let the Reader Understand: Reader-Response Criticism and the Gospel of Mark* (Philadelphia: Fortress, 1991). The finest survey and evaluation to date is that of Stephen Moore, *Literary Criticism and the Gospels: Theoretical Challenges* (New Haven: Yale University Press, 1989). My own study also falls within this category: Jerry Camery-Hoggatt, *Irony in Mark: Text and Subtext* (SNTSMS; Cambridge: Cambridge University Press, 1992).

[2]Thomas Long, *Preaching and the Literary Forms of the Bible* (Philadelphia: Fortress, 1989) 11.

When the scholar uses these texts as sources of information about historical events, persons, or views which lie behind them, he is forcing concerns which are subordinate in the text into a dominant position. This may be legitimate, for there are many purposes which a text may serve. However, it means that the scholar and the text are working at cross-purposes, and the information must be extracted in spite of the stubborn efforts of the text to speak in its own way. . . . One can properly claim to interpret a text only if he takes into account the intention embodied in the text. The interpreter . . . must recognize and respect the particular kind of event which is intended to take place between text and reader and clarify the nature of that event for others.[3]

Tannehill is right. How can we know what a native reader would understand from a text unless we do what a native reader would do with the text? How can we expect to read authentically until we first clarify the social and religious dimensions of early Christian life—who the reader of the text was, what the reader might have known or not known, and how the reader was expected to respond?

Perhaps the most important questions concern the connection between exegesis and exposition: Where do the results of the paradigm shift leave us regarding the tasks of preaching? Long suggests that the connection here is a natural one:

The writers of scripture faced a communication problem similar to the one encountered by the contemporary preacher—finding the most effective rhetorical shape for their messages. Recent biblical scholarship has, in fact, been attentive to the many rhetorical strategies the early writers employed. Nonetheless, while there is an abundance of talk in the preaching literature about the use of images, plots, arguments, and poetic devices, as they appear within *sermons,* there is not much help about what sense or use to make of those very same elements when they appear in the *texts* from which those sermons spring.[4]

The implication of Long's statement is that the shift in exegetical focus from the author to the reader may offer us new insights into the ways in which the text can shape and inform the task of preaching.

This, of course, raises the questions that will occupy our attention in the next major section of this book: What, exactly,

---

[3]Tannehill, *Sword of His Mouth,* 7.
[4]Long, *Preaching and the Literary Forms of the Bible,* 12.

do we do when we read? Is reading private and subjective? Or are its protocols widely shared? Can they be organized into a paradigm? These are large questions, and to answer them we will turn to a variety of disciplines: cognitive psychology, literary theory, reading remediation theory, and discourse analysis.

THE PRIMARY CHARACTERISTICS OF LANGUAGE

The starting point for an understanding of what we do when we read is the observation that the mind moves through its various tasks *strategically*—it functions most effectively when presented with problems.[5] Language is one of its primary tools for addressing problems, and much of what we think and say is strategic in intent. Language communicates information, opinions, attitudes, and points of view. It is used in an enormous variety of discourses—scientific, metaphorical, political, poetic, devotional. An argument could even be made that the tapestry of perceptions that makes up our world is woven of linguistic threads. Language sometimes does more than communicate information only. That "something more" is worthy of affirmation and understanding; no accounting of language can be adequate that ignores it. We also use language to persuade, alienate, confuse, humor, and entertain. Words are woven into the very woof and warp of the world.

And yet there is a more elemental sense in which the structure and character of language itself poses problems. The manner in which the mind addresses the larger, more complex questions of language is shaped and conditioned by the way it resolves the primary, elemental problems of language. What this means for our purposes is that the conventions and protocols of reading are conditioned and shaped by the properties of language itself. Any adequate understanding of how language works must begin here.

The five primary characteristics of language are these:

- *Language is selective.* It cannot present every detail of the story line without becoming unmanageable.

---

[5]See Wallace Chafe, "Some Things That Narratives Tell Us about the Mind," in *Narrative Thought and Narrative Language,* ed. Bruce Britton and A. D. Pellegrini (Hillsdale, N.J.: Erlbaum, 1990) 97.

- *Language is inherently ambiguous.* Because words must sometimes carry double meanings, language is always potentially ambiguous.

- *Language is polyvalent.* It carries meaning on a variety of levels—emotional, cognitive, social, personal.

- *Language has aural texture.* It sounds a certain way on the ear.

- *Language is linear.* It can only present its information in a specific sequence, one word after the other.

These are features of language as such, and therefore of objective, historical, or scientific language as well as imaginative and figurative language. The problems created by these features are overcome in various ways by various types of discourse. For example, scientific language tends to pare away ambiguities by using a rigidly precise technical vocabulary and by defining context in terms of standardized forms and commonly recognized scientific procedures. By contrast, literary language tends to *exploit* ambiguity to rhetorical advantage. Metaphorical and poetic language in fact may depend upon the reader's ability to associate competing and complementary dimensions of stress. Scientific language deals with the features of language in one way, while metaphorical language deals with them in another. Yet for both, the primary features are central organizing concerns. Since these are native to language as such, it is worth looking at them more closely.

Language Is Selective

The first characteristic of language is this: *Language is selective.* By this we mean that it cannot say everything. Something must be left for the reader to do. (The speaker who tries to say everything will soon discover that no one is willing or able to listen that long.) This means that there are "gaps" in the linguistic exchange. A writer is therefore forced to trust the reader to fill in the gaps in information from his or her own store of resources. But the reader is not free to fill in gaps willy-nilly. Gap filling is, in fact, informed and determined by the details which *are* included as well as by the cultural context within which the language is being used. The protocols by which we fill in gaps will occupy our attention in chapters 5 and 6.

Language Is Inherently Ambiguous

The second primary feature of language derives from the fact that language falls on the ear gate and not the eye gate. It is composed primarily of sound. Because the stock of sounds in any given language is necessarily limited, words must sometimes do double duty: *Language is therefore inherently ambiguous.* The task of interpretation requires that we have some way of "disambiguating," sorting through the options and arriving at a clear understanding of the speaker's intended meaning. The protocols by which we disambiguate will occupy our attention in chapters 7 and 8.

Language Is Polyvalent

Sometimes the ambiguities of language are intentional: *Language is polyvalent.* By this we mean that it strikes us on several levels. The inherent ambiguity of language suggests that several dimensions of stress may operate at the same time. When this happens, we may hear several things at once, as in wordplays, allusions, or double entendres. Some of the different dimensions of stress will strike us on several levels. Language may evoke responses that are purely intellectual or deeply emotional. It may make us angry, may entertain us, may demand that we make changes in the way we go about our business. The protocols by which we recognize and deal with polyvalence will occupy our attention in chapter 9.

Language Has Aural Texture

The fact that it falls on the ear rather than the eye also accounts for the fourth primary feature of language: *It has aural texture.* It sounds a certain way on the ear. The speaker's voice may be melodic or harsh, rhythmical or jarring, loud or soft. It may bark a sharp command or trail off into a sliding glissando. But those sounds are not incidental to meaning. Indeed, sometimes they represent critical dimensions of the linguistic exchange. The texture of sound can be used to convey the point of view from which the speaker asks that the story elements be judged good or bad. It can create and sustain mood and can suggest dissonance between the story's form and its content. The protocols by which we deal with aural texture will occupy our attention in chapter 10.

Language Is Linear

The final primary feature of language is this: *Language is linear.* By this we mean that it presents its information to the reader one word after another. Imagine for a moment that you have in front of you a coffee mug. All the properties of the mug are present to you continuously through time. Now imagine that you are describing the mug to someone over the telephone. You would have to begin somewhere and end somewhere. This involves making choices. Should you begin by identifying it as a mug? Which features should come first? The color? The size? The heft of it? Now imagine that you are on the other end of the telephone line. You encounter the features of the mug, but in a particular sequence. At any point along the way, you will only have the information that has been disclosed thus far. You may well guess at what is coming next, but your guess is always liable to be upset as more information is fed along the linguistic pipeline. The protocols by which we deal with sequence will occupy our attention in chapter 11.

IMPLICATIONS

We have surveyed five basic features of language. Language is selective, ambiguous, and polyvalent; it has aural texture; and it is linear. For our purposes, these together suggest two important implications for understanding the way in which the biblical writers have used language to interpret for us the meaning of the events they record.

First, *a story about an event simply cannot be the same as the event itself.* At each moment, the biblical writers had to make choices, and each choice affected the way the story would be understood. The writers had to decide what to include and what to leave out, in what sequence to disclose the details, what vocabulary to use, whether to create allusions to other literature, and whether and where to add explanatory remarks to help the reader understand what the story means. Luke did this, too, as he worked with his sources to give us our story of the anointing of Jesus. This means that the story is connected to the event in complex ways.

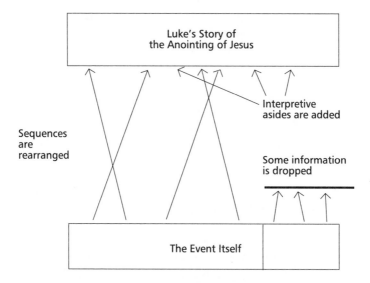

FIGURE 4.1: THE RELATIONSHIP BETWEEN STORY AND EVENT

Such decisions were not made randomly. Instead they were made on the basis of what Luke considered the inner significance that lay at the story's core. The content of the Gospel story was governed by the evangelist's sense of what the story meant—the story's point—and that fact itself means that the story is *the event refracted through an interpretive filter.* It could hardly have been otherwise. All stories interpret the events they record, even the most objective news story or the most carefully researched historical account.

At first it would seem that the primary features of language are difficulties to be overcome. It is a problem that language is selective, since the gaps in information leave open the possibility of misunderstanding. But a closer look reveals that these apparent difficulties are also opportunities for rhetorical strategizing. For example, the selectivity of language also means that the evangelist can withhold information to create intrigue or suspense. He can dawdle on apparently insignificant details to stress one element or to set the reader up to react to another element in a particular way. This, then, is the second implication for our understanding of rhetorical strategies: *The opportunities for rhetorical strategizing—the call to conversion—are resident in the nature of language itself.* The biblical writers took full advantage of them in the interests of furthering the gospel.

We have noted two significances of the primary features of language. First, the story is not the same as the event it describes. The evangelist shaped the telling according to what he believed to be the point of the story. Second, the primary and secondary features of language are not only obstacles to be overcome but also opportunities for rhetorical play. These two significances are actually closely related. By managing the reader's responses, the biblical writer invites the reader to share a particular point of view, a particular way of understanding the story of Jesus, and thus by extension also a way of understanding the claims the Gospel story makes on the reader's own life. It is in this way that the language of the Gospel becomes a vehicle of transformation. In the biblical stories we not only gain new information about the ways God works in the biblical world; we also come to view our own world in a new and different light. We enter the biblical story judging reality in one way, and we leave it judging reality in another. By managing the reader's responses, the evangelist makes the text a vehicle of transformation.

In this chapter we have surveyed rapidly the five primary characteristics of language. Each feature calls for its own kind of interpretive protocols. Each of those protocols in turn suggests an appropriate criterion for validity in interpretation. We will discuss each criterion in turn in the chapters that follow.

FINDING THE RIGHT PRESCRIPTION

What happens in the far more intricate cases of text-interpretation and what constitutes the key problem of hermeneutics is already foreshadowed in the interpretive process as it occurs in ordinary language. Thus the whole problem of text-interpretation could be renewed by the recognition of its roots in the functioning of ordinary language.

— Paul Ricoeur

SEEING WHAT ISN'T THERE

How We Fill in Gaps

Let us open this chapter with two folktales that together illustrate a central protocol of reading. The first is British and is very short:

> A man woke up terrified and reached for the matches so he could light a candle. The matches were put into his hand.

When I first heard this story it sent a chill shivering up and down my spine. In this chapter we're interested in the source of the chill. What happened here? What prompted the chill? Surely it was not because of something the story said. Instead the chill came because of some interpretive work I was asked to do on my own.

The second story is a New England folktale:

A city slicker went for a hunting trip with a guide in the Maine woods. Come morning time, the guide sent the slicker down to the pond to fetch a pail of water. In less than a minute, that slicker was back in the cabin, the pail rattlin' in his hand, and he was white as a sheet.

"Why're you so het up, slicker?" asked the guide.

"There's a bear down there in the pond, up to his belly button," said the slicker.

"Well, shucks," said the guide. "Don't you know he's just as scared of you as you are of him?"

"Well, then," said the slicker. "In that case the water wasn't fittin' for to drink anyhow."

This story is funnier. Why the laughter? Like the first, this one depends upon the reader actively working out images and conclusions that are only suggested by the story. These two stories together call attention to one of the elemental protocols of reading: We automatically fill in the gaps in what is said.

We seem to be impaled on the horns of a dilemma: We cannot leave the gaps unfilled, yet we are not free to fill them in in any way we choose. This suggests an important dimension of the literary experience: Differences between reader's responses are often based as much on what the text does not say as upon what it does! It does not take much insight to realize that the manner in which we fill in gaps accounts for a large part of the difficulties and challenges of interpretation. There are important implications here for preachers who may wonder why the same sermon will fall on deaf ears for the college professor in the back of the sanctuary, but be thunderously prophetic to the banker in the narthex and whisperingly personal to the lawyer who sits in the third pew, right side, three spaces in. As they listen to the language of the sermon, the professor, the banker, and the lawyer will inevitably fill in the gaps in differing ways, with differing degrees of interest and differing levels of skill. Any accounting of language and its functions must in some way broker a solution to this problem. Without an integrated under-standing of how we fill in gaps, we are left with a reductionist understanding of language, one that is unable to account for the wide range of understandings and misunderstandings that occur wherever communication takes place.

GAP FILLING AND THE PSYCHOLOGY OF LANGUAGE

Effective communication depends upon the fact that speakers expect their listeners to fill in the gaps in predictable ways. In fact, much of learning a language consists of learning the things that native speakers don't have to say. On the highest level, this fact has been called interpersonal consistency in interpretation. On a more basic level, it explains why my opening folktale about the city slicker and the bear usually elicits a laugh from an English-speaking audience but leaves an African cold. Interpersonal consistency in gap filling means that these processes are subject to rules and controls, just as the grammatical organization of sentences is subject to rules and controls. Gap filling is therefore patterned and not chaotic. If we could reconstruct those patterns, we would also be able to replicate the unfolding awareness of the story line that the biblical writers expected of their readers.

Notice that gap filling as I have been describing it is not the same thing as reconstructing what actually happened. From the standpoint of reading theory, we are interested only in uncovering the manner in which the reader of the text is expected to fill in the gaps as they are encountered, one after the other. Seen in this light, the combination of selectivity and linearity in language represents not so much an obstacle as an opportunity, something to be seized upon and used. The evangelist will use the gaps to manage the reader's understanding, setting the reader up for surprises, rhetorical turns, and insights. Much of what makes language elegant and much of what gives it its depth and power may be found in the way the mind deals with and overcomes the problems that the gaps create. Sometimes we have no choice but to read between the lines. But how?

Schemas

From a psychological point of view, the issue of gap filling centers on semantic memory. How is linguistic information stored in the mind? How is it accessed and used? What difficulties do we encounter, and how do we resolve them? The literature about semantic memory is growing rapidly, and is nowhere near complete. Even at this stage, however, there appears to be an emerging consensus that semantic memory is not stored as discrete units but as hierarchies of features, clustered around central organizing nodes. Cognitive scientists have employed the term "schema" to describe these hierarchies.[1] It is the schemas that enable the reader to fill in the gaps with appropriate information. For example, the semiologist Umberto Eco describes the ways in which basic dictionary meanings enable the reader to access additional supporting information:

> If the text says that /once upon a time there was a young princess called Snow White. She was very pretty/, the reader detects by a first semantic analysis of "princess" that Snow White is surely a "woman." The sememe "princess" is virtually much more complex (for instance, "woman" entails "human female," and a human female should be represented by many properties such as having certain body organs and so forth).[2]

If we were to elaborate a schema for Eco's comments about the term "princess," it might look something like Figure 5.1. Each node in the hierarchy provides access to subordinate nodes, and each of those in turn provides access to additional information yet further removed.

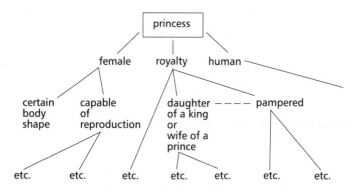

FIGURE 5.1: A SCHEMA FOR PRINCESS

[1]The literature on schemas is now mushrooming. See: M. Minsky, "A Framework for Representing Knowledge," in *The Psychology of Computer Vision,* ed. P. H. Winston (New York: McGraw-Hill, 1975); Patrick Winston, *Artificial Intelligence* (Reading, Mass.: Addison-Wesley, 1977); R. C. Schank and R. P. Abelson, *Scripts, Plans, Goals and Understanding* (Hillsdale, N.J.: Erlbaum, 1977); D. E. Rumelhart, "Schemata: The Building Blocks of Cognition," in *Theoretical Issues in Reading Comprehension,* ed. R. Spiro, B. Bruce, and W. Brewer (Hillsdale, N.J.: Erlbaum, 1980).
[2]Umberto Eco, *The Role of the Reader* (Bloomington: Indiana University Press, 1979) 18.

The Lexicon

Cognitive scientists employ the term "lexicon" to describe those schemas which are encoded into the reader's vocabulary. What is important here is that studies of the lexicon appear to confirm a structure very much like that suggested in Eco's comments about the term "princess." In 1969, Allan Collins and M. Ross Quillian conducted a series of experiments that measured the time it took for subjects to retrieve from memory the information necessary to determine whether a statement is true or false, for example, "A canary can fly."[3] The underlying assumption of the study was that the rule of parsimony can be applied to the mind: The mind will seek an economical organization of information. Rather than storing information as bits of unrelated data, the mind will organize the data into meaningful structures. The more central a fact is in the organization, the faster the retrieval time. For this to work, Collins and Quillian reasoned that the lexicon would be organized into complexes of features (Figure 5.2).

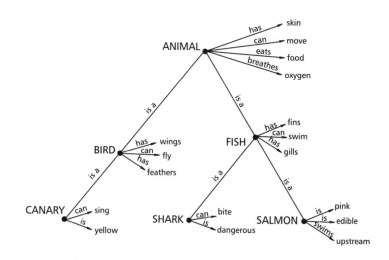

FIGURE 5.2: THE STRUCTURE OF THE LEXICON

---

[3] Allan Collins and M. Ross Quillian, "Retrieval Time from Semantic Memory," *Journal of Verbal Learning and Verbal Behavior* 8 (1969) 240–47.

A comparison of reaction times indicates that this is so. In order to determine whether or not a canary can fly, the subject first accesses one node, then a subordinate node, then another, following a pathway down through ever-refined configurations of information. The further removed the information stands in the hierarchy, the longer the question takes to answer. It appears that Collins and Quillian have charted out the schemas of the lexicon as measurable phenomena.

Here, then, was a simple and elegant solution to the problem of gaps in language: The basic information for gap filling is retrieved from the reader's lexicon. The lexicon is made up of schemas, which in turn are made up of hierarchies of features and not discrete items. In the course of the reading, the mention of each word automatically accesses a range of features, any one of which may later be assumed to be part of the reader's background understanding.

At this point we must pause for a refinement of terms. From what has been said thus far it would appear that there is a sort of one-for-one correspondence between schemas and words. Each word evokes one schema. But this is not exactly so. Instead, a single word may house several quite different schemas. The word "bug" may house a schema for "insect," a schema for "listening device," a schema for "type of automobile," and a schema for "something children do to parents who are trying to write books." There is relevance here for our understanding of the language of our story of the anointing in Luke. In 1859 John Lightfoot set out a number of possible uses—we would now say schemas—for the term with which Luke describes the woman. She is a "sinner," *hamartōlos*.[4] According to Lightfoot, a first-century Jewish woman who was a "sinner" could be guilty of any of the following:

- giving her husband food that had not been properly tithed

- allowing her husband to embrace her during her menstrual period

- failing to keep a vow

- acting loud and clamorous

---

[4]John Lightfoot, *A Commentary on the New Testament from the Talmud and Hebraica,* vol. 3, *Luke–John* (1859, reprint; Peabody, Mass.: Hendrickson, 1989) 85.

- doing her weaving in the street

- cursing her children

- cursing her husband's father in the presence of her husband

- falling into sexual immorality

This means that we need further clues before we can conclude that Luke's "sinful woman" was guilty of sexual sin or that she was a prostitute. In chapters 7 and 8 we will examine what those clues might be and how they enable the listener or reader to decide which schemas are intended by each word in the text. For now it is enough to note that sometimes there is rhetorical play between the different schemas housed under a single word. That rhetorical play is almost always untranslatable into a different language. Suppose the headline in the sports section reads:

MOTHER OF EIGHT SHOOTS HOLE IN ONE

This creates a kind of internal dissonance that is lost completely when the sentence is translated into, say, French or German. The reason for the loss of sense is that the interplay of synonyms, antonyms, and homonyms will be disrupted in the move from one language to another.

Schemas Are Only Partially Instantiated

As we shall see in chapter 7, there are limits to the amount of information we can process at any given time. This means that more complex schemas are only partially instantiated. They may be collapsed into their largest structures or extended almost indefinitely by the accessing and review of subschemas, which are nodes of information resident in the larger schemas.[5] If I asked you to visualize the supermarket in which you normally shop, likely you would do so in a large, generalized picture. Now visualize the meat counter and describe the layout of the chicken section. To make those changes you zoom visually to the subschema of "meat counter." You could zoom in once

---

[5]For a good summary, see ch. 2 of A. Sanford and S. Garrod, *Understanding Written Language* (London: Wiley, 1981).

again to describe the number of rows of chicken packages that are set out. Or you could zoom back to the larger frame of the market as a whole. If you zoomed out, however, the smaller schemas would be absorbed into the larger ones, which leads to a corresponding loss of detail.[6] This sort of movement goes on continually as we hear and process verbal information. We access schemas only partially, and then we follow whatever routes are necessary to access and develop additional information as we need it.

Context plays an important role in this process. Suppose I said,

The rubber ball shattered when it hit the ground.

This would certainly sound odd, because one of the primary features of rubber is that it bounces. That's all the information that is accessed. But suppose I said,

After it had been immersed in liquid hydrogen, the rubber ball shattered when it hit the ground.

This doesn't sound odd because the reference to liquid hydrogen calls up additional information about rubber. Rubber becomes brittle when exposed to extreme cold. Now—because of something in the context—we can say that this additional information is "instantiated." Sometimes inferences drawn from context may be enough to instantiate secondary information like this, but one has to have clear contextual—or grammatical or formal or thematic or syntactical—evidence to support that conclusion.

Schemas Are Built As Needed

Potentially, there are as many schemas as there are kinds of experience. In actuality, though, the number of available schemas is closely limited. Because we build them out of experience, the schemas with which we are most familiar will be more richly developed. Thus, while their number is potentially infinite, a catalog of an individual's actual lexicon of schemas

---

[6]There is a physiological reason for the loss of detail: The mind can manage only a small number of details at a time. See George Miller, "The Magical Number Seven, Plus or Minus Two: Some Limits on Our Capacity for Processing Information," *Psychological Review* 63 (1956) 81–97.

would represent a virtual contour map of his or her cultural range: birthday party, courtroom, ski lift, supermarket, wedding rehearsal, college hazing, football game. Ultimately this translates out to cultural norms. (We will turn to the matter of cultural norms in chapter 6.)

Schemas may be stereotyped and held in common by all native speakers of the language ("used-car salesmen"). They may be quite specific and created on the spot ("You know how boring old Professor Camery-Hoggatt can be."). Or they may be quite formal ("Dearly beloved, we are gathered here today . . . "). Whatever their origin, all of these are hierarchically ordered knowledge structures. One can hardly overestimate their importance for reading. They create enabling contexts upon which readers can draw for the information they need if they are to fill in the gaps properly. With only the barest of clues, the reader can access the schema in its entirety and then zoom in and out of its nodes of information to fill in gaps.

Schemas Enable Comprehension Itself

Not only do schemas provide additional background information; they have been shown to be integral factors in comprehension itself. Without the information they supply, the text may appear fragmented and incoherent. This was demonstrated in 1974 in a study by J. D. Bransford and M. K. Johnson.[7] In this study, subjects were given the following paragraph, then tested on their comprehension and recall of the paragraph's details:

> The procedure is actually quite simple. First you arrange things into different groups. Of course one pile may be sufficient depending on how much there is to do. If you have to go somewhere else due to lack of facilities that is the next step, otherwise you are pretty well set. It is important not to overdo things. That is, it is better to do too few things at once than too many. In the short run this may not seem important but complications can easily arise. A mistake can be expensive as well. At first the whole procedure will seem complicated. Soon however, it will become just another facet of life. It is difficult to foresee any end to the necessity for

---

[7]On this experiment see J. D. Bransford and N. S. McCarrell, "A Sketch of a Cognitive Approach to Comprehension," in *Cognition and the Symbolic Processes,* ed. Walter Weimer and David Palermo (New York: John Wiley and Sons, 1974) 206.

this task in the immediate future, but then one never can tell. After the procedure is completed one arranges the material into different groups again. Then they can be put into their appropriate places. Eventually they will be used once more and the whole cycle will then have to be repeated. However, that is a part of life.

Clearly, what is in view here is a particular schema, but which? Without appropriate guidance, the paragraph appears puzzling. Subjects in the study recalled only bits and pieces. A second group was tested on the same paragraph, only this group was provided with a name for the schema: "washing clothes." Now read the paragraph again. In the experiments conducted by Bransford and Johnson, comprehension and recall improved dramatically when the subjects knew in advance the names of the schemas they were reading about. The experience of reading this with and without an identifying schema shows just how deft the mind is at constructing appropriate nodes of information and using them as sources of background information for filling in gaps.

Schemas May Be Instantiated in a Variety of Ways

A speaker or author may use any of several strategies to evoke a particular schema. One can simply name the schema: "I was in the *supermarket* the other day." One can use technical jargon from the schema: "John was *stocking shelves,* and Sue was *checking.*" (When one technical term appears in the text, the reader's suspicions may be aroused, in which case the schema is partially instantiated. A second technical term will often be quite enough to bring the partial schema to full consciousness.)

Let us shift to an entirely different sort of schema. Consider the following:

"All rise."

"Your honor, I object."

"Do you swear to tell the truth, the whole truth, and nothing but the truth?"

"How do you plead?"

"The defense rests."

"We find the defendant guilty as charged."

These are all stock phrases from the schema "court trial." A native reader of English would know that and would need very little direct orientation to be sure. The schema, on the other hand, even though it is tacitly evoked, provides a world of orienting clues by which the reader can fill in the gaps in the language.

It is not at all necessary that the technical language be sustained or richly developed to evoke a specialized schema. The sign CHAINS REQUIRED is quite enough to evoke images of icy roads, with all the subordinate bits of information that those images carry with them. Very much of the gap filling activity of natural language is carried along on the back of technical jargon and stock phrases, and verbal competence can be largely measured by how ably one moves about in the world of features they evoke.

Schemas Interact with One Another

Schema theory also explains how vocabulary words interact with one another. This happens in two directions, one having to do with the ways in which they corroborate and limit one another, the other having to do with the ways in which smaller categories create access to larger ones. Often the realities of a schema connect it with larger, more inclusive schemas. The schema "tree" is an umbrella term and includes a greater possible range of features than does the schema "acacia." At the same time, the term "acacia" is more specific, and its features in the lexicon can be worked out in more concrete detail. The term "tree," however, is itself part of a yet larger category, "plant life." This is important. As we shall see, the larger category under which a particular schema is housed also provides important nodes of information upon which the reader can draw for filling in gaps. Since different languages organize realities according to different categories, they may well refract the details of the language through very different schematic grids. For an American Protestant the schema for "pig" almost certainly includes a node for "taste," which a Middle Eastern Moslem would find difficult even to imagine. The Moslem includes "pig" in a category that is tagged for taboo: Pigs are "animals that must not be eaten."

Schemas Are Sometimes Self-referential

We should also note that schemas are sometimes self-referential. That is, sometimes the important features have to do with the names or structures of the schemas themselves. Consider the following, from Robert Byrne:

> To err is human
> To purr feline.

A native speaker of English will easily recognize that the word "purr" was chosen because it rhymes with "err." In the same way, but more subtly, the word "feline" rhymes with the word "divine" from Alexander Pope's saying that lies behind Byrne's couplet: "To err is human, to forgive, divine." The allusion and the rhyme represent the controlling factors that determined the selection and arrangement of the words in the first place. The schemas are self-referential to the degree that their operative features include the sounds of the words themselves. This self-referential aspect of schemas may be the most difficult to translate from one language to another. The saying could be translated into another language quite without loss of syntactical or lexical sense, but the controlling factors that governed the selection and arrangement of the terms would be lost completely.

The same limitation is true in the movement from Greek to English. For example, the Greeks were fond of etching the following inscription on their drinking fountains:

> "Wash the sin as well as the face."

In terms of grammar and syntax, this is a fair translation. What it misses is that in Greek this is a palindrome.[8] It reads the same way in either direction (like "Anna" or "Apollo, Pa."):

N I S P O N A N O M I M A T A M I M O N A N O P S I N

If we approach the matter from the standpoint that the primary function of language is to convey information, the loss of the

---

[8]This example was taken from Bill Bryson, *The Mother Tongue: English and How It Got That Way* (New York: Morrow, 1990) 227.

palindrome is insignificant. If we approach it from the viewpoint that the effect on the reader is essential, and not incidental to meaning, the loss of the palindrome represents a significant loss indeed.

Schemas Differ from One Language to Another

Thus the schemas provide a way of cataloging ranges of features—which are necessary, which are not, which are central, which are more remote. These aspects of schema theory will later prove to be important when we consider the linguistic factors involved in the movement from one culture to another. When we simply translate word for word, we can easily overlook subsidiary nodes of information that are found in the schemas of the original language but not in the schemas of the receptor language. In the same way, literal word-for-word translation may overlook the secondary connections between the differing schemas housed within the same term. This happens when the complex activities of translation are reduced to a simple process of selecting a target term out of a number of options from the lexicon while ignoring the possibility that there is rhetorical play among the options.

It may be helpful to apply this discussion to the biblical literature itself, since that is our ultimate concern. One of the clearest ways in which schemas function is when they introduce analogies—"this is like that." Notice, however, that for an analogy to function correctly, the listener must have specific schematic competence. If the analogy says,

That went over like a lead balloon,

the reader must access schemas for "that" (the implied antecedent of the pronoun), for "lead," and for "balloon." The expression "lead balloon" is oxymoronic, and the reader knows it is not to be taken literally. What is in view is a crash. This gives a secondary meaning to the opening verbal complex, "went over."

By the same token, when Jesus says in Mark 10:15,

Whoever does not receive the kingdom of God like a little child, shall not enter it,

the listener must summon up a range of features for "receiving the kingdom of God" and for "child" and then must decide which features are shared between them. The difficulty here is that the features that are typical and obvious to an English speaker may be different from those which are typical and obvious to a speaker of Greek or Aramaic. In a short study of the homiletics of this verse, Richard White explores the ways in which the modern preacher can short-circuit the exegetical task by assuming that the unspoken spaces between the words are the same in English as in Greek.[9] Thus, "the preacher's fertile imagination and acculturation dictate a whole catalogue of virtues personified by the ideal child."[10] These include honesty, trust, dependence, obedience, innocence, and so forth. Yet—and here's the rub—"what everybody believed in first century Palestine is *not* what everybody believes now—at least not on this subject. . . . Jesus was assuming that everyone knew children were 'trivial,' 'weak' and 'poor,' 'having no standing' and 'come empty-handed like a beggar.' "[11] This emphasis on coming to the kingdom empty-handed is, of course, something we see quite readily in other passages of Scripture in which Jesus insists that the kingdom comes to the outcast. Why, asks White, do we miss it so often in this passage? The answer is that although the Greek term *paidion* really does mean "child" (and although this is an exactly proper translation), the Greek term accesses a very different schema, with a very different range of features.

IMPLICATIONS

This chapter has explored the ways in which the reader uses schemas as a resource for filling in the gaps in language. This suggests that the information encoded into the reader's lexicon is organized in complex and nuanced ways. Schemas may be collapsed into their component parts, may be self-referential, may by stylized and held in common by all native speakers of the language, or may be highly idiosyncratic. In whatever forms they appear, it is now clear that they are a primary means for

---

[9] Richard C. White, "Preaching between the Lines," in *The Best in Theology: Volume Two,* ed. Paul Fromer (Carol Stream, Ill.: Christianity Today, n.d.) 419–21.

[10] Ibid., 419.

[11] Ibid., 420.

filling in the gaps in the language of the text and are integral to comprehension itself.

For this reason, while schema theory offers a solution to the problem of how we go about filling in gaps in one language, it brings into sharp focus the serious difficulties we face as we interpret the Bible for a different cultural and linguistic setting. The discipline that examines the meanings of Greek and Hebrew terms is called lexicography. What we have seen thus far tells us that lexicography is significant not only because each word of the text may be theologically loaded but also because the schemas of the reader's lexicon are the reader's primary resource for filling in the gaps in the Bible's language. When we do lexical study, at the very least we must try and reconstruct the schemas that are instantiated by each new term in the text. This means that when we do our word studies, we must do more than just open a lexicon and pick from a list of translational options. We must also try to learn the full range of features that are possible for each term in the text. If we do not, we will have no way to fill in the gaps, no understanding of the range of schematic possibilities that were open to the original reader, no way to understand the natural readerly process of deciding between possible schemas. The rhetorical play that is created by the clash of schemas will be muffled or lost completely. On the other hand, if we take the range of features seriously, we very soon discover that the meaning of the biblical tradition is frequently shaped by considerations of rhythm and rhyme, sound and structure. Rhetorical play is everywhere.

But rhetorical play may run in different directions still because there are other resources for filling in gaps. We will turn to these in chapter 6.

How We Fill in Gaps 2

Social and Cultural Backgrounds

In the film *The Joy Luck Club* one scene was for me particularly arresting. Jing-Mei Woo—called June in America—has discovered that her mother once abandoned two infant daughters, June's half-sisters, on the side of a road in China. The mother dies without explaining to June why she would have done such a thing, and June has been left to wrestle with what this suggests about her mother's character. A major development in the plot is the discovery that the abandoned infants have survived and are still alive in China and that they believe their mother is still alive. June has been designated by the family to go in her mother's stead to tell her sisters in China that their mother has died. She wonders how she is to explain the abandonment. How, indeed, is she to understand it herself?

At this point, June's father steps in to retell the mother's story, not from an American point of view but from a Chinese one. The mother had been warned that the Japanese had invaded the province, and she had joined the stream of refugees trying to make their way to Chunking. Along the way she had contracted dysentery, and as she carried her children in slings from her shoulders, she had gradually weakened until she was certain she was going to die. But she also knew that if the babies were found in the presence of a dead body, no one would take them in because to do so would surely bring bad luck to the home. If she left them and went somewhere else to die, then they would have a better chance of survival. That is in fact what happened. She collapsed in the road and was later picked up by a hospital truck and given medical care. By the time she recovered, the babies were gone.

The point of this brief story is the heart of this chapter: Viewed through American eyes, to abandon one's children on the side of the road is unforgivable, an act of supreme selfishness or indifference. Through Chinese eyes, what June's mother did was a desperate act of heroism. It may, in fact, have saved the babies' lives. When June made this discovery, just before she embarked for China, it gave her a fresh appreciation for her mother, a kind of revelatory movement of compassion by which she came to understand what her mother had been through and how it must have been to have to take such a desperate and tragic step.

The point of this illustration doesn't stop there. Amy Tan wrote *The Joy Luck Club* for an English-speaking audience with American sensibilities. She knew that we would draw the same conclusions that June had and would view the abandonment of the children with the same scorn. Amy Tan knew we would default to our own cultural norms, just as June had. Thus, she withheld the father's explanation until the very end of the plot, where it springs on the audience like a trap. This is a stunning reversal, which the attentive moviegoer may experience without so much as noticing that it is the result of a carefully timed delivery of information.

CULTURAL LITERACY

With this observation we are brought to something sociologists have lately begun to call cultural literacy. There is some information that we expect of our readers simply because we share the same cultural environment. Amy Tan knew that we would default to certain norms, and she used that knowledge to entrap us.

Here are some of the ways those norms come packaged:

- rules and expectations of etiquette

- science

- procedures of production

- traffic laws

- information about how to deal with witches

- folk remedies

- information about agriculture, seasons, and the condition of the roads during the rainy season

- details about historical events, migrations, personal and social dynamics

- beliefs about society and about human nature

This list is endless. Readers draw freely from this body of cultural knowledge as part of their basic gap filling. This information, too, is organized as hierarchies of information—in schematic form—though those schemas may be larger and more complex in form than the schemas housed within the individual words of the lexicon.

Skill with cultural norms is a critical aspect of competent reading. There is no literacy without cultural literacy. Psychologists have established that this is so by studying the disruptions in reading protocols that occur when critical clues are missing. For example, in 1971 D. R. Dooling and R. Lachmann tested comprehension and recall for paragraphs such as the following:

> With hocked gems financing him, our hero bravely defied all scornful laughter that tried to prevent his scheme. Your eyes deceive you, he had said, an egg not a table correctly typifies this unexplored planet. Now three sisters sought proof, forging along

sometimes through calm vastness, yet more often over turbulent peaks and valleys. Days became weeks as many doubters spread fearful rumours about the edge. At last, from nowhere, welcome winged creatures appeared, signifying momentous success.[1]

A second group heard the same paragraph, only with a title: "Columbus Discovers America." Now read the paragraph again.

With hocked gems financing him, our hero bravely defied all scornful laughter that tried to prevent his scheme. Your eyes deceive you, he had said, an egg not a table correctly typifies this unexplored planet. Now three sisters sought proof, forging along sometimes through calm vastness, yet more often over turbulent peaks and valleys. Days became weeks as many doubters spread fearful rumours about the edge. At last, from nowhere, welcome winged creatures appeared, signifying momentous success.

Test results showed a dramatic difference in comprehension and recall. What this means, of course, is that the complicated work of gap filling absolutely requires adequate understanding of the historical and cultural schemas that are operative for the text in hand. At the same time, it suggests that when we fill in the gaps with information that the writer or reader could *not* have known, we will draw conclusions that the writer would not have intended.

Let us explore one additional example. In 1977 R. C. Schank and R. P. Abelson explored a different sort of schema under the rubric "scripts."[2] Schemas not only arrange facts; they also tell us what to expect of events. If the story begins by identifying the scene as "dinner out at a restaurant," the reader will likely know that this involves sitting together at a table, being approached by a waiter or waitress, ordering from a menu, and so forth. Usually these come in a predictable sequence. They are scripted activities, in which the characters are playing roles that were written and directed by society at large.

By contrast, in first-century Palestine the script "dinner party" was organized on a very different order. The primary movements of the anointing story rest upon the reader's knowledge of that script: When the guests arrive, they leave their

---

[1]D. R. Dooling and R. Lachmann, "Effects of Comprehension on Retention of Prose," *Journal of Experimental Psychology* 88 (1971) 216–22.

[2]Schank and Abelson, *Scripts, Plans, Goals, and Understanding.*

shoes at the door; there is an exchange of kisses; the host is obligated to see that the guest's feet are washed; guests recline at table, with their feet extended out behind them; village folk are permitted to observe from the perimeters of the room; and so forth. This is the script for our story of the anointing of Jesus. What gives the story its punch is the way it ends, by pointing out that the host has violated the norm and is himself therefore hardly "guiltless." Luke's reader does not know about the violation until the story's end; in the meantime the reader defaults to the norm and reads as though the host has fulfilled all of his responsibilities to his guest.

Although we are little aware of it, most of our social interaction is scripted out in these ways. Like other schemas, the scripts for social interaction are constructed with typicality as their primary organizing feature. The typicality means that the ritual dances of life are choreographed by social experience. We earn our place in the dance troupe by copying the principal dancers who went before us—where they wheel and turn, how they execute their pirouette, and when they stop and bow. In return for our trouble, we can proceed with the confidence that when we perform the pas de deux, we will be in step and our partner will not trip us. The problem is that when we read texts that were written to be read against the background norms of a different culture, our tendency to default to our own norms may lead to serious misunderstanding. The native readers of the biblical texts would have drawn quite different inferences from those reached by readers looking back through two thousand years of historical, social, and scientific development.

This point was brought home to me by a conversation I once had with a student. I knew something about the student that she did not know I knew: She was a single mother, her child was in the custody of the Department of Child Welfare, and she suspected that the child was being abused by his primary caregiver. She stopped me one afternoon by the drinking fountain and asked if I would explain to her the meaning of a verse in Mark: "Suffer the little children to come to me."

I asked, "What do you think the verse means?"

Her answer: "I think it means that little children are supposed to suffer and that that will drive them into the arms of Jesus."

It was painful for me to correct her misunderstanding. After all, her interpretation of that verse was part of what enabled her to deal with the problem she faced as a mother: Her child was being abused, and she had "claimed" this verse as a promise from God. All would turn out all right in the end. But I also understood something of the mental processes that had brought her to this place. She had defaulted to the *modern* English schema for "suffer" and by doing so had jury-rigged an interpretation that made sense to her but would probably have alarmed Mark very much.

What happened here is a paradigm for the way that our natural tendency to default to our own situation can straitjacket us into difficult and even dangerous misperceptions. The error lies in our assumption that what is taken for granted in our culture—what "makes sense" to us—is also what is taken for granted in the culture of the Bible. So long as we can make sense of the text on the basis of our own cultural norms, it may never occur to us that the reader for whom the text was intended may well have made a different kind of sense. To recall the image of the old woman/young woman in chapter 3, we may be seeing an old woman, while the writer is intending a young one.

For this reason, technological advances can create cultural cataracts that blind us to the trickery and dynamism of the text itself. In the *Testament of Job*—roughly contemporary with our New Testament or slightly before—there is an exchange between Job and his erstwhile friend Bildad. Bildad has been pressing Job for an accounting of the terrible things that have befallen him. Perhaps Job has lost his sanity. Bildad's interrogation becomes affrontive when he demands an accounting of the movements of the stars:

> "And again I say to you, if you are sound of mind and have your wits about you, tell me why we see the sun rising in the east and setting in the west, and when we get up early we find it rising again in the east? Explain these things if you are a servant of God" (*T. Job* 37.8).[3]

When I first read Bildad's question, I immediately envisioned the world as a globe, spinning on its course through the solar system. But Job is unable to provide that answer because he cannot even begin to envision a solar system. The science of his

---

[3]Translation R. P. Spittler, in J. H. Charlesworth, ed. *Old Testament Pseudepigrapha,* 2 vols. (New York: Doubleday, 1983, 1985).

day still saw the world as a flat plane with a vaulted dome over the top. At that moment, the question is a mystery.

Job responds with a similar mystery, one that we would also be able to answer without much difficulty. The account appears in the first person, on Job's lips:

> "Now then, so you may know that my heart is sound, here is my question for you: Food enters the mouth, then water is drunk through the same mouth and sent into the same throat. But whenever the two reach the latrine, they are separated from each other. Who divides them?"

> And Bildad said, "I do not know."

> Again I replied, "If you do not understand the functions of the body, how can you understand heavenly matters?"[4]

These examples can help us understand why it is important to investigate the social and cultural backgrounds of the Bible. From examples like these it is clear that such information is different from culture to culture. Yet within each culture, beliefs about the nature of the human experience are often taken for granted, as though everyone everywhere believed the same things we do.

The reason this is so is rooted in the psychological processes with which we build the schemas in the first place. We can gain some measure of clarity about those processes by revisiting from chapter 5 the discussion of schemas in the lexicon. The observations in that chapter were based on the research of Allan Collins and M. Ross Quillian.[5] Collins and Quillian concluded that the mind stores information in the form of ordered hierarchies of features—schemas. The reader instantiates whatever nodes of data appear to be appropriate at each point in the reading process. There was, however, a persistent problem with the structures of schemas as Collins and Quillian originally envisioned them. Initially the schemas were thought to be structured by logical subordination, much the way a scientist might organize his or her observations into ever narrower and more refined categories. But actual retrieval times suggested that the features of the lexicon are not

---

[4]*T. Job* 38.3–5, ibid.
[5]Collins and Quillian, "Retrieval Time from Semantic Memory," 240–47.

organized formally, according to logic, but informally, according to what is typical in experience. This discovery led to a clarification of the ways in which lexical information is stored away for later use. As we learn, we seek connections with what we already know. The connections are reinforced by repetition or by the vividness and clarity of the images they produce. The more frequent or more powerful the reinforcement, the more accessible the features will be. Morton Hunt describes the way in which new nodes of information are integrated into the lexicon:

> New material is added to this network by being plunked down in a hole in the middle of an appropriate region, and then gradually is tied in, by a host of meaningful connections, to the appropriate nodes in the surrounding network. That's why cramming for a test is so impermanent; it doesn't knit the new material into the existing web.[6]

The mind's ability to "knit the new material into the existing web" is truly amazing. A child does not need to see all cats in order to determine what is typical and what is not. One or two will do. This means, of course, that the network of schematic features is constructed ad hoc, rather than according to some rational plan.

There are implications here for our understanding of the nature of schemas. Features that are commonly observed, are reinforced in some way, or are particularly striking will be closer to the core of the network than will features that are uncommon or that the observer has been taught to overlook. Consequently, Collins and another researcher, Elizabeth Loftus, later modified the model to account for this aspect of the lexicon (Figure 6.1).[7]

The shift from organization based on logic to one based on experience is important if we are to understand what happens when we translate the text from Greek or Hebrew into English. Clearly, what is typical in one culture will not necessarily be typical in another. Very much depends upon the range and disposition of the reader's cultural experience. This means that

---

[6]Morton Hunt, *The Universe Within: A New Science Explores the Human Mind* (New York: Simon and Schuster, 1982) 107f.

[7]Allan Collins and Elizabeth Loftus, "A Spreading-Activation Theory of Semantic Processing," *Psychological Review* 82 (1975) 407–28.

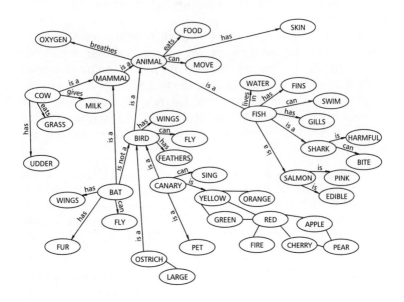

FIGURE 6.1: LOFTUS'S MODEL OF THE LEXICON

the schemas of Greek words will be organized differently from the schemas of corresponding English words. What is common and therefore central in Greek experience may be rare and therefore peripheral in English.

This aspect of language acquisition is made clear by a vignette told by Snell and Gail Putney in a discussion of the ways in which we take certain aspects of the world for granted:

> Our son grew up with a Siamese cat and when he was about three the only other cat in his limited world was also Siamese. Both had blue eyes, like all their breed. One day he saw a Persian cat padding toward him, and in the manner of three-year-olds he squatted down on the sidewalk to get a better look. The Persian also sat, wrapped her tail around her feet and regarded the boy. Suddenly he jumped up and ran into the house shouting, "I saw a cat with yellow eyes, Mommy! A cat with yellow eyes!"[8]

---

[8]Snell Putney and Gail Putney, *Normal Neurosis: The Adjusted American* (New York: Harper and Row, 1964) 6f.

The Putneys use this little story to point out that one takes one's perception of the world for granted until some disruption calls that sense of the normal into question. When their son discovered a yellow-eyed cat, "two things occurred to the boy: he became aware that all cats do not have blue eyes and he also became aware that *until that moment he had believed that they did.*"[9]

The point here, of course, is that what was true for their little boy is true for whole societies: Whole societies function with a large body of tacit, taken-for-granted beliefs about the world. Unless we are confronted with something that disrupts those beliefs, we will tend to take it for granted that people in other cultures believe them, too. Louis Wirth carries this point forward: "The most important thing . . . we can know about a man is what he takes for granted, and the most elemental and important facts about a society are those that are seldom debated and generally regarded as settled."[10] Yet what is taken for granted—and therefore unstated—may be quite the crucial matter in interpretation because it is the backdrop against which the interpreter can discover deviations. Deviations from the norm call attention to themselves and in that way create a subtle form of emphasis.

This taken-for-granted aspect of the world poses genuine challenges for the interpretation of the Bible because we naturally default to what is normal for our own culture. As we shall see in chapter 11, it is also an important factor in the literary strategies by which Luke tells us the story of the anointing of Jesus. Just as *The Joy Luck Club* reverses an established cultural norm, so also does the anointing story. As the story opens, the woman's behavior is described in terms that any ancient reader would find outrageous. The sensuality of it seems to dominate the opening verses. The reader is asked to share the same perspective as Simon the Pharisee. Yet by the time the story has ended, Jesus has reversed the cultural norm by giving the woman's behavior a radically different interpretation. To the extent that the reader has sided with Simon, the reader now must also share the judgment wielded by the reversal.

---

[9] Ibid., 7; italics theirs.

[10] Louis Wirth, preface to *Ideology and Utopia,* by Karl Mannheim, (New York: Harcourt, Brace, 1936) xxiv.

IMPLICATIONS

Let us pause here and explore the implications of chapters 5 and 6. One of the primary characteristics of language is that it is selective. For this reason readers must have some apparatus for filling in gaps. The mind solves this problem by drawing upon information that is stored in hierarchies, called schemas. Schemas may be as simple as individual vocabulary words about which the listener knows very little, or as encyclopedic as whole doctoral dissertations. The larger the schemas, the more unwieldy. Sometimes the reader can access them only partially, sliding down through the nodes of the hierarchy to focus in on the subcategories of information that are evoked by other clues in the context. The schemas are interactive, multifaceted, and sometimes self-referential.

A change in the structure of these schemas will lead automatically to a change in the interpreter's conclusions about the meaning of the text. As we fill in gaps, we have a natural tendency to default to the schemas, scripts, and other outside information native to our own culture, especially if we can make coherent sense of the text. This is a special danger if that outside information is information our culture takes for granted. A default to the schemas of our own culture can blind us to the possibility that a native reader of the original text might fill in the gaps very differently.

These affirmations, taken together, suggest a first criterion for validity in interpretation:

> *An act of reading is valid to the extent that it fills in the gaps of the text with the schemas that were operative for the culture in which the text was composed.*

The study of cultural norms is carried on by specialists working in a variety of disciplines, among them:

- *archeology,* which examines the physical remains left behind by historical processes

- *anthropology,* which examines the social dynamics of everyday life

- *sociology,* which asks the question of social dynamics on a larger, more comprehensive scale

- *comparative religions,* which compares standard beliefs and practices of one religion with those of another

What we have seen in this chapter suggests that all of these disciplines—along with lexicography—have something to contribute to our understanding not only of the biblical *world* but also of the biblical *text.*

Yet we are not free to pick and choose the background we supply for the text, nor are we free to fill in the gaps in the text in ways that "feel comfortable" to us. Gap filling is a controlled process and must be carried on within boundaries. As we have seen, gap filling can be incomplete, can be inaccurate, and can be carried too far. In chapter 7 we turn to controls.

GETTING TO THE GIST

How We Resolve Ambiguities

Let us begin with a story that illustrates the core of this chapter and chapter 8:

The pastor sat back heavily in his chair and wondered what he should do next. The woman was going to ruin him. What she was saying threatened to destroy both his marriage and his ministry. To understand his predicament, we must learn something of the events that had brought him to this moment.

The work at the church had become particularly burdensome in the last few weeks. There had been a major financial crisis, and a group of dissidents were lobbying for his removal. But he was a devoted pastor, who cared very deeply for his little flock. What agonized him most was the effect the troubles were having on his family. His work had taken him from home many evenings, and he knew that this meant his wife must spend her nights without him. She had come to refer to the church as "the other woman." She meant it as a joke, but the pastor knew that, in a sense, she was right. He was deeply committed to his ministry.

Still, whatever his commitments as a pastor, he was also an attentive and affectionate husband, and he missed his wife. In his yearning to be with her—and to reassure her—he devised a plan to help bridge the distance and punctuate her day with reminders that she was loved. Occasionally at first, then with increasing frequency, he began to hide little notes for her to find as she went about her work—a greeting card tucked in among the vegetables, a love letter in the linen closet. Sometimes he would wire flowers. He hinted of the day they would "run away together"—an upcoming vacation to the mountains they had long planned, and which they had grown to need now more than ever. Just the two of them; the children would stay with Grandmother.

Some women dream of a man like that. And so it happened that a crush developed in the heart of a troubled young woman in his congregation. Let us call her Mary Ellen. The fact that the pastor's devotion to his wife was unflagging only deepened Mary Ellen's infatuation. More than once she asked to see him—in his office, of course—for a "pastoral" visit. What could be more natural? She presented him with no reasons for the visits, but it was not hard to tell that she was troubled. Before long (was it the second visit? the third?) her remarks became more personal and more suggestive, until one day she made a clear and direct advance. The pastor dismissed her from his office with the uneasy feeling that he had not heard the last of her proposal. Mary Ellen continued to attend the church.

The pastor was now in a predicament. Should he tell his wife about Mary Ellen's advance? Should he tell the church board? At the very least, he instructed his secretary to schedule no more sessions with her, and he was careful never to be with her alone.

One day a parishioner canceled an appointment, and the pastor found himself free for the evening. He decided to surprise his wife with dinner out. His phone call didn't leave her much time: "Get a sitter for the kids, I'll be home in 15 minutes. I've made reservations for 7:00 at Antonio's."

"But dear . . . ," she said, and in her exasperation and delight she hung up the phone. Who would she call? The regular sitter was ill. The pastor's wife called Mary Ellen.

When her husband got home, he was upset. "Not Mary Ellen," he said. "She's so . . . troubled." He decided to break the girl's confidence and tell his wife of her advance.

"It'll be all right," his wife replied. "It's just for this one evening. We have so few evenings alone, and besides, she's already on her way. It's just for a couple of hours. We'll be home by 9:00. It'll be all right." And so it happened that the pastor and his wife spent a quiet evening at Antonio's, and Mary Ellen spent a quiet evening at their home.

The next day the pastor received an unexpected visitor in his study—Mary Ellen. She forced her way past the secretary and insisted on speaking with him alone. "You must come away with me," she said. "Right now. At once. If you do not, I will tell the church board that we have had an affair. Your career will be ruined."

"They will not believe you. I have not seen you now in weeks, and I have never been alone with you."

"I will say that we have been discreet and that now you have discarded me."

"It will be your word against mine."

"Then I will show them this." In her hand she held one of the love letters he had written to his wife. She read aloud:

My darling—

The hours are always longer when we are apart. The Other Woman keeps me so much a captive these days. It won't be long, now, though, I promise you. We will make our escape yet, and then it will be nothing but long and intimate evenings by the fireplace, just the two of us . . .

This is a true story. Or at least, I think it is true. Very much depends upon whom one believes. Read against one background, the letter gives us a pastor who is a caring, nurturing husband. Read against the other, he is a scoundrel who deserved what happened to him.[1] This story demonstrates an important concern of biblical interpretation: Words are ambiguous. We must have some way of sorting through the options as we fill in the gaps. This in turn makes clear the second major protocol of reading: While we must fill in the gaps, we are not free to do so in any way we choose. We must *disambiguate*. In this chapter and chapter 8 we will explore the protocols by which we choose between the various interpretive options.

These protocols are necessitated by two critical difficulties. First, the fact that language is ambiguous means that the reader may access the wrong schemas. This is not only possible for words and sentences; as we saw in our story of the pastor and Mary Ellen, it is possible for whole discourses as well. This means that standards of accuracy and completeness can be applied to this basic reading protocol. Writers expect readers to function within boundaries. Without boundaries, the reading process is chaotic and unpredictable. An argument could even be made that the act of communication rests upon a prior agreement—a kind of contract—to write and read, or speak and listen, according to a set of rules. Those rules represent the reader's mechanism for disambiguating, our way of sorting through the various options and focusing on the ones that are intended by the author.

Second, while a great deal of information can be encountered and processed preconsciously, only a limited amount can be elevated to conscious attention. This is rather like a bottleneck on a large highway. Some vehicles are able to get through, some must bypass the bottleneck on side routes, some are turned away altogether. The number of bits of information that get through the bottleneck at any given moment appears to be quite small, somewhere between five and nine "chunks" of information at a time.[2] This at least is the generalized conclusion represented in a famous article by George Miller on this

---

[1]The wife believed the pastor, but the church board believed the girl. The pastor spent the rest of his working life stocking shelves in a grocery store.

[2]A chunk of information is a cluster of facts gathered together into a single conceptual unit. For example, a telephone number contains seven digits but may be managed as a single chunk. The limitation we are discussing refers to the number of chunks that can be processed at any given time. See also Herbert A. Simon, "How Big Is a Chunk?" *Science* 183 (1974) 482–88.

subject.[3] In theory, a reader can supply an infinite number of details by drawing upon his or her knowledge of the lexicon and the other schemas that are evoked by the language of the text. But Miller's research shows that reference to an infinite range of features is just humanly not possible. The mind would very quickly become overburdened with supporting facts and would be unable to process anything new. Miller's conclusion is that the mind has a limited capacity for verbatim memory.

This physiological limit poses a critical problem that counterbalances the problem of gaps. Unless there is some mechanism for disambiguating, the informational logjam in the reader's mind stops the reading cold. Moreover, without a mechanism for directing traffic, the dynamic activities of language would be overburdened and ultimately crippled. A reader would have no way of knowing whether a writer was being literal or sarcastic. The entrapments of language would be destroyed. The play of features on which jokes and ironies depend would somehow play out. In the end, language would lose not only its clarity and economy but also its rhetorical power. In psychological terms, we must have ways of getting to the *gist,* or essence, of the text, and this means making decisions about what is and is not important.

In chapter 4 I pointed out that the gaps represent a problem for writers and readers to overcome. That problem presents the writer with opportunities to leverage the reader's perceptions. In the same way, the reader's activities of getting to the gist also enable the writer to achieve certain important rhetorical effects. Jokes work because the listener parses out a gist in one direction, only to have that gist turned on its head by the punch line. Metaphors and analogies work because we fill in gaps based on what we already know, in the process isolating gists that correspond to our perceptions of the metaphorical object.

We have identified two concerns—the fact that readers may access the wrong schemas and the fact that there are physiological limits to cognition. These two concerns suggest that we have to have some way of avoiding a traffic snarl, some switching mechanism, some way of directing traffic. This in turn requires preconscious decisions about what gets through and

---

[3]Miller, "Magical Number Seven," 81–97.

what does not. Only the gist is retained and carried forward. The question before us, then, is, how do we disambiguate, how do we get from the sentence to its gist?

BOTTOM-UP AND TOP-DOWN READING CONSTRAINTS

There are two general models of how these activities work. Cognitive scientists refer to these as "bottom-up" and "top-down" reading strategies. Of these, the models of bottom-up strategies are the older, and they also make the clearest common sense. According to the bottom-up models, reading takes place by induction, moving from the parts to the whole. The reader first makes out the letters, then the words, then the sentences. One reads, as it were, from the bottom up. Bottom-up reading strategies are informed and constrained in various ways: by syntactical markers; by the reader's knowledge of schemas; by nonverbal clues such as body language and the tone and texture of the speaker's voice. The syntactical markers enable the reader to decide on the relationships of the words to one another, and so, from the lexical schemas and the syntactical markers together, the reader makes out the sentences. In a similar but somewhat larger way, the reader strings the sentences together to construct paragraphs and then strings the paragraphs together into a meaningful accounting of the entire discourse.

Top-down reading strategies proceed in the other direction, moving from the whole to the parts. The reader begins with some idea of what the interaction is about. The idea may be very precise or it may be quite sketchy, but we almost never come to a text without some anticipations of what we will find there. As we shall see, those anticipations shape and sometimes distort what we do find. Most often this is an aid in reading, since it allows the reader to do some preliminary sorting of the available schemas. Like bottom-up strategies, top-down strategies are informed and constrained in various ways. These involve the integrated considerations of context, genre, and theme.

These, then, are the basic constraints that govern and inform the business of disambiguating and forming a gist:

This chapter will look at the bottom-up constraints, and chapter 8 will examine the top-down constraints.

Bottom-up Constraints	Top-down Constraints
the lexicon	context
syntax	genre
texture	theme
paralanguage	

FIGURE 7.1: BOTTOM-UP AND TOP-DOWN READING CONSTRAINTS

THE BOTTOM-UP READING CONSTRAINTS

The Lexical Possibilities

Chapter 5 explored the schemas of the lexicon as a possible resource for filling in gaps in information. But the lexicon also works to limit the reader's range of action. Here we want to explore how that limitation works.

On the surface of things, it appears that the reader simply sets about to identify the individual words and retrieve the appropriate lexical schema for each. This is simple only on the surface; in reality it is no small feat. It has been estimated that the human memory can store as many as 100 trillion bits of information.[4] The English-speaking adult may have a vocabulary as large as 50,000 to 75,000 words. One estimate has it that "the 500 most commonly used English words have an average of 28 dictionary meanings each."[5]

There are a number of theories about how we keep everything straight.[6] One theory is that the unfolding context leads the reader to anticipate what is coming next. Based on that anticipation, the reader partially activates clusters of "target"

---

[4]See S. Rose, *The Conscious Brain* (New York: Vintage Books, 1976) 269f. J. von Neumann (*The Computer and the Brain* [New Haven: Yale University Press, 1958] 63f.) had earlier estimated that lifetime capacity was as high as 280 trillion bits of information.

[5]Charles C. Fries, *Teaching and Learning English as a Foreign Language* (Ann Arbor: University of Michigan Press, 1945) 40.

[6]For a survey of the literature, see Mary Smyth et al., *Cognition in Action* (Hillsdale, N.J.: Erlbaum, 1987) 1–24, 161–80.

words. The presorting radically reduces accessing time so that comprehension is able to move along smoothly. The psychologists have studied this process in some depth because it seems to expose activities that are basic to all reading. In their summary of the literature, Smyth et al. have suggested that the opening structures of the sentence set up a configuration of target schemas that are already being "moved into place" as the sentence develops.[7] Consider the following illustration: The opening of the sentence

He went to the shops for some . . .

partially activates a possible list of target schemas: bread, meat, sausages, stamps, and so forth. If the sentence ends, " . . . for some windows," it can still be decoded, but the protocol takes slightly longer because one does not normally describe a window store as a "shop." The conclusion is that what comes earlier activates a cluster of "most likely" target words, which are then drawn closer to the threshold of consciousness, where they are more accessible. A rupture in this process causes a measurable increase in decoding time.

We experience this phenomenon informally when we find ourselves completing the sentence of some slow talker who just can't seem to come to the point. (I have a friend who seems to do this all the _____.) We also experience it when our initial projections of the meaning of a sentence are later subverted. Consider the following example:

The old dog the footsteps of the young.

This sentence usually requires a second reading. The reader first thinks the phrase "the old dog" is about an aging canine because it is slightly less common to use the adjective "old" as a substantive and the word "dog" as a verb. Thus, by a first analysis, the opening phrase of the sentence is taken for a common linguistic unit: definite article, adjective, noun. This yields a satisfactory configuration of features, and the reader draws upon his or her lexicon for a specific schema, "aging canine." The close of the sentence parses the opening phrase in a very different direction, and the reader is forced to retire the initial schema and replace it with another. For a moment, the

---

[7]Ibid.

two competing schemas exist alongside one another. That coexistence accounts for the momentary puzzlement that the reader experiences.

This explains why sometimes we hear what we want to hear, and manage to avoid hearing meanings that are difficult, dangerous, or distasteful. We keep uncomfortable information submerged by a prior, unconscious act of filtration, holding it away from the surface and therefore making it less accessible. If the sentence can be parsed in a more favorable way, we naturally take that course, sometimes never knowing that we have made a preconscious decision not to consider another, more difficult, possibility.[8]

This also explains why the immediate contexts of prior words in the sentence can limit the lexical possibilities available for later ones. The sentence

Pam went to see John.

yields a different gist than does the sentence

Yoko went to see John.

Wherever we understand the controls to be resident, it appears that redundancy of information is a central factor in how they work. A schema for the name "Yoko" is laid out alongside a schema for "John." The overlapping schemas share nodes of information, and those shared nodes are highlighted by the redundancy. In this way, the ranges of schematic possibilities complement and limit one another. When language is taken out of context, the schematic constraints are lost and the reader's activities of fixing meaning by redundancy are impaired. On the other hand, within a particular context the nodes of information from one schema may be reinforced by overlapping nodes of another.

Consider the following example, which appeared in the fall 1990 issue of the *Yarnspinner:*

> They're a crabby lot, stepmothers—at least the folktale variety— which is why some people today believe that their Draconian image should be revamped.

---

[8]There is a psychological reason for this form of personal dissembling. See Daniel Goleman, *Vital Lies, Simple Truth: The Psychology of Self-Deception* (New York: Simon and Schuster, 1985).

In this case, the adjective "Draconian" evokes a schema which at least aurally suggests vampires and dragons. To couple the adjective with the word "revamped" is to create a subtle but important wordplay.

We can see a similar play of schemas in our story of the anointing of Jesus. You will recall from chapter 5 that John Lightfoot listed a number of conditions that warrant the description *hamartōlos,* "sinner." A *hamartōlos* could be someone who was guilty of:

- giving her husband food that had not been properly tithed

- allowing her husband to embrace her during her menstrual period

- failing to keep a vow

- acting loud and clamorous

- doing her weaving in the street

- cursing her children

- cursing her husband's father in the presence of her husband

- falling into sexual immorality

Each of these is a possible schema for the term here. Most are missing from the English word "sinner." On what basis would the reader conclude that *hamartōlos* here refers to sexual sin and not some other objectionable practice? There are important contextual clues here that bring that last node to consciousness for Luke's reader, not least of which is the woman's unseemly behavior: She has let down her hair in public. Letting down the hair means little or nothing in English culture, but in the culture of Jesus' day it was an outrage and understood as an intensely sensual act.[9] The sexual nodes for the schema *hamartōlos* are therefore reinforced by those for letting down one's hair. This clearly suggests to the reader that the term implies sexual sin of some sort. The growing implication of sensuality provides the

---

[9]A convenient summary of the literature is found in Bailey, *Through Peasant Eyes,* 8f.

backdrop for a secondary nuance of the word "touching" in
v. 39. The Pharisee thinks to himself that this provides a test for
Jesus: "If this man were a prophet, he would know what sort of
woman this is who is 'touching' him . . . " The Greek word for
"touching" here is *haptesthai.* In Greek, *haptesthai* can be used
as a euphemism for sexual contact, as in 1 Corinthians 7:1: "It is
well for a man not to touch a woman."[10] (It even appears from
v. 39 that the Pharisee finds the touching even more offensive
than the exposed hair.)

Thus, in our story of the anointing, the term *hamartōlos*
must be read in the context of the woman's clearly offensive
behavior. Because of the secondary nodes of information implied in the previous schemas, the reader's natural inclination is
to elevate the sexual nuances of *haptesthai* to a dominant place.
This initial impulse is then punctuated by the way in which the
Pharisee finishes his thought: " . . . for she is a sinner." Thus, the
Pharisee's silent remark is powerfully loaded: "If this man were
a prophet, he would know what sort of woman this is who is
fondling him, for she is a *whore.*"

Syntactical Markers

The research described above establishes quite clearly that
words are easier to recognize and decode when they appear in
syntactically meaningful contexts. On the level of the sentences
themselves, those contexts are bounded by various syntactical
markers. Syntactical markers are the signals embedded within a
text that establish the grammatical relationships between the
words. There are four basic sorts of syntactical markers—affixes,
word order, function words, and punctuation. What goes on
with the other syntactical markers is perhaps more visible with
punctuation. Compare the following:[11]

Dear John,

I want a man who knows what love is all about. You are
generous, kind, thoughtful. People who are not like you
admit to being useless and inferior, John. You have ruined

---

[10] On this whole question, see Gordon Fee, *The First Epistle to the
Corinthians* (NIC; Grand Rapids: Eerdmans, 1987) 275.

[11] From *Games Magazine* (January 1984).

me for other men. I yearn for you. I have no feelings whatsoever when we're apart. I can be forever happy. Will you let me be yours?

Gloria

Dear John,

I want a man who knows what love is. All about you are generous, kind, thoughtful people, who are not like you. Admit to being useless and inferior, John. You have ruined me. For other men, I yearn. For you, I have no feelings whatsoever. When we're apart, I can be forever happy. Will you let me be?

Yours,
Gloria

The other syntactical markers play similar roles, though perhaps more subtly. We can easily see how they work by looking at some sentences in which their role is heightened. Consider Lewis Carroll's nonsensical poem, "The Jabberwocky," from Alice's further adventures in Wonderland, *Through the Looking Glass:*

> 'Twas brillig, and the slithy toves
>> Did gyre and gimble in the wabe;
> All mimsy were the borogroves
>> And the mome raths outgrabe.

On the surface of it, this is pure nonsense. Even Alice herself, who (apparently) dreamed it all up, could not make heads or tails of it. "Somehow it seems to fill my head with ideas—only I don't exactly know what they are!"[12] Later on, Humpty Dumpty provides her with a translation. But Humpty Dumpty translates only the semantic meaning of the words. (" 'Brillig' means four o'clock in the afternoon—the time when you begin *broiling* things for dinner.") The reason Humpty Dumpty does not need to explain the syntactical relations is that they are quite clearly marked by the affixes, word order, and function words. Stripped of the roots of the new words, one is left with only the syntactical markers:

---

[12] Lewis Carroll, *Through the Looking Glass* (New York: C. N. Potter, 1973) 120–23.

'Twas _____ , and the _____ s
  Did ____ and _____ in the ____ ;
All _____ were the _____ s
  And the ____ _____ _____ .

With only these markers in place, a native reader could easily identify which words are nouns, which are adjectives, which are verbs, which are singular, which are plural. The fact that the markers indicate English diction suggests that though this is nonsense, it is not total drivel. This is *English* nonsense. To achieve the same effect in, say, German, one would only need to translate the syntax. The vocabulary markers could be left intact:

> Es Brillig war, und die schlichte Toven
> Wirrten und wimmelten im Waben.

Peter Farb, to whom I am partially indebted for this translation, adds the comment: "Many languages of the world are true-life jabberwockies that have borrowed their vocabularies from other languages, yet maintain their identity because they preserve their own grammatical structures."[13] I have, however, modified Farb's translation slightly in the light of Humpty Dumpty's explanation to Alice ("Brillig" is not an adjective but a noun and so must be capitalized). If vocabulary words are the basic building blocks of sentences, syntactical markers must be the mortar that binds the words together into meaningful units.

Texture and Paralanguage

By "texture" we mean all of those extralinguistic clues which accompany and constrain vocabulary and syntax—the modulation of the voice, the tone, rhythm, intensity, and stress. By "paralanguage" we mean extralinguistic clues that come in the form of "body language"—gesture, facial expression, eye contact, proximity, and so forth.

In spoken language especially, texture and paralanguage serve as important signals and constraints that inform and govern the reader's attempt to disambiguate the speaker's intent. A shift in tone can signal that the sentence is a question

---

[13] Peter Farb, *Word Play: What Happens When People Talk* (New York: Bantam Books, 1983) 317.

rather than a statement, that the speaker is being sarcastic or ironic, or that the speaker is angry or feeling compassionate. A change of gesture or bodily position can change a sentence from a request into a demand. For this reason, texture and paralanguage are often used to intensify or soften the severity of what is being said. As we shall see in chapter 10, they can also serve as genre signals in their own right. For this reason, the constraints provided by paralanguage are extremely important, and we shall devote the entirety of chapter 10 to this question.

For now it is enough to note that the ancients were also extremely interested in such things. This may be difficult for us to see because texture and paralanguage are largely lost when a story is reduced to writing. Even so, Luke has provided hints about such things in our story of the anointing. When Jesus responds to Simon in vv. 44–47, Luke tells us that he *addressed Simon* but *looked at the woman*. This is a subtle touch, but it has the effect of softening the severity of his contrast between them. The words somehow feel gentler because of this gesture, and Jesus somehow seems more tactful. The paralanguage suggests that perhaps Derrett is right after all here: Jesus' response to Simon really was the soul of tact.

IMPLICATIONS

What we have discussed in this chapter suggests a single implication for our understanding of the kinds of questions we must ask if we are to understand the biblical text properly: *It is important that we understand the dual function of schemas.* We use schemas not only to fill in gaps and thus widen the range of information in the text but also to disambiguate and thus narrow the range of information.

The bottom line is this: As we do word studies during exegesis, we must keep these two functions constantly in mind. It is not enough to find out what the individual words mean by themselves, or even added together; we must also find out how they interact with one another to *limit* the range of meanings in the text. This consideration also extends to matters of grammar, texture, and paralanguage. Exegesis must not only occupy itself with interesting tidbits in which the syntax of Greek or Hebrew may differ from that of English. If we are to interpret properly, we must connect the bottom-up constraints—lexical possibilities, syntax, texture, and paralanguage—to form a unit in which the parts both extend and limit the whole.

None of this takes place in a vacuum. Instead, readers already begin interpretation before they see a single word or disambiguate a single sentence. To use the terms we have set out in this chapter, we come already equipped with the top-down reading constraints of context, genre, and theme. These constraints will occupy our attention in chapter 8.

8

How We Resolve Ambiguities 2

Context, Genre, Theme

I n chapter 7 we surveyed four bottom-up reading constraints—lexical meaning, syntax, texture, and paralanguage. These work in concert as the reader builds an interpretation of the discourse as a whole, from the bottom up. This is the older and more obvious model by which we understood the protocols of reading. It worked as a model because it could account for those reading protocols which are close to the threshold of consciousness and therefore more observable. It corresponds to the skills that we learn in school. It seems to make good sense. But as a model it was not without its problems. Some of our experiences of reading fall outside the boundaries here. For example, the following two sentences have the same grammatical structures, but very different meanings:

John was eager to please.

John was easy to please.

Native speakers of English know that in the first example, John is the one doing the pleasing, while in the second, he is the one being pleased. How do we know that? In this chapter we turn to the top-down reading constraints of context, genre, and theme.

When we use the term "top-down" to describe these constraints we imply a kind of counterbalance to the bottom-up constraints discussed in chapter 7. While the bottom-up constraints work from the parts to the whole, the top-down constraints work in the opposite direction. The reader begins with a sense of what the whole will be about, then corrects and adjusts that sense as additional clues come along. Psychological research has shown quite clearly that this is what happens. The mind begins the interpretive process even before anything has been said. The research has also shown that the mind's prior understanding significantly disposes us to see some things and to overlook others. It is now clear that activities of anticipation and correction play much more significant roles than was previously thought. Bottom-up reading therefore must be complemented by constraints that operate from the top down.

Reading theorists point out that top-down reading strategies are critical for the role they play in preorienting the reader. To revisit our metaphor of the traffic bottleneck from chapter 7, we could say that the top-down constraints are like the detour signs emergency road crews set up when there's trouble on the thruway. They direct the mind to deflect some options to side roads where they may be lost completely.

We shall explore the details of this process momentarily. For now it is enough to note that top-down reading protocols enable the reader to determine in advance the general frames of reference for the details of the text, and those frames of reference suggest sets of lexical possibilities. This makes for economy of movement and thus for the amazing speed with which the mind goes about its business. The lexical possibilities are already partially activated by the reader's anticipations of what is coming next. Even if these are not actualized in the reading process, they can serve as effective controls, governing and shaping the reading protocols on a subconscious, tacit level.[1]

THE TOP-DOWN READING CONSTRAINTS

Context

A primary top-down reading constraint is context. We have encountered context on a local level in our discussion of overlapping and reinforcing vocabulary words. The importance of context on a more global level has also been widely studied by the cognitive scientists, with largely consistent results: Incoming schemas are continually compared and overlapped with schemas brought in from the reader's knowledge of context.[2] Consider the following sentence:

I'm having trouble with my old man again.

This can mean any of several things, depending upon where it is uttered and who the speaker is. It would mean one thing coming from a fifteen-year-old boy on a street corner, another coming from a thirty-five-year-old woman in a laundromat, and yet another from a fifty-year-old man in his pastor's study.

The first and most general level of context is the knowledge of the world the reader is expected to have in hand. As we saw in chapters 5 and 6, the knowledge is arranged in schematic form, and inferences are sometimes drawn based upon what is and is not likely for that schema. For example, Donald Foss and David Hakes call attention to two sentences that have identical grammar but very different meanings:

The city council refused to grant the women a parade permit because they feared violence.

---

[1]On this whole question, see Kenneth Goodman, "Reading: A Psycholinguistic Guessing Game," *Journal of the Reading Specialist* 4 (May 1967) 126–35; and Frank Smith, *Understanding Reading* (New York: CBS College Publishing, 1982).

[2]For a survey and defense, see James McLelland, "Stochastic Interactive Processes and the Effect of Context on Perception," *Cognitive Psychology* 23 (1991) 1–44, esp. 4ff.

The city council refused to grant the women a parade permit because they advocated violence.

What is important here is that native readers of English always understand the antecedent of the pronoun "they" to be the city council members in the first sentence and the women in the second sentence. Why? The words "feared" and "advocated" are both verbs. Foss and Hakes explain: "The difference arises because of what we know about city councils, not because of some linguistic rule for interpreting pronouns."[3]

It is exactly the same sort of general world knowledge that enables the reader to understand the bumper stickers:

TOTO, I DON'T THINK WE'RE IN KANSAS ANYMORE

BLONDES PREFER GENTLEMEN

On a much narrower scale yet, context can be understood as the local literary context, that is, the constraints and possibilities suggested by everything that has gone before in this particular discourse. One body of research of special interest in this regard focuses on what cognitive scientists call garden path sentences. Garden path sentences work because of a psychological protocol called priming. Priming forces the reader's attention in one direction while masking other possibilities. Disambiguating contextual signals are removed to a place *after* the words they disambiguate:

> Cinderella sobbed bitterly because she couldn't attend the ball at the Palace. There were enormous tears in her brown dress.

One can effectively cripple the operative protocols of reading by simply locating the disambiguating word later. This crippling effect is measurable. In a 1981 study, Patricia Carpenter and Meredyth Daneman[4] traced the eye fixations of subjects as they read through homographs such as the following:

---

[3]Donald Foss and David Hakes, *Psycholinguistics: An Introduction to the Psychology of Language* (Englewood Cliffs, N.J.: Prentice-Hall, 1978) 151.

[4]Patricia Carpenter and Meredyth Daneman, "Lexical Retrieval and Error Recovery in Reading: A Model Based on Eye Fixations," *Journal of Verbal Learning and Verbal Behavior* 20 (1981) 137–60.

> The young man turned his back on the
> rock concert stage and looked across the
> resort lake. Tomorrow was the annual one-
> day fishing contest and fishermen would
> invade the place. Some of the best bass
> guitarists in the country would come to this
> spot. The usual routine of the fishing resort
> would be disrupted by the festivities.

Almost invariably, subjects fixate on the word "bass," then regress to the word "guitar," then return to the word "bass." This activity of regressive fixations reveals the presence of an error in lexical retrieval, and a subsequent repair. But why the error? Because the most immediate contextual constraints have primed the reader's expectations in one direction rather than another. The mental road crew heard all that talk about fishing and set up a detour that side-tracked the possibility that we were talking about bass guitars. Then the mind had to cut across the median to rejoin the flow of traffic.

The phenomenon of priming is frequently discussed in the psychological literature. There are direct implications here for such literary devices as foreshadowing and flashback. There are also sociological and hermeneutical implications here. The cultural repertoire we bring with us to reading can prime it in one direction or another, thus blinding us to other schematic possibilities that would have been perfectly clear to the reader for whom the text was originally prepared. In this way we are also blinded to the dynamic play between those schemas.

Let us consider for a moment what this business of priming might mean for our reading of the anointing of Jesus. The reader comes to the text primed by what has gone before in the narrative. The characterization of Jesus is already richly developed, in part by a dramatic interplay and contrast with the characterization of the Pharisees. Until the beginning of Luke 7 the reader's reactions to the Pharisees have depended almost entirely on inferences drawn from their behavior toward Jesus. The Pharisees as a group have been much flatter, a nameless class, but always suspicious of Jesus. They were put down when they questioned him for forgiving the sins of the paralytic who had been lowered through the roof (Luke 5:17–26). Later, when it looked like they were going to object to his healing a man's hand on the Sabbath, he impaled them on the horns of a theological dilemma by healing the man after asking, "Is it lawful on the Sabbath to do good or to do harm?" (6:6–11).

In our story Jesus is invited for the first time to dine at the home of a Pharisee.[5] It is not insignificant that the invitation comes just after the reader's earlier suspicions about the Pharisees have been given concrete and pointed expression in a narrator's aside: "The Pharisees and the lawyers rejected the purpose of God for themselves" (v. 30). Also in the immediate background is the imputed denunciation of Jesus as a "friend of tax collectors and sinners *(hamartōloi)*"[6] in v. 34.

Simon is not named until v. 40, in what appears almost as an afterthought. The effect is that when the story opens, he is simply designated "a Pharisee." In this way he is made to represent the Pharisees as a group and thus to bear the full condemnation that the reader has been trained to level against such people. When Simon invites Jesus to his house, the reader has been primed to expect that the Pharisee will challenge Jesus in some way and will be roundly answered. Whether or not the story fulfills these expectations remains to be seen. The point here is that the reader does not begin reading the story from a neutral position but begins primed by what has gone before. The narrator seizes the moment to sharpen his theological affirmations and give them a rhetorically significant thrust.

This sort of deft contextual stroke is often overlooked because we tend to read the Gospels piecemeal, which inevitably cripples the protocols that depend upon context to do their work. Attention to context implies sensitivity to sequence and thus to the linearity of language, to which we shall turn in chapter 11.

Genre

A second type of top-down constraint is imposed by genre. By "genre" we mean the basic "form" of the text or discourse.[7] (In biblical scholarship, the terms "genre" and

---

[5]He will be invited again in Luke 11:37, where he will break different cultural taboos and end up denouncing his host more directly than he does here!

[6]This denunciation comes on Jesus' lips and is addressed to the crowd (v. 24), but it is imputed to any who challenge Jesus for his outrageous relationships with unclean people. The repeated second-person plural ("you say this") in vv. 33 and 34 brings the matter closer to home and makes the charge more vivid.

[7]Admittedly, "genre" is a literary term. It has the disadvantage of suggesting that only formally defined, literary genres are in view.

"form" are used interchangeably.) Old Testament scholar John Barton defines "genre" as

> a conventional pattern, recognizable by certain formal criteria (style, shape, tone, particular syntactic or even grammatical structures, recurring formulaic patterns), which is used in a particular society in social contexts which are governed by certain formal conventions.[8]

Genre is recognizable by certain formal patterns, since these signal the reader about which form is in view and therefore also which interpretive conventions are appropriate. We read a poem differently than we do a recipe.

Genre combines elements of structure and content. For example, the genre "sonnet" is a highly defined form with a specific pattern: By definition, it is a poem consisting of fourteen iambic lines. The rhyme scheme of the Shakespearean sonnet is *abab, cdcd, efef, gg.* Typically, only specialists in a particular literary guild could supply that information without resorting to reference tools.

It is natural to think of genre more narrowly as *literary* genre. After all, the study of literature offers us a specific vocabulary and a refined sense of formal expectations. When we think of genre this narrowly, we miss the important role that genres play in the ordinary business of life. They are everywhere: jokes, recipes, speeches, conversations over dinner, wedding pronouncements, obituaries, the beginnings and endings of speeches, the specific details of footnotes. All are genres. All require appropriate interpretive conventions that must be mastered, just as vocabulary and syntax must be mastered if the reader is to understand the full import of the text in hand.

Genre controls reading in two ways. First, different genres permit varying degrees of latitude in filling in gaps. For example, the form "proverb" calls for a different sort of gap filling than does the form "newspaper report." Considerations of form dictate that a proverb is not to be taken literally in the same way

---

Cognitive scientists have tried to expand the basis of the discussion by developing alternatives, but to my mind, these are equally unsatisfactory. Eco, *Role of the Reader,* refers to "rhetorical and stylistic overcodes" (p. 19).

    [8]John Barton, *Reading the Old Testament: Method in Biblical Study* (Philadelphia: Westminster, 1984) 32.

that a newspaper report is to be taken literally. The "truth" of a proverb is to be found as its gaps are filled by reference to the immediate circumstances to which it is applied. The "truth" of a newspaper story is to be found as its gaps are filled with reference to the antecedent historical event that it describes. These two forms call for different sorts of gap filling, with different ranges of latitude. And the appropriate ranges of latitude must be learned, just as grammar must be learned. The rules differ from culture to culture.

A second way in which genre governs reading is that it primes the reader's expectations. In the following example, Umberto Eco discusses the ways in which the genre signals cue the reader on what to expect:

> /Once upon a time/ is an overcoded expression establishing (i) that the events take place in an indefinite nonhistorical epoch, (ii) that the reported events are not "real," (iii) that the speaker wants to tell a fictional story.[9]

These, then, are the two ways in which genre governs reading: It controls the reader's imaginative latitude, and it tells the reader what to expect. These two aspects of genre often work together. If the story begins,

> Once upon a time, Frog went to see Toad. They had coffee and donuts by the lake,

the reader feels no hesitation at all about imagining what is being described, because the genre "fictional story" indicates a wide range of readerly latitude. It would be somehow violent to the story to object that frogs do not have dealings with toads and that neither one eats donuts. The range of latitude and different controls on readers' expectations combine to suggest that different forms support different rhetorical effects. It is not by accident that recipes are written in spare, unadorned language or that the lush imagery of poetry is more suitable for expressions of love.

Because language unfolds its information one word after another, the reader cannot always know for certain which form is intended until an adequate body of genre signals has been established. Even so, the reader often begins with certain expec-

---

[9] Eco, *Role of the Reader*, 19.

tations, most of which are suggested by the context. (We are never surprised to hear a minister begin a wedding ceremony with "Dearly beloved . . . ") But those expectations require confirmation and are open to correction or subversion. Usually, an initial projection is made, then modified and developed as additional clues are taken in from bottom-up reading strategies.

We can see this projection, then reevaluation, in our discussion of the form of the anointing story. The suggestions from the scholars have been particularly disparate: Bultmann identified this as an "apophthegm," Dibelius as a "legend," and Burton Mack as a "chreia" (these are technical terms for different literary forms).

What would Luke's reader have thought? At first, it seems to me, the context would suggest that this is a "controversy story." The nuances of hostility laid down by the previous treatment of Pharisees (especially in this very chapter of Luke) prime the reader to expect a fight. And he or she is not disappointed, though the substance of the fight turns out to be different than expected because the woman's outrageous behavior intrudes on the reader's work and deflects attention away from the genre signals. The intrusion calls the reader's initial dispositions into question. In this way the reader is enticed into sharing the Pharisee's point of view in the controversy that is brewing. In the end, the very length of the story and the central position taken by the dialog suggest to the reader that this should be understood as a chreia. This, however, is not an easy conclusion to reach, and it takes considerable shifting of position before the reader can come to it. That shifting is part of what gives the story its rhetorical leverage over the reader.

Theme

A third type of top-down reading constraint is theme. By "theme" we mean the reader's overall grasp of the inner meaning of the story, his or her sense of what the story is about. Often it is the theme that makes the story memorable, because the reader builds an interpretation of the story as a whole by arranging its elements into a coherent framework. The theme is the core of the reader's interpretation. In a sense, the theme is to a story what the gist is to a sentence.

Psychological literature has repeatedly demonstrated that the reader's understanding of the theme is a critical element in comprehension and recall. For example, in an experiment conducted by J. D. Bransford and M. K. Johnson, subjects were given the following paragraph, with the title "Watching a Peace March from the Fortieth Floor":

> The view was breathtaking. From the window one could see the crowd below. Everything looked extremely small from such a distance, but the colorful costumes could still be seen. Everyone seemed to be moving in one direction in an orderly fashion and there seemed to be little children as well as adults. The landing was gentle and luckily the atmosphere was such that no special suits had to be worn. At first there was a great deal of activity. Later, when the speeches started, the crowd quieted down. The man with the television camera took many shots of the setting and the crowd. Everyone was very friendly and seemed to be glad when the music started.[10]

Tests showed good general comprehension of the overall paragraph but an extremely low rate of recall for the sentence about the landing. Even with cues, subjects had difficulty reconstructing the sentence.

A second group was given exactly the same paragraph, though with a different title, "A Space Trip to an Inhabited Planet."

> The view was breathtaking. From the window one could see the crowd below. Everything looked extremely small from such a distance, but the colorful costumes could still be seen. Everyone seemed to be moving in one direction in an orderly fashion and there seemed to be little children as well as adults. The landing was gentle and luckily the atmosphere was such that no special suits had to be worn. At first there was a great deal of activity. Later, when the speeches started, the crowd quieted down. The man with the television camera took many shots of the setting and the crowd. Everyone was very friendly and seemed to be glad when the music started.

For this group, the recall of the sentence about the landing dramatically improved. This experiment and others like it demonstrate quite conclusively that the reader's sense of theme represents a critical facet not only of memory but also—and more importantly—of comprehension itself.

The tendency to relate the elements of a story to a theme is intimately connected with the physiological limits of cognition

---

[10] J. D. Bransford and M. K. Johnson, "Considerations of Some Problems of Comprehension" (paper presented at the eighth Carnegie Conference on Cognition, May 1971).

discussed in the opening of the present chapter. The mind has a limited capacity for verbatim recall. Under ordinary circumstances verbatim recall cannot be relied upon to sustain stories of any length. We can bring this aspect of theme into clearer focus if we turn aside momentarily and look at theme as an aspect of composition. In oral composition storytellers will often learn only the themes of the story, then use those themes as a primary guide, constructing or reconstructing additional details as they need them (storytellers call this embroidering). This process can be quite complex. The themes will inevitably be larger and less differentiated than the details of the language itself. Because they involve inferences, imagery, and nonverbal memory, themes distribute the elements of the story through a variety of sensory storehouses. Readers go through this process in reverse. The gist of the story is recalled from a variety of storehouses, and the details of the story are reconstructed out of that gist. Thus, theme serves as a kind of mnemonic tracking device for the storage and retrieval of information.

IMPLICATIONS

We may be helped at this point with a diagram (Figure 8.1) to make some general remarks.

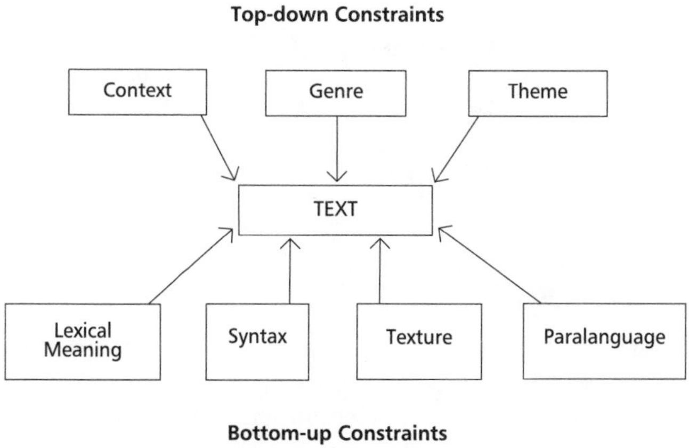

Top-down Constraints

Context	Genre	Theme

TEXT

Lexical Meaning	Syntax	Texture	Paralanguage

Bottom-up Constraints

FIGURE 8.1: THE CONSTRAINTS OF READING

We have seen that seven different constraints govern and inform the complicated business of disambiguating and of focusing down from the text to the gist. These constraints enable us to determine which schemas are intended and which features of the words are relevant at each point in our reading.

The constraints are employed simultaneously, rather than one after another. Because they operate simultaneously, they can overlap and reinforce one another, working interactively to conform the reader's decisions about which nodes of information are intended. This suggests that there are multiple pathways of disambiguating, all working at the same time. When the constraints are in alignment, the redundancy of signals suggests a coordinated matrix with which the reader can "triangle in" on the meaning of the individual words.

The key words here are "alignment" and "redundancy." It may be helpful to set this out in diagrammatic form. Let us consider that each of the constraints guides the reader's attention in a certain direction (Figure 8.2).

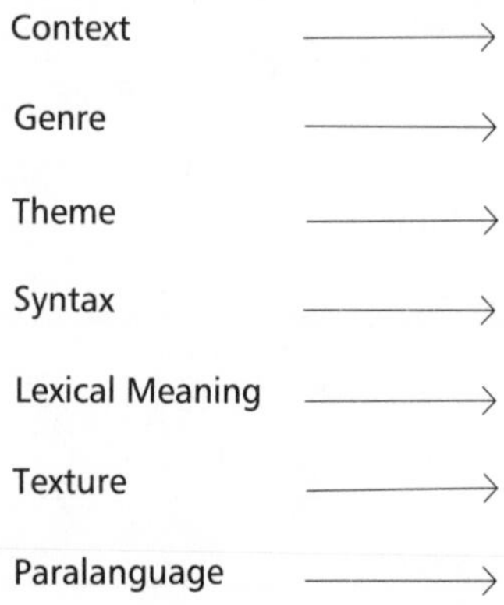

Context $\longrightarrow$

Genre $\longrightarrow$

Theme $\longrightarrow$

Syntax $\longrightarrow$

Lexical Meaning $\longrightarrow$

Texture $\longrightarrow$

Paralanguage $\longrightarrow$

FIGURE 8.2: CONSTRAINTS AND READER DIRECTION

When the constraints are in alignment, all the incoming textual signals agree. This produces redundancy of information as the various possibilities overlap. The redundancy permits the reader to make clear and confident decisions about which schemas are intended, which nodes of information are relevant, and which gists to build.

In chapter 6 we suggested a first criterion for validity in interpretation:

> An act of reading is valid to the extent that it fills in the gaps of the text with the schemas that were operative for the culture in which the text was composed.

The considerations we have discussed in chapters 7 and 8 suggest a second criterion for validity in reading:

> *An act of reading is valid to the extent that it takes into account the full range of constraints that govern the reading processes. It must do so in such a way that the interaction between the constraints yields an appropriate field of redundancies by which the reader can zero in on the nodes of schematic information that the author intends.*

What we have explored thus far suggests that the mental gymnastics of reading require sometimes dizzying displays of skill—leaps and bounds, layouts, backflips, and cartwheels—as the mind makes its way across the textual floor mat. The operative schemas here are "motion" and "multiplicity." As it works its way through the text, the mind compares syntax with context, correlates context with the ranges of meaning possible for the various schemas that the text evokes, checks these against cultural and linguistic norms, adjusts for paralanguage, feathers everything into an integrated sense of the theme, anticipates what is coming next, retrogresses to repair faulty understandings.

The interpreting mind is a mind on the move.

Done well, it is a dazzling performance, but that movement creates the possibility of leverage: Sometimes a skillful writer sets the constraints at odds with one another, to trip or entrap or entangle the reader. A text can lead the reader in one direction, only to change signals in midair and bring the reader down someplace totally unexpected. The result is rhetorical play, and it leads to a kind of double-exposure effect. In chapter 9 we turn to polyvalence.

9

DOUBLE EXPOSURE!

How We Recognize Polyvalence

Let us begin this chapter with the lyric from Garth Brooks's country song "Two of a Kind, Workin' on a Full House":[1]

> Yea, she's my lady luck
> Hey, I'm her wild card man
> Together we're buildin' up a real hot hand
> We live out in the country
> Hey, she's my queen of the south
> Yea, we're two of a kind
> Workin' on a full house

---

[1]This song is by Bobby Boyd, Warren Dale Haynes, and Dennis Robbins; it appears on Garth Brooks's *Friends in Low Places* album, ©1993, Garthart, Inc.

This lyric illustrates the basis for a third elemental protocol of reading: Language may be *polyvalent*. It strikes the reader on several levels, and those levels often play off one another. Since language is sometimes polyvalent, readers must have a mechanism for recognizing when this is so and for responding appropriately. In this chapter we address the question of how that feat of mental gymnastics is accomplished.

In chapters 7 and 8 I argued that the activities of reading are governed by the interaction of seven different reading constraints. When all the constraints are in alignment, the redundancy of information enables the reader to focus in on the specific schemas and nodes of information that the speaker intends. In this way the reader knows that he or she has established a satisfactory gist, which is then feathered into the reader's understanding of the discourse as a whole. In some types of discourse, it is extremely important that the constraints work in harmony this way. After all, the ambiguities of language can be dangerous, and there are moments at which they must be carefully pruned away. The redundancy of signals minimizes ambiguities. Thus, legal, scientific, and philosophical writing minimize confusion with the heavy use of technical vocabulary, with formally correct diction, with frequent qualifying remarks, and with precise attention to form. As we saw, the parts work together to form a consistent interpretive matrix of overlapping signals (Figure 9.1).

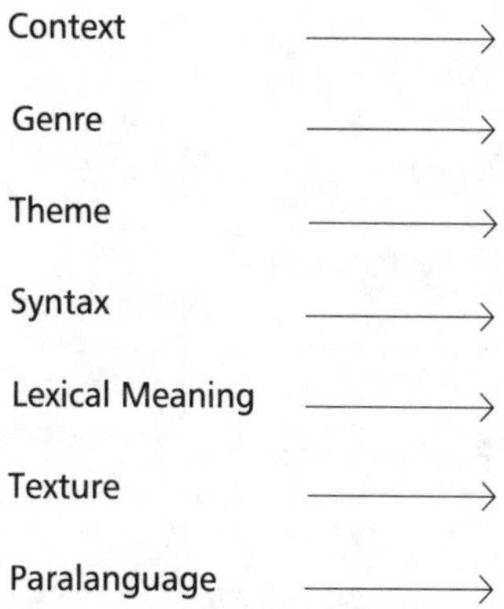

Context   ⟶

Genre   ⟶

Theme   ⟶

Syntax   ⟶

Lexical Meaning   ⟶

Texture   ⟶

Paralanguage   ⟶

FIGURE 9.1: CONSTRAINTS AND READER DIRECTION

When we move to literary language, however, things begin to get complicated. Textual signals may be permitted to run amuck. As the signals become mixed, they create ambiguities, secondary nuances, and multiple possibilities of interpretation.

> Literary language shows a preference for multiplicity and complexity, it exploits the double personal factor, makes use of connotation, allusion, suggestive ambiguities, it seeks out the unexpected novelty, the surprise, it transposes language to the realm of metaphor, imagination, symbol.[2]

If Luis Alonso Schökel is right, we can refine the way we pose the question of this chapter: How do we know when we have left off clear, unambiguous description and taken up "suggestive ambiguity, metaphor, imagination, and symbol"? Here we will argue that literary language achieves its effects by setting the various reading constraints at odds with one another. When the constraints are out of alignment, the resulting field of reference becomes much more complex and difficult to decode. In short, rhetorical dissonances are created by the interference of conflicting textual signals (Figure 9.2). Out of the conflict comes interference, and out of the interference comes a shift of readerly activity.

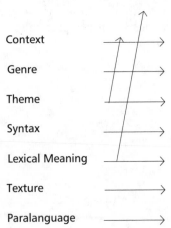

Context

Genre

Theme

Syntax

Lexical Meaning

Texture

Paralanguage

FIGURE 9.2: LITERARY LANGUAGE AND THE COMPLICATION OF CONSTRAINTS

[2]Luis Alonso Schökel, "Hermeneutics in the Light of Language and Literature," *Catholic Biblical Quarterly* 25 (1963) 380.

OVERCODING[3]

This is what happened with the song on page 116. The allusions to card playing appear as secondary nodes of information, slightly below the reader's conscious awareness. If any single line were isolated from the others, the reader would be unlikely to identify the technical language of card playing. When the tacit references to card playing are taken together, however, they overlap and, in that way, reinforce one another enough to raise the imagery above the reader's threshold of consciousness:

> Yea, she's my *lady luck*
> Hey, I'm her *wild card* man
> Together we're *buildin' up a real hot hand*
> We live out in the country
> Hey, she's my *queen* of the south
> Yea, we're *two of a kind*
> *Workin' on a full house*

Even though the imagery is brought to consciousness, it is not sufficient to displace the primary gist of the lyric—a man bragging about his woman. These two gists then stand in conflict, and the listener plays one back and forth upon the other.

The kind of rhetorical play we have been describing is called overcoding. One might say that the secondary imagery of a card game is overcoded on top of the primary image of a man and a woman. Overcoding works because the various mental systems for disambiguating—the seven top-down and bottom-up reading constraints—function interactively and thus at the same time.

We can gain a measure of clarity about how this all happens by turning aside momentarily to draw an analogy with computer science. Suppose we describe the mind as consisting of discrete "information systems." One such system would deal with hearing, another vision, a third taste, a fourth touch, and so on. A number of studies indicate that the systems do not function independently of one another. Instead, they are interactive. One of the earliest and most famous of these studies was

---

[3]I have taken over the term "overcodes" from Eco, *Role of the Reader*, 19.

conducted in 1935 by J. R. Stroop.[4] Stroop asked subjects to read cards on which were printed the names of the colors—red, blue, green, and so forth. The cards for the control group were printed all in black, while those of the test group were printed in opposing colors. That is, the word "red" might be printed in blue ink, the word "blue" might be printed in green ink, and so forth. What Stroop discovered is that the presence of an opposing color interfered with perception, making it more difficult to read. It is harder to read the word "red" when it is printed in green ink. The only way to account for the difficulty is to posit interference between the verbal and the visual processing systems. That interference is called the Stroop effect, and it has been explored and extended by a large body of experimental literature.[5] Interference makes information processing much more complex, and the complexity is reflected in additional processing time.

Verbal Interference

In his experiments with mixed stimulus, Stroop introduced dissonance between two different information systems—visual and verbal. But a similar sort of interference can also occur within a single system. The famous optical illusions of M. C. Escher are created by dissonant signals within the visual system. Dissonant verbal signals can interfere with one another in a similar way. The needed mental gymnastics call for increased concentration and more intensive effort. It may be this which gives oxymorons and wordplays their characteristic ability to confuse and dazzle:

> A lie is an abomination to the Lord, and an ever present help in time of trouble.

This illustration achieves its effect by drawing upon several different types of schemas. First, there are two partial allusions to the Bible, drawn from the reader's repertoire of cultural knowledge. Second, "ever present help in time of trouble" subverts the original quotation by attributing the help to the lie,

---

[4] J. R. Stroop, "Studies of Interference in Serial Verbal Reactions," *Journal of Experimental Psychology* 18 (1935) 643–62.

[5] For a survey, see Kathryn Spoehr and Stephen Lehmkuhle, *Visual Information Processing* (San Francisco: W. H. Freeman, 1982) 242–45.

rather than to the Lord. The interference will frustrate the reader's attempts to reconcile the competing schemas, so the reader will hold them in creative tension. The tension is pleasurable, so the reader laughs.

The mind appears to react to interference immediately in one way, slightly later in several other ways. The immediate response is to do a double take, reviewing and checking for errors. We can see this cross-checking at work when we have to retrogress to correct errors of understanding. The experiments with garden path sentences discussed in chapter 8 demonstrate this reparative activity very clearly and graphically:

> I was afraid of Ali's powerful punch, especially since it had already laid out many tougher men who had bragged that they could handle that much alcohol.[6]

Here, contextual signals ("Ali") prime the reader to target one meaning for the word "punch," and this appears to be confirmed by the reference to "tougher men" being "laid out." At the end of the sentence, though, the disambiguating term "alcohol" calls for retrospection and repair.

Richard Lederer calls attention to the following slips of the pen by otherwise competent writers of newspaper headlines:[7]

MEN RECOMMEND MORE CLUBS FOR WIVES

DEFENDANT'S SPEECH ENDS IN LONG SENTENCE

POLICE SQUAD HELPS DOG BITE VICTIMS

The first step, then, is retrospection and repair. Sometimes we discover that the difficulty persists, however, and then we must use other strategies. One such strategy is simply to discount the constraint that is causing the problem and distribute the control across the other constraints. If someone mumbles, we may use context to clarify and enhance the incoming stimulus, and in that way make an educated guess about what must

---

[6]For this I am indebted to Herbert Clark and Eve Clark, *Psychology and Language: An Introduction to Psycholinguistics* (New York: Harcourt Brace Jovanovich, 1977) 81.

[7]Richard Lederer, *Anguished English* (Charleston: Wyrick, 1987) 56–66.

have been said. If we hear someone we know say something that is completely out of character, we may filter out the difficulty and, using other controls to focus in, produce a sentence that sounds similar but has a more acceptable or likely meaning.

Sometimes elements within the discourse indicate that we should expect the overcode, that it is part of the speaker's rhetorical intent. This happens most clearly with genre signals. When my friend David slaps me on the back in the washroom and says,

> "Did you hear the one about the two old ladies who took a fifth of whisky to the ball game?"

everything I know about the body language (slap on the back), the context (washroom, rather than board room), and David (funny guy), suggests that there's a joke coming. That expectation is validated by the genre signal ("Did you hear the one about . . . ?"). In the joke there will be dissonances, and I will know to let them stand rather than resolve them in one direction or another. He has posed the question. I know from the genre signals that the appropriate response is to claim ignorance.

> "No [I tell him]. What about the two old ladies who took the fifth of whisky to the baseball game?"

He follows up with the punch line:

> "At the bottom of the fifth the bags were loaded."

These overcoded rhetorical plays are hard to translate into another language because a translator has to choose one gist or the other but is seldom able to render both. If I repeat David's joke in class, two groups will not laugh—those who heard the joke before ("You heard that from David, didn't you?") and the foreign students ("What?"). Foreign students may understand every word and every syntactical relationship but still miss the verbal play because they do not know enough about baseball. If I explain the joke, it will somehow cease to be funny. Typically, humor is the last thing one masters when one learns a foreign language because humor requires highly refined sensitivities about what the speakers of the language consider normal.

This phenomenon appears also to be rooted in an elemental facet of human nature. As we saw in chapters 7 and 8, when we read, we base our interpretive decisions on redundant signals from overlapping reading constraints. When we learn a foreign language, we place ourselves in the position of needing to master all seven of the reading constraints. If we do not, we will miss the dissonances that occur when one of the constraints is out of whack with the others. Because we are newcomers, if we hear something out of whack, we will tend to distrust our perception of that one constraint and fall back on the strategy of discounting our perception of the one and distributing the burden of control over the remaining six. By its very nature this shift requires that we soft-pedal the dissonance or dismiss it out of hand. Since humor often involves dissonance between two equally legitimate gists, we may reach what appears to be a perfectly satisfactory interpretation of the sentence. Just as in garden path sentences, we may even resolve the dissonance without being aware of having done so and thus also without even considering that it might be intentional.

When we turn to the biblical literature, the implications are startling. For many interpreters they are disturbing. There, too, specific nuances of the text are often dictated by the play of ambiguous language, but the cultural information upon which the play depends is buried beneath almost two thousand years of cultural and historical rubble. In many ways, the biblical world is like a lost civilization, waiting to be excavated. For the pastor, who must worry more about the immediacies of ministering to a living, breathing congregation, the amount of work involved can be overwhelming. The natural tendency is to treat the biblical literature as though it is simple, straightforward prose, with all of its signals in alignment. For more than one pastor, the scholar's insistence on exegetical digging very quickly becomes a source of frustration and distress.

But there is a positive side to this difficulty. Once the rubble has been removed, we discover that there is more wit in the Bible than our English translations lead us to believe. In Aramaic, Jesus was sometimes enormously funny, and when he was angry, his wit could be devastating. Sometimes—just often enough—the loss of easy clarity is more than repaid by the exhilaration of discovery and by the realization that Jesus was somehow more warmly human, with a wider range of emotions and greater prophetic pointedness. Whatever else, Jesus was fully in touch with the headaches and heartaches of life.

WORDPLAY

The fact that Jesus delighted in wordplay was first popularized by Elton Trueblood.[8] Trueblood focused primarily on the dissonances between the subtle and the preposterous that seem to characterize the sayings of Jesus. He attended only secondarily to the play between culturally coded schemas. Since then, a number of major studies have appeared. Not least of these is a survey by Jakob Jonsson.[9] In the terms we have been developing in this book, Jonsson makes it clear that the characteristic sayings of Jesus often achieve their effect by juxtaposing dissonant schemas or by setting form and content at odds. The conflicting schemas evoke conflicting images that are difficult to resolve into a unified gist. The result is thus more rhetorically powerful, and therefore also more memorable.

For example, when Jesus says, "It is easier for a camel to go through the eye of a needle than for a rich man to enter the kingdom of God" (Mark 10:25), the saying juxtaposes largest things and smallest things.[10] The resulting incongruity is perhaps grasped best by Frederick Buechner:

> In desperation the rich are continually tempted to believe that they can solve these problems (happiness, meaning, purpose) . . . with their checkbook, which is presumably what led Jesus to remark one day that for a rich man to get to Heaven is about as easy as for a Cadillac to get through a revolving door.[11]

---

[8]Elton Trueblood, *The Humour of Christ* (New York: Harper and Row, 1964).

[9]Jakob Jonsson, *Humour and Irony in the New Testament Illuminated by Parallels in Talmud and Midrash* (1965; reissue, Leiden: Brill, 1985).

[10]I am well aware that there is a popular interpretation of this passage that understands "eye of the needle" to refer to a "gate within the gate" of an oriental city. This is largely fanciful. A second approach is based on the fact that the Greek words for "camel" and for "rope" differ by a single letter—*kamēlos*||*kamilos*—a coincidence that is exploited by a few late manuscripts (f[13, 28]) at Mark 10:25. (Perhaps Jesus really said "rope.") Against both of these possibilities, we must note there are numerous rabbinic parallels suggesting that what is in view is a literal camel and a literal needle (on which see William Lane, *The Gospel according to Mark* [NIC; Grand Rapids: Eerdmans, 1974] 369f.). This is, according to Jonsson, an example of "excellent paradoxical humour" (*Humour and Irony in the New Testament,* 110).

[11]Frederick Buechner, *Wishful Thinking: A Theological ABC* (New York: Harper and Row, 1973) 81.

Jonsson has seen a similar kind of gentle humor in our story of the anointing of Jesus. This is yet another interpretation, though it is consistent with J. Duncan M. Derrett's view that Jesus' response to the Pharisee was "the soul of tact." According to Jonsson, Jesus sees through the host, and "in a friendly and humorous way he rebukes him by comparing him—the host—with the sinful woman, . . . letting the Pharisee judge himself by answering a question."[12] There are subtle and important silences here, not least of which is that the conclusion is left for the host to draw:

I entered your house,

A   You gave me no water for my feet,

B   but she has bathed my feet with her tears
         and dried them with her hair.

A   You gave me no kiss,

B   but from the time I came in she has not
         stopped kissing my feet.

A   You did not anoint my head with oil,

B   but she has anointed my feet with ointment.

Therefore I tell you,

B   her sins, which were many, have been forgiven;
         hence she has shown great love.

A   but the one to whom little is forgiven little, loves little.

The host is tricked by a double shift: The sequence (A-B-A-B) is reversed, and the accusation ("you gave me no . . . you gave me no . . . you did not . . .) is depersonalized and moved from the second person ("you") into the third person (lit. "he who is forgiven little, loves little"). These are delicate touches. The opening contrast may seem to point an accusing finger, but the final line turns the hand around into a gesture of invitation.

---

[12] Jonsson, *Humour and Irony in the New Testament,* 155.

ALLUSIONS

We can also see interference at work in the rhetorical play of allusion. What effect does allusion have upon the reader in the reading process? Allusions work like other forms of background information, though they do more than simply provide an environment within which the reader can parse sentences confidently. Instead, an allusion accomplishes its effects by calling up a secondary frame of reference and superimposing that on top of the primary frame. The two frames work together to create a kind of verbal double exposure. We saw something similar in our discussion of the song "Two of a Kind, Workin' on a Full House." Interference between the frames prevents their resolution into a unified gist. The reader's mind plays back and forth between the two images, and as a result, the activities of decoding are slowed and made more complex.

Let us consider another example. In Dinesh D'Souza's controversial evaluation of political correctness in the American university system, there appears this rather eloquent allusion to T. S. Eliot's poem "The Love Song of J. Alfred Prufrock":

> At the prestige schools, such as those of the Ivy League, impressive domes and arches give off a distinct aroma of old money and tradition. Across the lawns the scholars come and go, talking of Proust and Michelangelo.[13]

In order to recognize the allusion, the reader must already know Eliot's poem. Notice that the parallels between the original and the allusion are quite subtle. They begin at first with only a simple pattern of ordinary words that fall into a recognizable rhythm:

Eliot	D'Souza
In *the* room	Across *the* lawns
the women	*the* scholars
come and go	*come and go*
talking of	*talking of*
	Proust and
Michelangelo	*Michelangelo*

[13] Dinesh D'Souza, *Illiberal Education: The Politics of Race and Sex on Campus* (New York: Free Press, 1991) 1.

The opening rhythm introduces the allusion, the reader accesses what he or she knows of the poem, then the reference to Michelangelo nails it down tight. The resulting interference is a kind of verbal double exposure that deepens the punch of the punch line.[14]

We can see something of this overcoding effect in Mark's description of John the Baptist (1:6):

> Now John was clothed with camel's hair,
> with a leather belt around his waist,
> and he ate locusts and wild honey.

This description appears very near the opening of Mark's narrative. Even so, already a number of allusive elements have primed a complex of schemas concerning the appearance of the Messiah. The reference to Isaiah in v. 2a combines with the conflated quote from Malachi and Isaiah in vv. 2b–3 to evoke a series of visual images, all of which suggest the eschatological prophet Elijah. Along with the quote from Malachi 3:1,

> "See, I am sending my messenger ahead of you,"

the reader is likely to access the more specific information of Malachi 4:5:

> "Lo, I will send you the prophet Elijah before the great and terrible day of the LORD comes."

Even though this reference may not be fully instantiated, it serves as tacit background to the material that follows. Verse 6 nails the connection down solidly by describing John in the exact same language as a description of Elijah found in 2 Kings 1:8:

2 Kings 1:8a	Mark 1:6
[Elijah was] a hairy man, with a leather belt around his waist.	Now John was clothed with camel's hair, with a leather belt around his waist.

---

[14] The rhetorical effect of allusions is more potent than that of quotations, precisely because quotations are more focused, call for a different type of readerly work, and are not overcoded on top of the primary frame.

For Mark's reader the allusion is clear. The narrator has identified the figure in the desert as John the Baptist, but the reader
knows from the description that it is also Elijah the Tishbite,
herald of the coming Messiah.

STRUCTURAL OVERCODES

Interference also plays a role in a rhetorical effect I call
structural overcodes. These work much like allusion by creating
a kind of mental double exposure in the reader's experience,
though their effect is achieved through a different route. Instead
of overlaying secondary images by alluding to an existing literary or oral tradition, structural overcodes overlay the secondary
images by using technical vocabulary from a different frame of
reference.

We saw in chapter 5 that schemas from common knowledge can be evoked in any of three ways. The frame of reference
can be named ("icy road"), inherent features can be described
("cars were skidding everywhere"), or technical language can be
used ("chains required"). Any one of these strategies can be
used to evoke the range of features that are inherent in the
frame, "icy road." Sometimes, though, the frames can be set at
odds, as in this bumper sticker:

CHAINS REQUIRED
WHIPS OPTIONAL

As with allusions, the dissonance creates an oscillating play
between primary and secondary frames. In the play, one schema
is overcoded on top of the other. The reader is invited to hear
both and to let them stand in tension.

Something similar can occur when the reader employs the
technical language of one frame of reference within the elaboration of details from a different frame. The resulting play of
images can deepen the rhetorical power of the primary frame. A
good illustration, though a very subtle one, may be found in
Mark's telling of the stilling of the storm (4:35–40). In this story
the situation has become desperate. The disciples are at the
limits of their strength, and Jesus even more so. He sleeps on.
When they awaken him, he rises from his sleep and addresses
the wind: "Peace! Be still!" (v. 39). In English these are gentle,

reassuring words: "He whispers to me, 'Peace! Be still.'" But the schemas of the Greek hold nodes of information that are lost completely in English translation. Howard Clark Kee has shown that this is technical language for exorcism.[15] Consider the effect created by superimposing such language over the top of the story. The language of exorcism gives the story a more frightening aspect, with thundering hints of the demonic. Mark seems to be suggesting that the battle being fought and won here is a supernatural battle, one with cosmic significances. In this way he primes his reader for the full-scale confrontation with the demonic in the story, about the pigs and the wild man, that follows in chapter 5. The effect is electric. The informed reader can hear the howling of demons in the background even before the story of the Gerasene demoniac begins.

Irony

We must remember that, for the reader, the elements of the story are communicated through the medium of the narration. The characters inside the story cannot hear the narrator at all, and they are completely unaware of the narrator's explanatory asides to the reader. The reader therefore always works with a different repertoire of background information than what is available to the characters inside the story. The distinction between the reader's perceptions and the characters' perceptions brings us to a very different sort of rhetorical dissonance. This is the stuff of irony.

There are several sorts of irony—tragic irony, comic irony, and so forth—but what they have in common is that they are constructed out of the difference between what the reader knows and what the characters inside the story know. A character in the story will drop a double-edged comment, something that can be parsed just as easily in either of two directions. Because the contextual constraints operative for the characters are different from those operative for the reader, the reader will often be aware of nuances and implications that are lost on the characters. The characters, after all, are stuck inside the story the way a figure is stuck inside a painting. From inside the

---

[15] Howard Clark Kee, "The Terminology of Mark's Exorcism Stories," *New Testament Studies* 14 (1967–68) 232–46.

painting, one cannot see the frame. The reader, however, is not stuck inside. The reader can observe not only the constraints operative for the characters but other constraints as well. Many of these other constraints are mediated through the narrative exchange itself—authorial asides, orienting remarks, overcoded language, a different sense of context, and so forth. Others may deal with what has already transpired within the story. In either case the reader's understanding may be overcoded on top of the understanding that would have been available to the characters inside the story. For the reader, the two levels stand in tension, and the rhetorical play oscillates back and forth between them. This oscillating effect may serve apologetic or theological ends because it forces the reader to rethink what has gone before or to understand what follows in a particular light.

Ironic tensions may also overcode emotional and rhetorical nuances on top of the primary frame. An example is in the story of the sacrifice of Isaac in Genesis 22. Abraham is called upon to sacrifice his only son on Mount Moriah. The reader is permitted to overhear God's instructions to Abraham in v. 2:

> Take your son, your only son Isaac, whom you love, and go to the land of Moriah, and offer him there as a burnt offering on one of the mountains.

Isaac does not hear v. 2. In this way the narrator overcodes Abraham's slow march to Moriah with intimations of horror that are completely lost on Isaac. The march to Moriah is a dirge. The boy's innocent question in v. 7 is all the more bittersweet for its innocence:

> The fire and the wood are here, but where is the lamb for a burnt offering?

The poignancy and horror are made almost unbearable by the many references to the blood relationship between the two men: "Take your *son*, your only *son*, Isaac, *whom you love*" (v. 2); "and Abraham took the wood of the burnt offering, and laid it on Isaac his *son*" (apparently Isaac is to carry the wood for his own execution; the treachery of it! [v. 6]);[16] "and Isaac said to his *father* Abraham, 'My *father*!' And he said, 'Here I am, my *son*' "

---

[16] To my mind, v. 6 is the most horrifying moment in the entire story.

(v. 7). When Isaac finally asks about the lamb for the burnt offering, Abraham replies with an ambiguity in v. 8. Isaac hears:

> God himself will provide the lamb for a burnt offering, my son.

The reader hears:

> God himself will provide the lamb for a burnt offering: my son.

It is not simply that the reader hears one thing and Isaac another. The reader hears both and is horrified by Isaac's innocent question and Abraham's dissembling response.

There may be ironies at work in our story of the anointing, too, though if there are, they are of an unusual type. To understand them we must turn aside briefly. Ordinarily the reader is the holder of the privileged information, and someone inside the story is the ironic victim, because readers know things that the characters cannot. Readers can learn what happens in other scenes, and they can hear orienting information that is dropped while the ironic victim is "offstage." They can be informed about the other characters' inner thoughts. Readers also have access to the narrator's asides and explanations. In Mark 4:41, after the stilling of the storm, the disciples cry out, "Who then is this, that even wind and sea obey him?" They have no way to answer that question. It will take until 8:29 before Peter finally blurts out his confession that Jesus is the Christ, and even then he misunderstands what that confession means. Mark's reader, however, knows that Jesus is the Christ right from the beginning of the story, since the Gospel of Mark opens with this superscription: "The beginning of the good news of Jesus Christ, the Son of God." Because the reader has the superscription, he can answer the question that the disciples cannot.

Sometimes the leverage is reversed and the orienting information is withheld from the reader until the story is well along. When this happens, it is the reader's knowledge that is proven defective. The direction of the irony is reversed. An excellent example occurs in director George Roy Hill's film *The Sting,* starring Robert Redford and Paul Newman. Hill intersperses scenes that are real with others that the characters have staged as part of a con operation. The plot line is essentially ambiguous, though this does not become clear until the very end, when the viewer discovers that some of the scenes that he thought were real were in fact staged, while others that appeared staged were real. The viewer is the ironic victim.

This appears to be what has happened with our story of the anointing of Jesus. The story gives reasons for the woman's behavior, but not until the very end. By that time, the reader has made judgments and formed reactions. In this way the timed disclosure of information may have created a reverse irony. The reader's reactions mirror those of the Pharisee. To the extent that this happens, Jesus' response to Simon the Pharisee is subtly but effectively directed to the reader, too.

Genre

Genres with Mixed Content

Another way to achieve rhetorical dissonance is to over-code conflicting genre signals. Remember that the reader's anticipations are governed in advance by the top-down constraints of context, genre, and theme. Those constraints contain instructions about such things as the reader's imaginative latitude, which conventions are appropriate, and what the reader should expect next. In psychological terms, they prime the reader's expectations in one direction while masking other possibilities. Ordinarily, the priming effect of genre is consistent with the text's context and theme. When this happens, the consistent signals confirm that the reader is on the right interpretive track. Sometimes, however, a writer can set genre at odds with the other reading constraints. The result is rhetorical trickery. One morning on my way to work, I heard the following statement on the radio:

> Darkening toward evening, with 100 percent chance of dark by nightfall. Clearing by morning.

A native speaker of English knows automatically that this is a play upon the genre "weather report." In this case, there is interference between the actual content of this "weather report" and the standard content of a real weather report. In order for the interference to work, the writer must assume a specific schematic competence, which the reader or listener is expected to have in hand. The reader who does not know about the standard genre misses the play entirely. On the other hand, the reader who does know hears the one against the backdrop of the other. This creates a fluctuating interference between the two. The genre signals prime the reader's expectation in one direction, while the content primes the reader's work in another direction.

Mixed Genres

A similar effect can be achieved by mixing genres themselves. If we begin, "Once upon a time," the reader knows that what is coming is a fairy tale. The reader's expectations are primed in a particular direction, and the reader knows to hold in check any objections from "normal" experience. Lots of things happen in fairy tales that cannot happen in real life. In literary terms, the reader "willingly suspends disbelief." We might go on, however, to create an example story or a morality tale. The reader who has suspended disbelief is more likely to be taken in. In this way, readers can be "had" before it has dawned on them what has happened.

Scripture is filled with examples of this sort of entrapment. A primary illustration is the story of the ewe lamb that Nathan the prophet told King David after that shameful debacle with Bathsheba (2 Sam 11–12). The story begins as a hypothetical legal case: "What would you say about a rich man who stole his neighbor's only lamb, which he loved, to prepare a meal for a visitor?" (12:1–4). The way Nathan poses the question signals the king that he is asked to make a legal judgment, but he does so in such a way that it masks the similarities between the case and David's act of treachery against Uriah. David's anger is kindled, and in a burst of righteous indignation he blurts out his verdict:

> As the LORD lives, the man who has done this deserves to die (v. 5).

This is a clear irony, not at all unlike the irony in which Oedipus the king unknowingly pronounces judgment against himself for the murder of his wife, Jocasta's, first husband:

> This murderer, no matter who he is, is banished
> from the country where my power and my throne
> Are Supreme.[17]

David's verdict is in before Nathan names the defendant: "You are the man," he says to the king (v. 7). David has been set up

---

[17] "Oedipus the King," trans. Kenneth Cavander in *Sophocles,* ed. Robert W. Corrigan (New York: Dell, 1968) 77.

by Nathan's deceptive use of genre signals. He was only too willing to suppress the similarities between Nathan's "legal case" and his own abuse of power.

The reader of 2 Samuel has a different experience from David's. For the reader, the parable of the ewe lamb is housed within the larger story of the murder of Uriah. The larger story establishes a contextual frame around the smaller one, and the reader comes to Nathan's parable fresh from a report of David's treachery. That proximity overrides the apparent distance between the two stories, thus giving David's moral blindness a particularly ugly spin. When David blurts out his judgment against the villain in Nathan's parable, the reader's immediate reaction is to delight in the irony of David delivering his own comeuppance. Even kings who dance before the Lord are not above the law!

IMPLICATIONS

We have been exploring the ways in which dissonant signals interfere with one another. When the various constraints fall out of alignment, the language may be changed into a subtle but effective vehicle of transformation.

The implication for the exegesis of Scripture is clear: If, on the one hand, we read the text only in the light of genre and ignore context and theme, or if we consider only context and ignore theme and genre, we will be unable to detect the conflict of clues that signals the presence of wordplay, irony, and plays on genre. We will see only the flat picture and miss the verbal double exposure. On the other hand, if we attune our sensitivities more broadly, if we look for redundancy of signals and places where that redundancy is somehow violated, we will discover that the Bible is a book rich in wit and wisdom, a complex tapestry of human pathos, divine revelation, seething anger, and downright good humor.

In chapters 6 and 8 we set out two criteria for validity in reading:

> An act of reading is valid to the extent that it fills in the gaps of the text with the schemes that were operative for the culture in which the text was composed.

An act of reading is valid to the extent that it takes into account the full range of constraints that govern the reading processes. It must do so in such a way that the interaction between the constraints yields an appropriate field of redundancies by which the reader can zero in on the nodes of schematic information that the author intends.

The considerations we have explored in this chapter suggest a third criterion for validity in reading:

> *An act of reading is valid to the extent that it responds appropriately to the conflicts and tensions that occur when the constraints of context, genre, theme, syntax, lexical possibilities, and paralanguage get out of alignment. It will also respond appropriately to signals that are overcoded by allusion and by the rhetorical play of mixed forms.*

The last several chapters have dealt with one or another of the primary features of language: Language has gaps, is ambiguous, is polyvalent. As we have seen, each characteristic of language requires a corresponding configuration of skills: Readers fill in gaps, disambiguate, respond to polyvalence. Authors know that readers do this, and they strategize the presentation of the facts to take advantage of these natural readerly activities. They may withhold information, may prime the reader in one direction (thus masking other possibilities), may overcode their language with suggestive associations. So "readerly work" is many-sided. It operates on several levels. Some of the levels are rational and deal with information, while others are more emotional and deal with affective responses. In chapter 10 we address the affective domain.

10

ADDING THE SOUND TRACK

How We Respond to Aural Textures

When William Wordsworth was a young man, he took a walking tour of the Swiss Alps. Before he returned home, he wrote the following poem. Notice the way the shifting textures of the poem mirror the shifting textures of the scene that the poem describes:

Alpine Storm

'Tis storm; and hid in mist from hour to hour
All day the floods a deeper murmur pour.
And mournful sounds, as of a spirit lost
Pipe wild along the hollow blustering coast.

> 'Till the Sun walking in his western field
> Shakes from behind the clouds his flashing shield.
> Triumphant in the bosom of the storm
> Glances the fire-clad eagle's wheeling form;
> Eastward, in long perspective glittering, shine
> The wood crowned cliffs that o'er the lake recline;
> Wide o'er the Alps a hundred streams unfold,
> At once to pillars turned that frame to gold;
> Behind his sail the peasant strives to shun
> The west that burns like one dilated sun,
> Where in a mighty crucible expire
> The mountains, glowing hot, like coals of fire.

As the poem opens, the diction is heavy with labials—*m* sounds predominate. The softly aspirated sounds of the *h* evoke the formless, billowing image of the mist that has settled along the coastline. The term "murmurs" is heavily onomatopoeic. The poem itself fairly mourns. The off-rhyme—"hour/pour," "lost/ coast"— deepens the sense that something is awry. As the sun appears and the rain stops, the diction shifts to the sharper, brighter sounds of the sibilants, palatals, and dentals—*s, p,* and *t.* At the same time, the off-rhyme is replaced by true rhyme, as though something wrong has been brought back into balance. The final line brings the poem to a kind of formal closure. There's something eminently satisfying in the way the sound trails off like that:

> Where in a mighty crucible expire
> The mountains, glowing hot, like coals of fire.

With this illustration we are brought to an entirely different aspect of the linguistic exchange: aural texture. By "aural texture" we mean all those dimensions of language which are resident in the sound of the words themselves. These include both the texture of the language and the changes of the speaker's tone—the modulation of the speaker's voice, pitch, rhythm, stress, and volume. Closely related to aural texture is paralanguage. By "paralanguage" we mean such extralinguistic features as gestures, facial expressions, eye contact, and changes in the way the speaker moves his or her body. Clearly such things are important facets of natural language. If I respond to your greeting by turning my back on you, my silence may not be a word, but it is most surely a statement. A come-hither look in the eye can transform an ordinary conversation into an opportunity for adventure . . . or disaster. In chapter 7 I argued that aural texture and paralanguage constrain reading in important ways. In this chapter we explore further dimensions of these constraints.

AURAL TEXTURE

Let us identify two extremes. On the one extreme is the rational, ordered, cognitive side of language, evoked and sustained by the formal properties of grammar and vocabulary. On the other is the visceral, gut-wrenching, soothing side of language, evoked by the sounds of the words. The first is more visual, the second more auditory. Significant dimensions of meaning are resident in the sheer palpation of the words themselves. At first glance it appears that texture affects only the second of these two extremes. This is an impression I do not believe will survive closer scrutiny. Instead, the two extremes are bridged by the mental linkage between the two hemispheres of the brain. Texture not only evokes emotional responses; it also serves as a kind of backup reading constraint, buttressing and clarifying the other reading activities. Texture intensifies visual imagery, clarifies syntax, telegraphs genre, and enables memory. In a moment we will survey these one at a time. For now it is enough to note that understood in this way, "meaning" includes not only the full range of rational and emotional reactions evoked in the listener but also the penetrations and interactions between them.

Texture Intensifies Visual Imagery

Consider the meaning of the word "wicked" in the sentence,

The axe was *wicked* sharp.

Here, the word has no meaning of its own. Rather, it functions as an intensifier of the adjective "sharp." Verbal texture does precisely that. It intensifies the effect of the other dimensions of meaning. Sometimes verbal texture is sharp, pointed, staccato. At other times it is a blunt instrument, incapable of precision on its own but useful as a cudgel when that is what is needed to drive one's point home. This phenomenon is the result of the interpenetration of visual and auditory language processing.

That is, it is a consequence of psychological interference. In chapter 9 we examined the significance of interference under the rubric of the Stroop effect: Visual and auditory information-processing systems interpenetrate. The "intersystem hookup" between sight and sound extends even to the textures of the language itself.

It may be for this reason that the sounds of the language can intensify the visual images the reader is able to construct. If the diction of the story includes an onomatopoeic sound for action—a "whoosh" or a "splash," for example—the very sound reinforces the sense of movement drawn from the lexicon and in that way makes the visualization of the appropriate schema more immediate and vivid. The clash and clamor of consonants can evoke the rolling thunderclap. The whispered hush of the voice speaks to us of breezes and palm trees. If the storyteller growls out the words of the antagonist in the story, the listener is more apt to visualize an angrier, more hostile face. Thus, important dimensions of our responses to linguistic texture lie on the most primitive level of interpretation: They are visceral and not cognitive; they are sanguine and instinctive, and they may affect us on levels of which we are only dimly aware.

Texture Clarifies Syntax

The notion of texture as intensifier invites us to return to the other side of the bridge between viscera and vision: the cognitive side. When a sentence is written out on the page, there are punctuation marks to indicate syntax. When the same sentence is spoken aloud, the clues must come in the form of stress, tenor, and the modulation of the speaker's voice. On the sentence level, the placement of stress on one word over another can change a statement to a question, or a question to a command. In Ovid's story of Echo and Narcissus, for example, Echo the wood nymph has fallen hopelessly in love with the boy Narcissus. He, of course, dismisses her advances with a taunt:

I would *die* before I would give you a chance at me!

She responds, as she must, by echoing back his very words, but she inflects the words differently to communicate her own nuances:

. . . *I* would give *you* a chance at *me*!

Echo repeats the boy, but the change of inflection transforms his words from a rejection into an invitation.

Texture Telegraphs Social Context and Genre

This business of complicating nuances extends more broadly to signal the social environment against which the language should be interpreted. The shape of the sounds constrains and informs the drawing of inferences and can help fix context and therefore intent. One arena in which this is particularly evident is the way we identify professional and formalized situations by the presence or absence of particular forms of diction. Consider the diction of the court bailiff profession. This is characterized by a flat, intoning voice, delivered at a fairly high register:

> All rise. The court is now in session, the honorable Judge Roy Bean presiding.

There is also a professional diction characteristic of ministers, which Peter Farb describes: "a narrow range of pitch, frequent use of monotone, overpreciseness of pronunciation, regular rhythm, fairly slow tempo, and deep resonance of the voice."[1] For many listeners this diction is one of the characteristic signs of the sermon; language from the pulpit that does not have that diction simply does not feel like a sermon at all.

There are other signals. Preachers from the American South are more apt to exploit the syncopated rhythms and parallel structures of intoning, as in this excerpt from the sermon "Go Down, Death," by James Weldon Johnson:

> Weep not, weep not,
> She is not dead;
> She's resting in the bosom of Jesus
> Heart-broken husband—*weep no more;*
> Grief-stricken son—*weep no more;*
> Left-lonesome daughter—*weep no more;*
> She's only just gone home.[2]

Intoning is the rhythmical repetition of balanced phrases. In the eyes of some, an unintoned sermon is no sermon at all. This tells

---

[1]Farb, *Word Play,* 70.
[2]James Weldon Johnson, *God's Trombones: Seven Negro Sermons in Verse* (New York: Viking Press, 1953) 27.

us something else: Texture sometimes telegraphs genre. When it does so, it activates a range of expectations and corresponding interpretive conventions, just as other genre signals do.

Texture Enables Memory

We should also note that texture enables memory. Anyone who has attempted to memorize poetry recognizes that rhythm and meter seem to fit like keys into whatever unlocks the storage units of the mind. It may be that the self-referential aspects of language that are embodied in texture have the same effect as the overcoding we discussed in chapter 9. In places where texture is a clear component of meaning, a satisfactory gist will need to include the texture as a factor. This can only happen if the gist remains close to the verbatim language of the text itself. Thus, texture can limit the degree of abstraction to which the reader can go, keeping everything close to the exact details of the text itself. There are two reasons this is so. First, the patterns of the texture are over-coded on top of the words themselves. In that position they ensure that the gist of meaning the reader constructs will be closer to verbatim memory. Second, textures create an important secondary pathway of access into the memory. If both pathways are used at once, or if we toggle back and forth between them—as happens when we find ourselves reconstructing the lyric of some half-forgotten melody—it becomes easier to retrieve the words themselves.

SOCIOLINGUISTIC PERSPECTIVES

We have thus far explored language as though its properties were somehow private—encoded by a speaker, transmitted in a text or a spoken word, decoded by a reader or listener. All of that may be true, but it is not the whole truth. The whole truth must reckon with the fact that language is a medium of exchange by which we pay the membership dues exacted by our group. We seldom talk and listen alone. Instead, we gather in company. We use language as a tool for gaining social leverage or for cementing our place in the social edifice we call culture. We seldom merely report facts, and even when we do report facts, it is often as part of a campaign to persuade someone else to accept our interpretation of what the facts mean.

The discipline of sociolinguistics emerges from concern for this more interactive dimension of language. As we move from the level of the word to the level of the sentence and then beyond that to the level of discourse, we can see that the roles played by texture and paralanguage grow increasingly complex. In the same way, as we move beyond the details of the discourse itself to the social environment in which its implications are played out, those roles make yet another movement toward greater complexity.

We have engaged this discussion before. In chapter 6 we examined the role of socially located frames of reference as the enabling context from which the reader or listener can fill in gaps in information. There we discussed technical vocabulary and jargon. Technical language can evoke an entire common frame of reference and in that way provide a world of features upon which the reader is expected to draw. But this is not the only way to do this. Texture and paralanguage do it as well. The example of the intoning voice of the preacher is a case in point. We could name a dozen instances in which professional diction signals the presence of a special province of language—sports announcers, courtroom bailiffs, newscasters, barkers in side shows, and so forth. These special provinces in turn determine the listener's expectations. Policemen speak differently when they're functioning in official capacities. Politicians, too, sometimes speak with a different tongue when they speak to the voting public. Thus, texture enables the reader or listener to access appropriate frames of reference within which the discourse is to be understood.

Verbal Dueling: The Tournament of Tongues

Sometimes these frames of reference indicate moments of tension. Language also has winners and losers. Perhaps nowhere is this more evident than in something social scientists identify as "verbal dueling."[3] Duels can take place on any number of levels, from punning to the posing of riddles, to arguing, to

[3]See Farb, "Verbal Dueling," in *Word Play,* 107–28.

outright formal debate.[4] Peter Farb notes that even the opening of a conversation involves a kind of duel: A competition occurs to see who will speak first. On this elementary level, nonverbal cues may be everything. "The role of the speaker is almost always determined by cues from eye contact, facial expressions, and gestures rather than from words."[5] When the duel is more intense, it is sometimes accompanied by more extreme expressions, by which we largely keep track of when and how we have scored a hit. (This is so unless, of course, one has learned the skill of deadpan delivery, which can change the rules and give the canny dueler a decided advantage.)

Most verbal duels involve trivial matters of position and status in the social interaction itself. Sometimes, though, the stakes are much higher. Consider the following conversation between the African-American doctor Alvin Pouissant and a white policeman in Jackson, Mississippi. Exactly fifteen words are exchanged between them:[6]

"What's your name, boy?" the policeman asked.

"Doctor Pouissant. I'm a physician."

"What's your first name, boy?"

"Alvin."

Here is clearly a contest with a winner and a loser. That much is evident in the vocabulary. But anyone familiar with the speech patterns of the American South can also easily supply the accompanying texture and paralanguage. The policeman's voice has an edge to it. His eyes are focused squarely on Pouissant's face. Pouissant phrases his first move very carefully to assert the status claim of his education without pushing the policeman to the limits. He gives only his title and surname. The policeman's countermove rejects Pouissant's title as irrelevant and discounts his surname. He ups the ante by sharpening the edge to his

---

[4]There is an enormous body of literature on riddles. For a summary and an annotated bibliography, see Roger D. Abrahams and Alan Dundes, "Riddles . . . ," in *Folklore and Folklife: An Introduction,* ed. Richard M. Dorson (Chicago: University of Chicago Press, 1972) 129–43.

[5]Farb, *Word Play,* 107.

[6]See Pouissant's article in the *New York Times Magazine,* August 20, 1967, 53.

voice. It is too much. Pouissant capitulates, and in doing so, he turns his eyes down and drops his voice away. In reporting this conversation, Pouissant tells us that his final response, "Alvin," was given with "profound humiliation."[7]

Let us imagine that there were others present at this scene, say, Pouissant's wife and nine-year-old son in the car and two or three good ol' boys watching from the curb. A duel that is fought in the presence of an audience takes on a different aspect. The crowd not only observes the duel; in a real and meaningful way, it participates in it. The presence of onlookers raises the stakes by intensifying the status issues involved. This makes a significant difference in the thrust and parry, and the duelers play not only to win but also to save face or to score a hit with the crowd.

Texture and Reading the Bible

Thus far we have discussed texture as we experience it when we speak English. It hardly bears mentioning that there are important implications here for the way we read the languages of the Bible. When we raise the matter of texture in the reading of the Bible, we are confronted immediately with a set of thorny problems. First, the sound patterns of the biblical languages are now pretty much lost. It is well known that the scholarly pronunciation of the biblical languages is an artificial construction. The biblical text itself seldom gives away clues about where and how stresses are to be placed. Second, even if we could recover with certainty the sounds of the biblical text, we cannot know for certain how those sounds would have affected a first-century reader because the interpretation of texture is learned and not innate. Anything learned is subject to change, to elaboration and decay. Thus, we should take seriously the caution urged by Farb: "Contrary to what many people believe, no speaker can judge the emotions expressed by a speaker of an unknown language just by noting his paralanguage. . . . Each speech community has its own rules for the expressive use of paralanguage."[8] No one can tell immediately what the texture and paralanguage of a foreign culture must

---

[7]For a discussion of the sociological dimensions of this conversation, see Joshua Fishman, *Advances in the Sociology of Language* (The Hague: Mouton, 1971) 21f.

[8]Farb, *Word Play,* 69.

signal. How much more of a problem this is when we approach the literature of the Bible, from which we are removed by almost two thousand years.

Even bearing this caution in mind, however, we can still make some responsible conjectures. Most of the scholarly questions raised about the sayings of Jesus have been formulated as part of the larger historical-critical agenda. Which elements of the tradition are more primitive? Which are accurate? In this vein, a not uncommon observation is that the rhythm and texture of the Jesus sayings contributed to their survival. But this attention to the historical-critical questions may divert attention from the effect Jesus' love of wordplay would have had on the gallery of onlookers who thronged about him. In this matter, we are offered guidance by our discussion of verbal dueling. According to Matthew Black, who offers a general summary, the Aramaic voice of Jesus is "soft and gentle in the kindly sayings, as in the promise to the heavy-laden, inexorable and hard in the sayings about Offenses [sic], strongly guttural and mockingly sibilant where hypocrites and 'the rest of men' are contrasted with the Christian disciples."[9]

Black's comment may be illustrated from our story of the anointing of Jesus. In chapter 9 we reported Jakob Jonsson's position that Jesus' response to the host was "friendly and humorous." Jesus turns the tables on the host, inviting him to compare himself with the sinful woman but stopping just short of an accusation. He does this by shifting from the first person to the third person:

A "You did not . . .
B   but she did . . .
A   You did not . . .
B   but she did . . . .
A   You did not . . .
B   but she did . . . .

B   Therefore her sins . . . are forgiven,
A   but the one to whom little is forgiven loves little."

---

[9]Matthew Black, *An Aramaic Approach to the Gospels and Acts,* 3d ed. (Oxford: Clarendon Press, 1967) 185.

This subtle shift may be buttressed by a wordplay. Black has pointed out that in Aramaic the term for "sin" and the term for "debt" are the same: *hobha*. The Pharisee's private thought is that the woman is a "sinner," a *hayyabhta*. In response, Jesus tells a story about what it is like to be deeply in debt, *hayyabh* (or *bar hobha*).[10] In a later comment, Kenneth Bailey builds upon Black's observation: "Jesus uses this wordplay both to compare and contrast the sinful woman (*hayyabhta*) with her sin (*hobha*) and Simon who is socially in debt (*bar hobha*) and has failed to love (*habbebh*)."[11]

As the consonants and vowels roll back and forth upon one another, the gallery is treated to the play of sounds. It would have been obvious to any of Jesus' listeners, and the crowd in the room would have been delighted.[12] Even if this is true in Aramaic, however, it would have been lost completely on Luke's Greek-speaking reader. But at least in Aramaic the play of reiterated consonants would have rendered the psychological processes more complex. The lilt in Jesus' language lingered longer in the listener's mind.

Can it be any wonder that he was a champion of the little guy? In the thrust and parry of the duel, the sword of his mouth was wicked sharp.

IMPLICATIONS

Let us now pause to gather together the substance of this chapter. Linguistic textures, paralanguage, and other extralinguistic cues control the reading exchange much the way the more formalized reading constraints control the reading process. They indicate syntax. They help the reader or listener identify social context, level of discourse, genre, and context. They signal the status of the speaker and intensify the visual and visceral dimensions of the speaker's language. Rhythmical and

---

[10] Ibid., 181–83.

[11] Bailey, *Through Peasant Eyes,* 13.

[12] One aspect of this interpretation should give us pause. The original objection—which forms an important component of the wordplay—is contained within the unuttered thoughts of the Pharisee. It would have gone unheard by the crowd but certainly not by Simon, to whom the response is directed.

alliterative dimensions of texture aid verbatim memory by re-sisting resolution into a gist, and—in the context of verbal dueling—they demonstrate skill.

In the previous chapters of this section, we have set out three basic criteria for legitimacy in reading. The first concerned the manner in which the reader fills in gaps. The second concerned the way in which the reader governs the reading process, through top-down and bottom-up reading constraints. The third concerned the recognition of dissonance and overcoding as the constraints are set at odds with one another.

The considerations we have explored in this chapter suggest a fourth criterion for validity in reading:

An act of reading is legitimate to the extent that it accounts for the visceral responses evoked by paralanguage and texture and also to the extent that it governs its activities by recognizing and observing the controls that texture and paralanguage provide.

It is not enough that these activities take place during reading. It is just as important that they take place in a specific sequence. In chapter 11 we turn to timing.

11

FRAME AFTER FRAME

How We Deal with Sequence

In their introduction to psycholinguistics, A. Sanford and S. Garrod offer the following series of statements:

John was on his way to school.

He was terribly worried about the math lesson.

He thought he might not be able to control the class again today.

It was not a normal part of a janitor's job.[1]

---

[1]Sanford and Garrod, *Understanding Written Language,* 114.

For each word an appropriate schema is accessed, and at appropriate moments the schemas are compared and evaluated. Within the constraints of context and so forth, the reader focuses down on whatever nodes of information seem likely and from these constructs a gist. The difficulties in reading this series indicate that the prior readerly work was defective in some way, and the reader is forced to retrogress and make corrections.

Of course, it is not that the gists were defective. The series was designed to evoke the response of retrogression and correction; that's part of what makes it an interesting example. Its disruptions are only evident if the reader has constructed the gists in a particular sequence. If the reader reads the sentences in some other order, the disruptions are lost and the illustration loses its potency. This demonstrates, quite clearly I think, the next major protocol of reading: Language is linear, and because it is linear, we must assemble its significances in the sequence in which they appear in the text.

In this chapter we consider the effect of sequence on the text's rhetorical impact. Psychologist Daniel Goleman describes a childhood fantasy in which "reality"—the stuff that appeared to be brute, unmediated experience—was like a series of movie sets constructed just for him, just outside the boundaries of awareness.

> This Herculean task was accomplished by some group or force outside my ken. I imagined a huge, unseen horde of workers feverishly—but silently—at work constructing these sets as I approached, and just as feverishly dismantling them and storing them away as I left. All this work was guided by hands I never could see directly, and with purpose and motives I never could know.
>
> That childhood fantasy, I have since come to realize, is rather a close metaphor for the workings of our minds.[2]

What Goleman has in view here is the psychological reality that we live in a "world" that our mind constructs, a world that may or may not correspond to the actual world of objects and events. The imagery is also a helpful metaphor for the ways in which we access, deploy, and then retire the schemas of language. A "horde of secret workers" is feverishly—but silently—at work constructing gists as we need them, and just as feverishly

---

[2]Goleman, *Vital Lies,* 74.

dismantling them and storing them away when we do not. Whenever we interact with language, the sets, or schemas, are constructed one *after* another, and the manner in which the earlier work is carried on establishes the range and latitude for the work that comes after.

John was on his way to school.

John must be a student.

He was terribly worried about the math lesson.

Yep. He is a student.

He thought he might not be able to control the class again today.

No. I was wrong. John is a teacher.

It was not a normal part of a janitor's job.

Wrong again. I've been had.

This process, hardwired as it is into the psychological machinery of the mind, has serious and extensive consequences for our understanding of the linguistic exchange and therefore also for what we do when we interpret the Bible. Since the construction of each gist is controlled by what has gone before, the sort of gist we have in hand from an earlier point in the reading process both enables and limits what we make of material encountered at a later point.

The fact that the gists are constructed one *after* the other is a necessary consequence of the linearity of language. Biblical language is like other language in that it can only present its cues to the reader one after the other. Like the other elemental characteristics of language—gaps, ambiguity, and so forth—linearity poses its own special challenges for authors and readers. In the same way, those challenges also create corresponding opportunities for the biblical writers to leverage their readers in various ways.

STORY TIME AND DISCOURSE TIME

One way in which writers leverage their readers is to rearrange the sequence of the schemas and in that way manipulate the series of gists the reader is able to construct. This means that time passes differently in a story than it does in real life. For example, consider the problem faced by a narrator who wishes to portray two events that in real life happened simultaneously. A TV director might simply split the screen or toggle back and forth between the two scenes. It is difficult for a narrator to do that without confusing the reader. A simpler solution is to tell one event first, then tell the other afterward with a notation ("Meanwhile, back at the ranch," or some such thing). While in real life the events happened at the same time, in a narrative they are encountered by the reader one *after* the other. This sort of linguistic phenomenon leads literary scholars to make a distinction between "*event* time"—which describes the time, sequence, and duration of the actual event—and "*story* time"— which describes the timing, sequence, and duration of the story about the event.[3]

It is clear that the two sorts of time behave according to very different rules. Story time can speed up and slow down in a manner that the time of the actual event cannot.[4] Story time can also reverse itself. A narrator is under no obligation to present the facts of the story in the actual sequence in which they occurred. Consider the following New England folktale:

> My Uncle Henry and Aunt Mehetabel had an argument here last Christmas. Seems he didn't buy his mother-in-law a Christmas gift this year. And that got Mahitabel all het up. 'Course, she was het up last year, too, 'cause then he bought the old woman a cemetery plot.

---

[3]While the literary critics have widely recognized this reality, they have employed an equally wide range of terms to describe it. A. A. Mendilow (*Time and the Novel* [New York: Humanities Press, 1952] 65–71) distinguished between "chronological time" and "fictional time"; Gerard Genette (*Narrative Discourse: An Essay in Method* [Ithaca, N.Y.: Cornell University Press, 1980] 33–86) distinguished between "story time" and "narrative time." Seymour Chatman (*Story and Discourse* [Ithaca, N.Y.: Cornell University Press, 1978] 62f.) distinguished between "story time" and "discourse time." I have learned the most about this topic from Menakhem Perry, "Literary Dynamics: How the Order of a Text Creates Its Meanings" *Poetics Today* 1 (1979) 35–64.

[4]This may not be beyond challenge. Albert Einstein is said to have remarked that "when you sit with a nice girl for two hours, it seems like two minutes; when you sit on a hot stove for two minutes, it seems like two hours. That's relativity."

So this year, when Mahitabel started in on him, Henry just stood up, looked at her, and said, "Now, Mahitabel. Why should I buy your mother a gift this year when she didn't use the one I gave her last year?"

Part of what makes this story work is the way the comment about last year's gift has been stuck in the center. This sort of out-of-place sequential element is called an analepsis. The story has this temporal sequence:

Introduction of the problem this year

Analepsis to last year

Return to this year

The story could well have been told in its correct "historical" sequence—event time—but it would have been less vivid. The rhetorical effect is increased because the analepsis introduces an element of surprise and brings the mention of the cemetery plot into closer proximity to the punch line.

Of course, this example is just a folktale. But narrators of real events also sequence the disclosure of information to heighten or channel the rhetorical effects. The radio commentator Paul Harvey tells a story about a grocery clerk who was loading packages into a customer's car when he happened to notice that another customer had left a bundle on the roof of her car. As the second car began pulling out of the parking lot, the clerk began running after her and yelling, but she had her window up and couldn't hear him. Just as she pulled out of the parking lot and into the avenue, the bundle slid off the roof, and the clerk reached out and caught the baby just in time.

This story achieves its effect by a combination of two psychological phenomena—priming and masking. We have encountered priming several times before in the course of our study, particularly in the exploration of garden path sentences:

Cinderella was sad because she could not attend the ball. There were big tears in her brown dress.

Masking

What we have seen is that the priming enables the writer to highlight what is important and in that way to guide the reader's unfolding perceptions. This is an integral part of the coordination of top-down and bottom-up constraints we examined in chapter 7. At the same time, the manner in which the reader's anticipations are primed also deflects attention away from other interpretive options. Cognitive scientists call this darker side of priming masking. Since the writer leads and the reader follows, the writer can lead the reader into missteps. By manipulating the priming effects, the writer can make some gists appear more likely than others, and in that way set the reader up for a fall. The reader's perceptions are masked against the hidden possibilities.

Jokes often depend upon masked features, as do white lies. I am leaving the house, already ten minutes late for a meeting at work. The telephone rings. When I hear the ring, I experience a momentary relief, then a private inner battle: I now have a "truthful" way of apologizing for my tardiness. I can say (quite accurately, but also quite deceptively), "I'm sorry I was late. The phone rang just as I was leaving the house." I know that the listener will make all the necessary connections and draw the quite incorrect conclusion that I am late *because of* the phone call. If the white lie works, I will have masked the full truth.

Masking can take place in a number of directions. One can hold back disambiguating cues or manipulate the top-down reading constraints. Or one can mask possibilities by intruding distractions into the normal flow of thought. Paul Kolers offers the following analogy: A clerk in a store is attending to the needs of his customer when he is interrupted by a second customer, who demands immediate attention. When the clerk returns to the first customer, he may have difficulty recalling where he was in the transaction. This is an example of "backward masking."[5]

Foreshadowing and Foretelling

With the related concepts of priming and masking, we can make some observations about the cognitive experience that

---

[5]Paul Kolers, "Some Psychological Aspects of Pattern Recognition," in *Recognizing Patterns,* ed. P. Kolers and M. Eden (Cambridge, Mass.: MIT Press, 1968). For an extensive discussion of related literature, see M. T. Turvey, "Constructive Theory, Perceptual Systems, and Tacit Knowledge," in *Cognition and the Symbolic Processes,* ed. W. B. Weimer and D. S. Palermo (Hillsdale, N.J.: Erlbaum, 1974) 165–80.

attends such literary strategies as foreshadowing, foretelling, and flashback. *Foreshadowing* prepares the reader to anticipate later experiences in particular ways. The reader does not necessarily know that foreshadowing is taking place, however, because he or she may be completely unaware of upcoming turns in the plot. Instead, the foreshadowing becomes fully potent only when its effects are evinced by their later fulfillment. A good example from our literature is the way in which Mark's Gospel prepares the reader for the death of Jesus. Everywhere there are clues that the course Jesus is following is going to lead ultimately to disaster. The arrest of John the Baptist in Mark 1:14 may already have suggested overtones of tragedy.[6] The authorities reach the decision to put Jesus to death as early as 3:6. The rejection at Nazareth in 6:1–6 carries that decision forward. Jesus responds with a subtly ambiguous remark in v. 4: "A prophet is not without honor, except in his own country, and among his own kin, and in his own house." When John the Baptist is executed in 6:14–29, the reader is fully primed to hear the horror there as a deepening anticipation of the fate that awaits Jesus. The horror of John's death casts a kind of pall over the narrative as a whole, and when we find Jesus dangling on the machine of his death, we cannot help but hear the story of John still echoing in the background.

Foretelling works much like foreshadowing, except that it stands much closer to the surface of the narrative. It may take the form of direct prophecy, placed on the lips of some character in the story, or it may come directly from the narrator. In Greek drama, foretelling was often performed by the chorus, which played the role of narrator and addressed the audience directly.

Entrapment

We have been discussing the elements of timing that contribute to the dynamic movements of the language—priming and masking, foreshadowing and foretelling. All of these temporal dimensions of language provide occasion for entrapments

---

[6]This is especially so if, as is sometimes argued, the expression *paradothēnai* here means "to be handed over to execution." This possibility is suggested by Mark's grammar, and—remember—Mark's reader would not have had the other Gospels around to suggest otherwise.

and seductions. In a major discussion of reader-response criticism and the Synoptic Gospels, James Resseguie defined entrapment this way: "Entrapment occurs when a reader is led to make premature conclusions—probably conclusions based on assumptions he already holds—and then is forced to discredit those assumptions and reverse his conclusions."[7] Resseguie provides an example of entrapment that illustrates the point quite nicely. In Luke 22:24–27 a dispute arises among the disciples over the question which of them was the greatest. Jesus offers an analogy in v. 27:

> Which is greater, one who sits at table, or one who serves? Is it not the one who sits at table?

Here, customary practice "entices the reader to make a premature, and as it turns out an incorrect response: 'The one who sits at table.' "[8] That initial response is confirmed by the grammatical structure of the question that follows: "It's the one who sits at table, isn't it?" The trap is set. The disciples can only respond in the affirmative. With his final comment Jesus springs the trap and calls the disciples to a kind of repentance. His words fall like a bombshell:

> But I come among you as one who serves.

Resseguie claims, I think wrongly, that "entrapment is rare in the gospels."[9] What he has in view may be the smaller, more focused instances of entrapment, in which the reader is set up and then brought down within a few quick strokes. In a larger sense, however, entrapment may be a fair way of describing the overarching movements of the Gospel as a whole. What better way to describe a body of literature that continually leads the reader to a fresh encounter with Christ?

---

[7] James L. Resseguie, "Reader-Response Criticism and the Synoptic Gospels," *Journal of the American Academy of Religion* 52 (1984) 314.

[8] Ibid., 314.

[9] Ibid., 314. Jeffrey Staley describes a similar phenomenon under the term "victimization" in John 4 (*The Print's First Kiss: A Rhetorical Investigation of the Implied Reader in the Fourth Gospel* [SBLDS 82; Atlanta, Ga.: Scholars Press, 1988] 95–118), and Andrew Lincoln offers this reversal of expectations as a fundamental aspect of the irony that ends Mark's Gospel ("The Promise and the Failure: Mark 16:7, 8," *Journal of Biblical Literature* 108 [1989] 290f.).

TIMING AND THE ANOINTING OF JESUS

With these observations in hand, let us turn for a moment and explore some of the dimensions of timing as they apply to our story of the anointing of Jesus. For purposes of comparison, let us set this story against a reconstruction of the underlying historical event. Our survey of the history of the discussion makes it clear that this is difficult to do with any certainty. For this reason, I have arbitrarily selected Kenneth Bailey's reconstruction.[10] Bailey does not combine the story with the anointing in Bethany, and he reconstructs the events entirely from clues found within Luke's version.

According to Bailey, the actual events most likely followed this sequence:

1. Jesus—apparently—preached a sermon that impressed Simon the Pharisee,[11] who invited him home for a meal.

   1.1 At this time (or perhaps sometime earlier) the woman had experienced forgiveness for her sins and had prepared a kind of libation to express her gratitude (see v. 47, which could be read to imply that she had already been forgiven).

2. Jesus entered the house and reclined at table.

3. The doors were left open, and the townspeople were allowed to enter.

   3.1 After Jesus entered the house, the woman learned that he was there,[12] and followed him. Verse 45 implies that she must have arrived very soon after him.

4. Something went awry. The host withheld the traditional social pleasantries—water for the guest's feet, a kiss, and oil for his face. By doing so, he delivered a serious insult to his guest.

5. The woman decided to make up for the host's rudeness by supplying what he had overlooked. This is an extremely emotional gesture, and she "breaks down and literally washes his feet with her tears."[13] This latter act—the weeping and the

---

[10] Bailey, *Through Peasant Eyes,* 1–21.
[11] Ibid., 3.
[12] Ibid., 7.
[13] Ibid., 8.

washing of the feet—is unplanned and spontaneous, and she has no towel! Her solution—tender and affectionate, but easily misunderstood—is to let down her hair to dry his feet.

6. Simon's calculated snub has been thwarted by the gesture, and his response—lost on the crowd but not on Jesus—is to deepen his sense that Jesus is not worthy of the title "prophet."

Let us stop here. After this, the sequence of the actual events merges with that of Luke's story. The attractiveness of this elaboration is that it provides a helpful reconstruction of the woman's motives and it explains why what she does appears to be a mixture of planned expressions (the libation to express her gratitude), deep emotion (the tears), and social awkwardness (she lets down her hair).[14] We should note also that it is almost impossible to locate the date or the place of the underlying historical event. This is a tradition that "floated free."

Now let us compare the sequence of Bailey's reconstruction of the event with the sequence of Luke's telling of the story. When Luke takes over the tradition, he places it in a specific literary context. That context forms the basis for the top-down constraints that will govern the reader's perceptions of the details as they unfold. Within this same chapter he has included an extensive condemnation of the Pharisees and lawyers who had "rejected the purpose of God for themselves" (v. 30) and who had condemned Jesus as a "glutton and drunkard, a friend of tax collectors and sinners" (v. 34). These background notes prime the reader to expect a controversy of some kind, and they shape the reader's disposition toward the Pharisee.

To achieve this effect, Luke reorganized the scene's sequences very differently from the historical sequence of what actually happened (Figure 11.1). Two odd but subtle twists stand out. First, Luke has withheld the name of the Pharisee until v. 40. Why hold it back? Andre Legault felt that it was an "involuntary, spontaneous, unconscious insertion."[15] But such an insertion would indicate that Luke knew Simon's name. (Surely he knew Simon's name when he began composing the

---

[14]To my mind, Bailey may be right that she was moved by compassion to make up for Simon's discourtesy toward his guest, but this—or its contrary—is incapable of demonstration from the evidence as we have it.

[15]Legault, "The Anointings in Galilee," 144.

story only four verses earlier.) Whatever its compositional source, the rhetorical effect of withholding the name is that the host at the banquet is made to serve as a *representative* Pharisee. Thus, the suspicions that the reader has already generated about Pharisees are brought to bear on the opening of this story.

Event Sequence	Story Sequence
Sermon	Sermon
Invitation	Invitation
Townspeople come in	Townspeople come in
The host snubs Jesus	_____
The woman anoints Jesus' feet, weeps, washes his feet	The woman anoints Jesus' feet, weeps, washes his feet
The host objects	The host objects
Jesus responds by referring to the host's snub,	Jesus responds by referring to the host's snub,
"Simon . . . "	"Simon . . . "

FIGURE 11.1: EVENT SEQUENCE AND STORY SEQUENCE

The second displacement is that there is absolutely nothing in the opening verses to suggest a motive for what the woman does. If Simon were guilty of social improprieties—as indeed he may have been—the reader is completely unaware of that fact until the story is well along. Again, Luke surely knew of the improprieties when he began composition. Nonetheless, by withholding any clue that there is something wrong, he allows the reader to default to the norm and assume by inference that all is well and good. In this way, Luke effectively prevents the reader from making any but the worst sense of the woman's clearly outrageous behavior.

Thus, by holding something back, Luke invites the reader to draw a more disturbing impression of the woman. He reinforced this judgment by deftly but effectively overcoding the description of the woman's behavior with subtle sexual innuendo. Let us look at this process a little more closely. As we have seen, the context primes the reader to expect a controversy of some sort, with the Pharisee as Jesus' opponent. When the woman appears, it intrudes on that expectation. As the story opens, there are clear and frequent elements suggesting instead that all the improprieties lie with her. When she is described as a sinner, *hamartōlos,* in v. 37, the schematic connections with the *hamartōloi* in v. 34 are immediate and clear: The reader can expect that Jesus will prove to be a friend of such a person. Yet the woman behaves scandalously. The reader is very likely to default to the schema "prostitute" when he encounters the term *hamartōlos* here. When she caresses Jesus' feet and then punctuates that act by letting down her hair in public, the effect strains the reader's credulity to the breaking point. There are good reasons for what she does, but the reader does not know them because Luke has held them back until a later point in the narrative. The reader's initial dispositions toward the Pharisee, the woman, and Jesus are "backward masked," and another perspective emerges with a jolt.

That jolt has a sobering aftershock: Perhaps Jesus himself is implicated here. After all, he does nothing to stop the woman. Were it not for the woman's tears, the eroticism of it would simply be too much. She continues to kiss Jesus' feet.[16] The plot complicates. The reader's confusion and hesitation grow. The tension increases until v. 39, in which the reader finds herself shadowing the inner thoughts of the Pharisee: "If this man were a prophet . . . " In this way the complication of the plot is mirrored by complicating factors within the reader's own mind.

Closure

If we think of loose ends as plot complications and tied-up ends as resolutions of plot complications, then it becomes clear that not all such matters are adequately resolved. Not every narrative makes sense. Sometimes the sense must be made by the reader. But this does not mean that the reader is always satisfied with what he or she has been asked to do. The complication within the reader's mind has important implications for our understanding of what we do when we read. If the

---

[16] Note the imperfect verb, "she was kissing" (*katephilei*), in v. 38!

reader's internal complications are not adequately resolved, he or she is left with unfinished business, unfinished readerly work.

Perhaps this is why some narratives have the power to force us beyond the surface of historical reports into ever deeper and more penetrating perceptions. The literary critic Laurence Perrine discusses this rupture of superficiality in terms of "happy" and "unhappy" endings. Literature that is designed merely to entertain will neatly tie off its plot complications, resolving everything into an aesthetically satisfying denouement. Literature that is designed to make us think more deeply will leave us with unfinished readerly work.

> The unhappy ending has a peculiar value for the writer who wishes us to ponder life. The story with a happy ending has been "wrapped up" for us: the reader is sent away feeling pleasantly if vaguely satisfied with the world, and ceases to think about the story searchingly. The unhappy ending, on the other hand, may cause him to brood over the results, to go over the story in his mind, and thus by searching out its implications get more from it.[17]

Here it is worth stepping aside to apply these observations to the matter of preaching. In some kinds of sermonic situations, the hallmark of good preaching is clarity, and the rule of thumb for achieving clarity is repetition: Tell them what you are going to tell them, tell them, then tell them what you told them. In my view, this may be an appropriate strategy for some situations but not for others. When the needs of the congregation call for consolidation, for comfort, and for encouragement, perhaps redundancy and full closure may be exactly right. But when the situation calls for confrontation, for growth, and for transcending limits, it may be appropriate to ask challenging questions even when these cannot be adequately resolved. Unresolved sermonic complications stir up messy business and leave the listener with unfinished work to do. When we take that step, we sometimes find that the congregation remembers not the sermon itself but the difference of thinking that the sermon elicits. It is a risk we sometimes need to take, if only because it is a risk the biblical writers sometimes took before us. But it is a risk we must take with our eyes open to the discomfort we may be causing our congregation.

---

[17] Laurence Perrine, *Story and Structure* (New York: Harcourt, Brace and World, 1959) 66.

IMPLICATIONS

Let us summarize this chapter with a quote from an eminent literary critic, Menakhem Perry, who points out that the problem of linearity in language creates exactly that window of opportunity rhetoricians require if they are to time the disclosure of information.

> The nature of a literary work, and even the sum total of its meanings, do not rest on the conclusions reached by the reader at the end-point of the text-continuum. They are not a "sifted," "balanced," and static sum total constituted once the reading is over, when all the relevant material has been laid out before the reader. *The effects of the entire reading process all contribute to the meaning of the work: its surprises; the changes along the way; the process of a gradual, zig-zag-like build-up of meanings, their reinforcement, development, revision and replacement; the relation between expectations aroused at one stage of the text and discoveries actually made in subsequent stages; the process of retrospective re-patterning and even the peculiar survival of meanings which were first constructed and then rejected.*[18]

In the previous chapters of this section, we established a series of criteria for validity in reading: Reading must fill in gaps with appropriate schemas; must observe appropriate constraints; must recognize the dissonances that occur when the constraints call for different, conflicting conclusions; and must respond appropriately to the cues of aural texture and paralanguage. What we have learned in this chapter suggests a fifth and final criterion for validity in reading:

> *An act of reading is valid to the extent that it takes the sequences of the text seriously, where appropriate bracketing out any knowledge of any upcoming turns that would have been impossible for someone reading naturally and integrates such activities into a dynamic, fluid whole.*

With this criterion in hand, we are brought round to the point at which this major section of our book began: Reading is an act of strategy, it involves movement and direction, and both the

---

[18] Perry, "Literary Dynamics," 41; italics added.

movement and the direction are important factors in the leverage the author holds over the reader. The same is true of preaching. The proclamation of the gospel involves not only the direction and movement of the sermon but also the direction taken in the congregation's response. Out of that movement—dynamic, directional, strategic—comes precisely that window of opportunity which the preacher can use to challenge a congregation to deeper and more fulfilling encounters with the Word. We shall turn to those concerns in the chapters which follow.

12

RHETORIC OF TEXT, RHETORIC OF SERMON

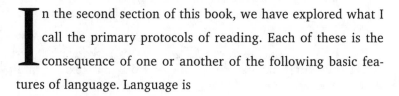

In the second section of this book, we have explored what I call the primary protocols of reading. Each of these is the consequence of one or another of the following basic features of language. Language is

- selective
- ambiguous
- polyvalent
- aural
- linear

For this reason, when we interact with language, we must have some way to

- fill in gaps
- disambiguate
- recognize and respond to dissonances and conflicts between the reading constraints
- respond to aural textures and accompanying paralanguage
- unscramble sequences, anticipating what is ahead and correcting our anticipations against the actual details of the text as they unfold, one word after the other

Each of these suggested a corresponding criterion for validity in reading. An act of reading is valid to the extent that it

- is informed by an appropriate set of schemas, scripts, and contextual and cultural information and is capable of recognizing the interplay between the nodes of information that are resident in the schemas
- takes into account the full range of constraints that govern reading—context, genre, theme, lexical possibilities, syntactical possibilities, and paralanguage
- accounts for the rhetorical effects created when those constraints are set at odds with each other—overcoding; the slowdown of reading as interference makes reading more complex; the enhancement of memory when overcoded and allusive language resists resolution into a gist
- accounts for the visceral responses evoked by paralanguage and texture and governs its activities by recognizing and observing the controls that texture and paralanguage provide
- takes the sequences of the text seriously, bracketing out any knowledge of upcoming turns that would have been impossible for someone reading naturally, and integrates these activities into a dynamic, fluid whole

The closer the reader conforms to criteria such as these, the closer his or her responses will be to those that the text was originally designed to evoke in its intended readers.

Exegesis is the process—or combination of processes—by which we reconstruct what those reading experiences might have been. In this chapter we want to pull these various processes together into a single framework. Traditionally the formal study of the Bible has had a more or less analytical bent. The interpreter isolates some element—say, historical context, word study, or cultural background—for detailed analysis. This is like unraveling the strands of a rope and looking at them individually, and it is a helpful procedure because it can give us a fix on the variety of things we must know if we are to read well. But something more must happen. The rope must be rewoven and viewed whole. To do that, the reader must move to a level of involvement that entails more personal investment and is more integrative of the text as a whole.

THE RHETORIC OF THE TEXT—
ENTICEMENTS AND ENTRAPMENTS

With this we are returned to matters that occupied our attention in chapter 6, though on a higher plane of complexity and sophistication. Although as readers we do not normally dismantle texts into component parts, nevertheless we encounter any text piecemeal because its language is selective and linear. The reading activities are designed to make whole sense out of something inherently fragmentary and cumulative, and they can make heavy demands upon the reader's gap-filling skills. The result is something Wolfgang Iser identified as "asymmetry" between the text and the reader.[1] The opening and closing of gaps, entrapment, and the disclosure or withholding of orienting information all combine to keep the reader just a bit off balance.

If we are trained to analyze the text into its component parts, the imbalances and entrapments are an offense to be done away with. Indeed, that seems to be the nature of systematic inquiry itself. Truth, to be truth, must be internally coherent. Truth is *factual,* it has to do with what is or isn't so. The problem is, sometimes the biblical text simply pushes the envelope of our understanding of what constitutes truth. Truth is

---

[1]Wolfgang Iser, *The Act of Reading: A Theory of Aesthetic Response* (Baltimore: Johns Hopkins University Press, 1978) 163–79.

also *transformational.* One does not have to read very far before it becomes evident that the writers of the Bible occasionally time the disclosure of information to entrap the reader into new visions of the way God's thumb leaves its print on human affairs. The tendency of the text to keep the reader off balance is a problem for the critic who would reduce the meaning of the Bible to the objective information it yields, but it is an asset to the reader who seeks a transforming encounter with the word of God. The God of the Bible does not argue with us, like a lawyer; God woos us, like a great cosmic lover. If the Bible is a play for our souls, it is a rhetorical play—a Word play—that intrigues and entices our minds as well.

This seems to be entirely in keeping with our nature, with the nature of our minds. Wallace Chafe suggests that rhetorical play is part of what keeps the mind moving, pushing it to make its strategic responses.

> Although the mind possesses schemas that help in [its] model building activity, it is at the same time especially well equipped to react to inputs that conflict with its schematic expectations. Without such inputs it enters a state of boredom; with them it enters a state of excitement that prepares it to reject the sources of disturbance. Hence, the only successful narratives are those that provide a conflict of expectations.[2]

This is also in keeping with the nature of language itself. According to Iser, the asymmetry is the natural consequence of the gaps in information. The gaps trap the reader in a shifting middle ground between familiar repertoire and unfamiliar narrative world. When properly timed, the lack of symmetry creates suspense, it foreshadows, it entices, it seduces the reader, all the while creating the impression that what the reader is envisioning is the stuff of the narrative world itself, purely and innocently grasped.

But the constraint must be evenhanded. The author must leave room for the reader; he or she must "halve the matter amicably." There are several dimensions of that shifting equilibrium. We will look at only two of these because they are important but often overlooked aspects of reading and are critical if we are to understand what gives the biblical text its rhetorical power.

---

[2]Chafe, "Some Things That Narratives Tell Us about the Mind," 97.

Asymmetry in the Reader's Identification with Characters

In tracing out the sources of the reader's dissonance, some theorists place the emphasis on the internal psychological processes of identification with the story's characters. In a provocative essay Robert Hellenga describes a favorite device for teaching literature.[3] He has his college coeds read a poem written through the eyes of a young man who is anticipating the successful seduction . . . of a college coed. The poem is graphic and explicit. The first reaction is usually distaste and even anger (as perhaps it should be). Hellenga's purpose, however, is to force them to experience literature as a vehicle through which they can try on other identities, can see through someone else's eyes: "Many of my female students discover that whatever their feelings about the character—the universal lover—the role is an extremely interesting one to try on, to look *through*."[4]

It is the capacity to see the world through someone else's eyes that interests us here, since it introduces a variety of psychological interactions we may have with literature. We get under the skin of the characters in a story, and we do so by injecting ourselves into the gaps that are left in the story line. This happens when the characters are only partially sketched in. Because language is selective, the characters will naturally be underdeveloped. This native feature of language provides the reader with the elbowroom that is necessary if he or she is to squeeze inside the character and feel what it is like to move around as someone else. Thus, narrative and poetry create something George Poulet called "a magical object that allows the interiority of one human being to play host to the interiority of another."[5] At the same moment, the reader can bring that

---

[3]Robert Hellenga, "What Is Literary Experience *Like?*" *New Literary History* 14 (1982) 105–15. For a discussion of levels of identification within the biblical literature, see John Darr, *On Character Building: The Reader and The Rhetoric of Characterization in Luke-Acts* (Louisville: Westminster John Knox, 1992) 31.

[4]Ibid., 111f.

[5]George Poulet, "Criticism and the Experience of Interiority," in *Reader-Response Criticism: From Formalism to Post-Structuralism,* ed. Jane Tompkins (Baltimore: Johns Hopkins University Press, 1980) 41–50. This quote is found in the editor's remarks on p. xiv.

imagined character home, to view the reader's own difficulties through the character's eyes.

This, it seems to me, is very much what Angela did in response to the homily in Henry Mitchell's interpretation of the story of the anointing. You will recall that the homily was delivered in a summer camp setting. Angela had been a bit too free with her affections, and the boys had talked. The chaplain had so structured his telling of the story that Angela could enter empathically into the experience of the woman and in that way also come to share in her sense of forgiveness. When Jesus championed the woman against the Pharisee, he championed Angela, too. The result was transforming, but it could not have been so if Angela had not squeezed inside the skin of the woman in Mitchell's story. Only by an act of identification could she come to understand the woman's redemption as the key to her own.

An important dimension of practical theology is apparent in this kind of intimate involvement with the characters described in Scripture. The effect on Angela may surely justify the means, if only because the way it extends the story is congruent with the story's central point. When David abuses Bathsheba and murders her husband, Uriah, clearly there are universal lessons to be learned. When the psalmist cries out before the Lord, are not his cries echoes of the cries all of us have uttered in the depths of our souls?

Gap Filling as the Resolution of Internal Conflict

Whenever we deal with literature, the identification with characters is one of the driving factors that move the drama forward. At least, this appears to be so on the surface of it. Some theorists would press the metaphor further. One does not identify completely with this or that character against the other characters; rather, one identifies partially with several characters. For this reason, the complication of the plot raises a mirroring ambivalence within the reader's subconscious mind.

In a comment on the story "Sinbad the Seaman and Sinbad the Porter," analyst Bruno Bettelheim describes the psychological dynamics by which the listening child stretches into these two incarnations of Sinbad. Sinbad the Seaman is the swashbuckling adventurer, given to the fantastic, the life beyond the humdrum safety of the palace walls. For Sinbad the Seaman, "palace" is another word for "prison." Sinbad the Porter is his counterpart, overtaken with the responsibilities and burdens of reality and afraid to venture beyond the palace walls. For Sinbad the Porter, "palace" means "fortress" and "place of security."

> The fairy tale helps us to understand ourselves better, as in the story the two sides of our ambivalences are isolated and projected each onto a different figure. We can visualize these ambivalences much better when the instinctual id pressures are projected onto the intrepid, immensely rich voyager who survives when all others are destroyed. . . . The opposite, reality-oriented ego tendencies are embodied in the hard-working, poor porter. . . . When the fairy story indicates that these two very different persons are actually "brothers under the skin," it guides the child toward the preconscious realization that these two figures are really two parts of one and the same person; that the id is as much an integral part of our personality as the ego.[6]

This, it seems to me, is more like what must have happened to the boys in Mitchell's report of the chaplain's campfire homily and its effect on Angela. The boys took advantage of the girl and then exposed her to ridicule. But the chaplain took pains to structure the homily so that the listener's empathies for the woman (and thus implicitly for Angela, too) are fully developed. The boys are also asked to make this movement of empathy. Yet their personal history demands that they also see themselves in the men in the story, perhaps most especially in the self-righteous "bigshot from the church" who "couldn't see nothin' but her body neither." The result is that the boys must split their identification processes. They empathize partially with the woman, partially with Angela, partially with the men. The dissonance developed in the plot is mirrored by a corresponding dissonance within the boys. It is very difficult to get off this hook. There is no way out except self-judgment and repentance.

If we were to contrast Angela's hearing of the story with that of the boys, we would have to say that hers was perhaps the more intense, while theirs was the more complex. In either case, the business of identifying with the characters forms part of the locomotive that drives the reading process forward.

---

[6]Bruno Bettelheim, *The Uses of Enchantment: The Meaning and Importance of Fairy Tales* (New York: Alfred Knopf, 1976) 85.

Entrapment

We may agree with Bettelheim in deriving the tension from internal psychological dissonance; we may follow Iser in placing the tension between the familiar and the unfamiliar of the text and its repertoire. We may find tension between the narrower details of the theme and the wider panorama of the horizon. In the end, though, we will not need to choose between them. These factors will be emphasized to different degrees in different pieces of literature and by different readers at different times. Whatever tack we take, the balances and imbalances occupy central governing positions in the aesthetic experience. Those positions are elevated in importance to the extent that we acknowledge the reader as an active participant in the linguistic exchange.

Identification, Entrapment, and the Anointing of Jesus

What we have seen suggests that there may be important differences and interconnections between literature that is inspired and literature that is Inspired, between the aesthetic experience of insight and the religious experience of revelation. Even so, these are not mutually exclusive movements. The entrapment that so naturally takes place in reading is sometimes the very stuff that calls our ordinary experience of the world into question. From time to time it seems that the Divine Storyteller intrudes into our little earthbound dramas and, by a subtle complication of our plot, transforms them into a vision of something higher.

Even a story about a whore at a banquet may yet turn out to be a transforming moment. For this reason, there may be more than aesthetic sensibilities at work when the reader is asked to split off his or her loyalties, to identify partially with the Pharisee, partially with the woman, partially with Jesus. To the extent that the reader is now asked to share the point of view of the Pharisee, he or she is also asked to hear Jesus' rebuke in vv. 41f. and again in vv. 44–47:

> A certain creditor had two debtors; one owed five hundred denarii, and the other fifty. When they could not pay, he canceled the debts for both of them. Now which of them will love him more?

You did not . . .
> But she did . . .

You did not . . .
> But she did . . .

You did not . . .
> But she did . . .
>
> Her sins . . . are forgiven

He who is forgiven little, loves little.

These words to the Pharisee are words to the reader, as well. This is something completely overlooked by those historians who would peer through the story at the historical event but who would dismantle the story to do so.

As for the question whether or not Kenneth Bailey is right that the host had behaved badly toward Jesus, it is clear that this has become a secondary concern by the time it is raised in vv. 44–46. Once the reader reaches that moment in the story, the question of the host's social improprieties is no longer relevant. Instead, the host's own spiritual condition is brought to the foreground, for he—and perhaps the reader with him—is asked to confront his own spiritual grandiosities. We return to Bailey. Bailey would have us know that, following as they do the parable of the two debtors (in vv. 41f.), the indictments of Simon in vv. 44–46

> reflect far more than formal inadequacies as a gracious host. Rather they indicate deep levels of pride, arrogance, hardheartedness, hostility, a judgmental spirit, slim understanding of what really defiles, a rejection of sinners, insensitivity, misunderstanding of the nature of God's forgiveness, and sexism. The most damaging criticism of all is the fact that Simon witnessed the woman's dramatic action and still labeled her as a "sinner" (v. 39).[7]

This is the indictment Jesus has leveled against Simon, only more subtly, I think, than Bailey would have us believe. The fact that Jesus looks at the woman as he corrects Simon softens the blow of it. By an equally subtle shift of timing, Luke has invited the reader to ride along on Simon's coattails and hear the same indictment against himself, at least insofar as its terms apply. This entrapment, I believe, is the rhetorical core of the story and the legitimate starting place for the construction of a sermon:

---

[7]Bailey, *Through Peasant Eyes,* 18f.

All too often our condemnation of others proceeds from our failure to recognize our own need for grace.

If we begin with the notion that the reader's mind must fill in gaps by drawing on its own resources, it is difficult to avoid the implication that the reader has great interpretive latitude in how to go about doing this. Much of our experience of the rhetorical play in a text appears to be the product of the *reader's* imagination and creativity. Indeed, it seems to be axiomatic in reader-oriented interpretation that the reader is a kind of collaborator with the author in the creation of textual meaning. Yet this must not be made to mean that the text is fixed and the repertoire of schemas and constraints is up for grabs. Even if we affirm that meaning emerges from the interaction of the text and its repertoire, the constraints of reading—context, genre, theme, and so forth—continue to serve as effective controls over the reader's latitude.

This is so because the author or redactor would expect the gaps to be filled out in particular ways. The observation that schemas are constructed on the basis of typicality refers to what is typical at the moment of the text's origin and not necessarily to what is typical in the experience of the modern reader. This is the way in which the words of the text are *expected* to convey meaning. Just as writers depend upon our knowledge of grammar, so also they depend upon our filling in gaps in predictable ways. Thus, the primary protocols we have discussed govern the construction of discourses in the same way that the rules of grammar govern the construction of sentences.

In large measure, this means that the words tie the text to categories that are specific to the intention of the author in a particular social and cultural moment. If we would enter the world of the text empathically we must be prepared to do so within the framework of the prior knowledge and protocols that were operative at that moment. If the schemas channel our interpretations in some ways and not in others and if the schemas tie the text to a particular cultural moment, then we are, in effect, eavesdropping on a conversation meant originally for someone else. If we are to understand that conversation, we must reconstruct the arrangement of schemas and respect the constraints that the original author and reader would have shared. When they are observed, the reader is available to be moved in particular ways by the rhetorical structure of the text.

THE RHETORIC OF PREACHING—
ENTICEMENTS AND ENTRAPMENTS

It is here that the tasks of reading and the tasks of preaching converge. In chapter 2 I suggested that the business of preaching involves two interrelated tasks—exegesis and exposition. The bridge between these two steps is one of the most difficult transitions for a preacher to make. In a significant discussion of homiletical style, Eugene Lowry identifies a kind of third stage, somewhere between the "I've got it" of the exegesis and the "I've got it" of the sermon. During this time the preacher toys with ideas, playing them back and forth to see which one offers the best hope of a successful sermon. Eventually one idea emerges and takes definite form; in a word, the sermonic idea "gets" the preacher as much as the other way around.[8]

How does this happen, and—more importantly—how does it happen successfully? What occurs when the sermonic idea genuinely engages the inner life of the preacher and the congregation? Lowry's answer to this question is to reshape the conception of the sermon from one of *content* to one of *emplotment*. By making this shift, the preacher comes to see the sermon not as a thing but as an "event-in-time," with a timed disclosure of details: "Because a sermon is an *event-in-time—* existing in time, not space—a process and not a collection of parts, it is helpful to think of sequence rather than structure."[9] What interests the listener and focuses the listener's attention, says Lowry, is the "homiletical bind," which is the point at which the human predicament requires the divine response. The sermon moves from the homiletical bind through a series of transformations, arriving ultimately at resolution.

This implies an antecedent problem: How does one get to the homiletical bind? For Thomas Long, the bind can be discovered in the genre of the text.[10] Long is explicitly concerned with the rhetorical strategies by which genre invites the reader to new insights. Those new insights provide the essential structure

---

[8]Eugene Lowry, *The Homiletical Plot: The Sermon as Narrative Art Form* (Atlanta: John Knox Press, 1980) 17f.

[9]Ibid., 25. The emphasis is Lowry's.

[10]Thomas Long, *Preaching and the Literary Forms of the Bible* (Philadelphia: Fortress, 1989).

of the sermonic idea—Lowry's homiletical bind. The point of
preaching is not simply to find out what the text meant and then
repeat that but, rather, to hear the text afresh, asking what
claim its truth makes upon the present.

> Preaching does not involve determining what the text *used* to
> mean and then devising some creative way to make that meaning
> pertinent to the contemporary scene. Preaching involves a con-
> temporary preacher closely attending to a text, discerning the
> claim that text makes upon the current life of the community of
> faith, and announcing that discovery in the sermon.[11]

It is clear that for Long the movement from text to sermon is a
controlled process. But where is the locus of control to be
found? The answer to this question lies in the close attention the
preacher must pay to the rhetorical structure of the text. Thus,
the text itself provides the basis for the control.

The transition from text to sermon is moved along by a
series of questions that, says Long,[12] help to maintain the inner
connections between exegesis and exposition:

- 1. What is the genre of this text?

- 2. What is the rhetorical function of this genre?

- 3. What literary devices does this genre use to achieve its
  rhetorical effect?

- 4. How in particular does the text under consideration, in its
  own literary setting, embody the characteristics and dynamics
  described in questions 1–3?

- 5. How may the sermon, in a new setting, say and do what the
  text says and does in its setting?

Thus, the homiletical bind is governed by the genre of the text.

This is not the only way to arrive at a sense of the
homiletical bind, however. Eugene Lowry's solution rests in
the preacher's willingness to encounter the larger themes of
the gospel itself. This contains a subtlety. Every theme, he
says, implies a corresponding need, a difficulty. The text is
addressed to a human situation, and that human situation
itself poses the possibility of tension, challenge, struggle, and

---

[11] Ibid., 34.
[12] Ibid.

resolution. Texts by nature involve conflict. For example, says Lowry, "if . . . I am considering the possibility of a doctrinal sermon on the Trinity, the preliminary question to be asked is, What problem or bind does the trinitarian formula resolve?"[13] The homiletical bind is therefore governed by the theme of the text, insofar as that theme engages issues that are also important for us.

Both Lowry and Long are right, at least partially so. What we have seen is that the dynamics of reading include not only the information and constraints of theme and genre but, more important, the interplay between them. The rhetorical structure of the text is generated by the interaction of context, genre, theme, and the play of textual elements against the repertoire of cultural information that the reader is expected to have in hand. On the other hand, Lowry and Long are right to call for a richer interaction between exegesis and exposition. Long, in particular, makes it clear that this is the point at which reader-oriented interpretation is best able to join the conversation with preaching. *Attention to the responses asked of the reader provides the essential clue to the underlying rhetorical structure of the text itself and thus also to the rhetorical structure of the sermon.*

There are two further concerns. First, the congregation may have heard it all before. The cherished memories of beloved verses may have been rubbed bald of challenge by the constant mental fingering over time. For some listeners the overfamiliarity is the greatest single obstacle to hearing the claim of the gospel as a fresh alternative to the competing claims of our culture. Fred Craddock explores the problem of "preaching and teaching the faith to persons who have already heard." Craddock points out that this may be a special difficulty for seminarians and others who are involved in the professional study of religion: "How much more pressing, albeit more difficult, is the challenge to help them hear what they hear every day, to learn what they already know, to be apprehended by that material with which exams are passed."[14]

Second, the sermon is itself a literary form, with a usual specific context. Preachers can assume that their congregations

---

[13] Lowry, *Homiletical Plot,* 19.
[14] Fred Craddock, *Overhearing the Gospel* (Nashville: Abingdon, 1978) 26.

will bring with them an established framework of interpretive conventions. This is not to say that the preacher is obligated to operate within those conventions; but to ignore them is to court misunderstanding and confusion. Sometimes the preacher can drive home a point by violating the conventions, since a violation of convention creates a subtle form of stress. In this vein, Lowry suggests that the well-crafted sermon will often include a reversal of expectations: "The process of reversal as presented in a sermon can be likened to the action of pulling the rug out from under someone. Often it is necessary to *lay* the rug before one pulls."[15] Of course, it is not always appropriate to go pulling rugs out from under the people who are under a pastor's care. Sometimes the reversal must be milder, like a seduction, and sometimes it must be based on a clear rational argument. But when it *is* appropriate, the shock of reversal can often be accomplished by a violation of conventional sermonic form. The sermon on the good Samaritan in chapter 14 is a case in point. This sermon was preached at a Presbyterian Church in which the pastor was well known for his expositional style. By presenting my sermon as a narrative instead of a systematic exposition, I was able to catch the congregation unaware. I believe that the sermon was more effective because it diverged from the style to which the congregation was accustomed. In this case, as in the other examples in the third section of this book, I have shaped the homiletical structure of the sermon by playing the rhetorical structure of the text against the conventional structures I knew my congregation expected to hear.

---

[15] Lowry, *Homiletical Plot,* 56.

TRYING ON THE LENSES

13

THE ANOINTING OF JESUS

Exegesis and Exposition

In chapter 12 I suggested that the homiletical structure of the sermon could play upon the congregation's repertoire of norms in the same way that the text plays upon the norms the reader was expected to bring to the reading. This is what I did with the sermon on the anointing of Jesus in chapter 1. Here I propose that we trace the exegetical and rhetorical considerations that led to this sermon. In this way we can turn the matter of reading around yet one more time and look at the integration of elements that produces the rhetorical bind of the text. At the end of the chapter, we will reflect on the reasoning processes occurring between the "I've got it" of the exegesis and the "I've got it" of the exposition and in this way show how I attempted to use the rhetorical bind of the one to create the homiletical bind of the other.

THE RHETORIC OF THE TEXT—
TOP-DOWN READING CONSTRAINTS

You will recall from chapter 8 that the top-down reading constraints are in place from very early on in the reading process. There are three: context, genre, and theme.

Context

Context governs interpretation in two ways. First, it permits the reader to supply additional information, and second, it constrains gap filling by directing the possibilities of interpretation in specific directions. It thus works dialectically, both expanding and limiting the psychological processes of gap filling.

The circumstances for which Luke wrote and the date of composition remain a matter of debate. What is not disputed, however, is that Luke has a heavy emphasis on the poor, the outcast, and the disreputable.[1] His well-known emphasis on women can be understood as something of a piece with these concerns.[2] Over against these, Luke also pays considerable attention to the Pharisees, not out of concern for their social role but because they seem to epitomize a kind of piety that he forcefully and explicitly rejects. The parable of the Pharisee and the tax collector, which will come later in the reading process (17:9–15), seems to reflect balances and contrasts that are at the heart of our story of the Pharisee and the sinful woman. One might well say that our story prepares for that one, that the resonating themes of the first story deepen and reinforce those

---

[1]For a summary of the discussion, see Robert Karris, "Poor and Rich: The Lukan *Sitz im Leben*," in *Perspectives on Luke–Acts,* ed. Charles H. Talbert (Edinburgh: T. & T. Clark, 1978) 112–25.

[2]The literature here is enormous and growing rapidly. For a good summary discussion, see Letha Scanzoni and Nancy Hardesty, *All We're Meant to Be: A Biblical Approach to Women's Liberation* (Waco: Word, 1975), esp. 215f.

of the second. In both stories is an implied contrast between two different sorts of alignment. The question is not how one defines sinfulness but, rather, whether one is willing to align oneself with the forces of redemption.

Luke has taken pains to set the reader up for just this question. We noted this concern in our discussion of literary context as a reading constraint. The Pharisees have appeared several times already in the narrative, always taking a hostile attitude toward Jesus and his apparently freewheeling attitude toward the law. In 5:17–26, the story of the "rooftop paralytic," he challenged the Pharisees for their unexpressed objections to his pronouncement that the sins of the paralytic were forgiven. In 6:1–5 it was the Pharisees who objected when the disciples plucked heads of grain on the Sabbath; and in 6:6–11 again it was the Pharisees who objected when Jesus healed the man with the withered hand.

Laced through many of these stories is a subtle underlying theme: Jesus has the ability to read the private thoughts of his antagonists. That this is a significant theme in Luke is signaled by the fact that it is presented as the fulfillment of a messianic prophecy in 2:35 on the lips of Simeon, the old man at the temple. There are numerous places in Luke where Jesus reads the thoughts of his opponents (5:21f.; 6:8; 9:47; 24:38). By the time the reader reaches our story of the anointing, he or she has already encountered this theme on two occasions, one of them in the immediately preceding chapter. These references prime the reader's expectations and in this way highlight the little exchange in vv. 39f.

> Now when the Pharisee who had invited him saw it, he said to himself, "If this man were a prophet, he would have known who and what kind of woman this is who is touching him—that she is a sinner."
>
> Jesus spoke up and said to him, "Simon, I have something to say to you."
>
> "Teacher," he replied, "Speak."
>
> "A certain creditor had two debtors; one owed five hundred denarii, and the other fifty. When they could not pay, he canceled the debts for both of them. Now which of them will love him more?"
>
> Simon answered, "I suppose the one for whom he canceled the greater debt."

The reader's expectations are also primed by the immediate literary context of chapter 7. In particular, there is a marked and persistent contrast between the judgmental piety of the Pharisees and the redemptive piety of Jesus. This contrast is drawn into sharp relief in vv. 29f. Jesus has just announced that John came as a harbinger of the Messiah and that even so, "the least in the kingdom is greater than he."

> ²⁹ And all the people
>> who heard this,
>> including the tax collectors,
>> *acknowledged the justice* of God,
>>> because they had been baptized with John's baptism.
> ³⁰ But
>> by refusing to be baptized by him,
>> the Pharisees
>> and the lawyers
>> *rejected God's purpose* for themselves.

The balances between the verses here can hardly have been accidental:

Verse 29	Verse 30
Who heard this	But the
And all the people	Pharisees
including the tax collectors	and the lawyers
acknowledged the justice	rejected God's purpose
of God	for themselves,
because they had been baptized	by refusing to be baptized
with John's baptism.	by him . . .

The chief purpose of the balances is to highlight the contrast between the two attitudes toward redemption.

This balancing contrast is carried forward in vv. 31–35. These verses open with a rhetorical question directed at "the people of this generation," though the context makes it clear that the "Pharisees and lawyers" are specifically in view:

> ³¹ "To what then will I compare
>> the people of this generation,
>> and what are they like?
> ³² They are like children
>> sitting in the marketplace
>> and calling to one another,

> 'We played the flute for you, and you did not
> dance;
> we wailed, and you did not weep.'
> [33] For John the Baptist came eating no bread
> and drinking no wine;
> and you say,
> 'He has a demon';
> [34] the Son of Man has come eating
> and drinking,
> and you say,
> 'Look, a glutton
> and a drunkard,
> a friend of tax collectors
> and sinners'!"

Here again, it is not so much the Pharisees and the lawyers who are called to the reader's mind but the specific disposition toward redemption they are made to represent.

All of this forms the backdrop of our story of the anointing of Jesus. Everything is brought to focus in the enigmatic saying in v. 35, just before our story begins: "Wisdom is justified by her children." As Charles Talbert points out, this saying refers to the attitude of God's people toward God, rather than the other way around. To "reject the purpose of God," as the Pharisees and lawyers have done (v. 30), is to reject God himself.[3] To reject God: this is shallow theology indeed! If it does not invite the judgment of God, at the very least it invites the judgment of the reader. In this way the word "Pharisee" has been given a negative spin.

Theme

Thus we are introduced to questions of theme. As a top-down reading constraint, theme represents the reader's anticipations of what the story will be about. These invite the reader to summon up preliminary schemas, which then act as "grids" in forming and shaping gists of the details as they unfold. A sense of theme is often in place even before the reading itself begins.

So it is here. The contextual constraints all suggest that something is brewing. The negative spin on the word "Pharisee"

---

[3]Talbert, *Reading Luke*, 84.

and the problematic associations of the word *hamartōlos,* "sinner," combine to tip the reader off that the theme here will be cut from the same cloth as the contrasting attitudes toward piety set out in the immediately preceding pericopes. What is brewing is a fight; there's controversy in the air.

Genre

Genre, like theme, controls reading in two ways. First, it gives the reader clues about what to expect next and in that way governs the reader's anticipations. Second, it governs the reader's interpretive latitude. Some genres provide wide latitude, others restrict latitude quite narrowly.

In our story of the anointing, the genre signals are quite loose. Eventually the story will appear to mix several forms under the overarching structure of a chreia,[4] but since chreias are sometimes freely composed, the genre signals are imprecise. The reader is aware that the story will take the form of a controversy of some kind.

It will prove to be rhetorically significant that the opening details of the story do not directly support that expectation. In fact, it appears at first that the story will present the Pharisee in a positive light. He invites Jesus to his home to supper, and the fact that Jesus reclines at table suggests that the occasion is being treated as something special. We will return to this detail momentarily.

THE RHETORIC OF THE TEXT—
BOTTOM-UP READING CONSTRAINTS

The top-down constraints of context, theme, and genre are largely in hand from the beginning of the reading process. By contrast, the bottom-up reading constraints are evoked by the dynamic processes of the reading itself. These are interactive and so must be treated together. For this reason, we shall examine the text verse by verse.

---

[4]For a good brief discussion of chreias, see Buchanan, *Jesus,* esp. ch. 2, "Rhetoricians, Historians, and Literary Forms," 43–74.

Verse 36

One of the Pharisees asked Jesus to eat with him, and he went into the Pharisee's house and took his place at the table.

Nothing here suggests that there is anything amiss. The reader will later be told that the host has failed to observe the social niceties of kissing his guest, anointing the guest's face, and washing the guest's feet. For now, however, there is no hint of improprieties. The reader defaults to the norm. The fact that Jesus "reclined" at table—*kateklithē*—suggests a rather more formal affair. Jesus will have left his shoes at the door. This is part of the standard script and does not need to be stated.

The reader will also later be told that the host's name is Simon (v. 40). For now, however, that piece of information is withheld, and the host is simply identified as a Pharisee. This enables the reader to make a clearer and more generalized connection with the schema for "Pharisee" that has been generated and critiqued earlier in the narrative. The unnamed host is made to serve as a representative of a particular brand of piety, much more than an individual with a name and a history.

Thus, the stage is set.

Verse 37

And [behold], a woman in the city, who was a sinner, having learned that he was eating in the Pharisee's house, brought an alabaster jar of ointment.

With "behold" (in Greek; cf. RSV) the action begins. A woman of the city appears, a *hamartōlos,* a "sinner." At this stage it is still unclear to the reader what is meant by the term. The fact that the same term occurs in v. 34 in connection with "tax collectors" suggests that she simply represents the *am-ha-aretz,* the unlettered and uncouth "people of the land" whose failures of legal piety are the subject of the contrasts earlier in the chapter. Thus, the range of options is still quite broad. Syntactical constraints do not aid the reader's attempt to narrow the field. One might well translate, "tramp," or even "lowlife."

We are not told how the woman has gained access to the house. This may simply reflect a Middle Eastern custom of allowing one's neighbors to drop in on dinner parties. This is a handy way of impressing the neighborhood with the importance of one's connections. The reader may still expect the controversy, though on very general terms.

Verse 38

She stood behind him at his feet, weeping, and began to bathe his feet with her tears and to dry them with her hair. Then she continued kissing his feet and anointing them with the ointment.

The expectation of a controversy is here disrupted—in psychological terms, it is "backward masked"—by the strange, outrageous behavior of the woman. We are not told her motivation, at least not yet. A good deal of speculation has risen over it. What was her reason for doing such a thing? Why did she let down her hair? Why anoint Jesus' feet, rather than his face? Was she already forgiven, or was she seeking forgiveness? No one can deny that these are legitimate and important questions. But they are not likely to have occurred to Luke's reader at this stage in the reading process, for two reasons. First, there is the sheer, unexpected, and vivid imagery of her action. It is nuts, perfectly shocking. Second, the language is unmistakably overcoded with sexual nuances. These lie just below the surface of the vocabulary, but the secondary nuances reinforce one another until they erupt into the reader's conscious mind. If she had only let down her hair, it would have been enough. To that signal the reader adds erotic echoes from the term for "kiss"—*kataphileō*. The fact that she kisses Jesus' feet rather than his mouth guarantees that these echoes will remain secondary, perhaps even tertiary, but even then they are not erased completely. Instead, they are highlighted by the sensuality of her gesture of letting down her hair. Thus, the play of schemas creates a strong secondary impression of sexual impropriety. It is this secondary impression which then consolidates and clarifies the meaning of the term by which she was first described in the previous verse: When the text says she is a *hamartōlos,* it means that she is guilty of sexual misconduct. Perhaps she is even a prostitute.

For whatever reason, Jesus does not interrupt her. Luke indicates as much in the way he has structured the syntax of the sentence. She "*began to bathe* his feet with her tears." This is a periphrastic imperfect—a roundabout way of signaling that the action is to be viewed as continuous. Thereafter, all the verbs are simple imperfects—"she *was bathing* his feet," "she *was drying* his feet with her hair," "she *was kissing* his feet," "she *was anointing* [his feet] with ointment." The fact that Jesus does not interrupt her will reappear as a factor later in the story; the imperfects in this sentence prepare for the later reference. The action seems to go on and on. The woman's behavior presents a serious difficulty for the host. The only element softening its sensuality is her weeping.

In this way the woman's behavior intrudes upon the constraints of context and theme, deflecting the reader's attention away from the expectation of a fight. There are so many puzzlements and open-ended gaps in v. 38 that the reader cannot help but be shocked by the spectacle. Yet the constraints of context and theme continue to lead in another direction. The result is rhetorical tension between conflicting constraints. The reader must choose one set of constraints or the other, or—barring that—hold everything in tension until the story resolves everything in its own way. The tension is very great.

It seems to me that the shock of the woman's behavior is more dominant. This is because it is more immediate. The contextual signals and the thematic expectations have been distanced now by an intervening verse, one that has masked the expectation of controversy and permitted the reader to assume that everything is well with the Pharisee. Thus, the focus of attention is on the scandal of it, and the reader is subtly invited to join the Pharisee in his shocked reaction. If this is so—and it is certainly possible—then the reader will mirror the unexpressed condemnation privately voiced by the Pharisee in v. 39.

Verse 39

Now when the Pharisee who had invited him saw it, he said to himself, "If this man were a prophet, he would have known who and what kind of woman this is who is touching him— that she is a sinner."

This verse picks up and consolidates the nuances of sexual impropriety that were hinted after in vv. 37f. The words for sexuality now become much more direct. Instead of *kataphilei,* "she is kissing him," we now have *haptetai,* "she is fondling him." The verb is in the present tense, and—like the imperfects in v. 38—may imply continuous action. The sexual nuances are now much closer to the surface. They are reinforced and made explicit by the repeated reference to the woman as a *hamartōlos,* a "sinner," which now clearly refers to some sort of sexual guilt. For the host, it is a most embarrassing spectacle. The reader mirrors the same sentiments.

One other element commends the Pharisee's point of view: He has been discreet about his objections. The imperfect verbs in v. 38 suggested that the woman's unseemly behavior had been going on for some time. Jesus had permitted it without objection. A host would naturally think of his other guests and the sorry impression all this would leave on the neighbors. Silence implies consent. The embarrassment would now be almost beyond bearing, but the host has said nothing, has made no public accusation.

There is an interesting and subtle rhetorical strategy at work here. Since the reader is now mirroring the thoughts of the Pharisee, the writer can use these thoughts to clarify and then correct a kind of grandiosity on the reader's part. The Pharisee has set out a kind of criterion for establishing Jesus' prophetic identity: "If this man were a prophet he would know who and what sort of woman this is who is touching him." How is Jesus to know such things? Perhaps he is to read her mind? This much is not said explicitly, but the mention of the term "prophet" at least suggests that the Pharisee expects some sort of clairvoyance. Since the theme of Jesus reading minds has been established already in Luke's narrative, the reader would hardly have come to some other conclusion. This is a cunning way of shifting the reader's point of view to rhetorical advantage.

The Pharisee makes one other assumption. A true prophet would not allow himself to be fondled by such a woman. The reader who shares the restrictive piety resident in the Pharisee's point of view would also share this assumption. This may well be the very heart of religious boundary marking in the Judeo-Christian tradition.

Verse 40

Jesus spoke up and said to him, "Simon, I have something to say to you."

"Teacher," he replied, "Speak."

Simon's name is here introduced for the first time. Why withhold it until now? One cannot say for sure. To my mind, it has at least this rhetorical effect: The opening verses have been a trap. Having once identified with the Pharisee's point of view, the reader has no choice but to continue in that role. Kenneth Bailey points out that the expression translated, "I have something to say to you," is a common way of introducing an unwelcome, blunt speech.[5] Something unpleasant is coming. If the reader has any inclination to retreat to impersonal generalities about "those Pharisees," the fact that Simon is now addressed by name cuts the retreat off short.

The Pharisee continues his posture of public deference to Jesus. His response opens with an expression of respect: "Teacher, speak."

Verses 41–42

"A certain creditor had two debtors; one owed five hundred denarii, and the other fifty. When they could not pay, he canceled the debts for both of them. Now which of them will love him more?"

A good case could be made that Simon would have missed the indictment implicit in this brief puzzle. It would be clear enough that the "larger debtor" is to be identified with the woman, but who is the "lesser debtor"? Surely not himself. He has, after all, done nothing wrong. He has objected, but he has kept his objections to himself. Neither Jesus nor his guests could have read his mind. Certainly Jesus could not have read his mind; if he could have, he would have known that the woman who was touching him was a sinner!

Yet there was something troubling about the manner in which Jesus has addressed him in v. 40: "Simon, I have something to say to you." Could it be that Jesus thinks that *he* has done something amiss?

If the story had ended here, neither the Pharisee nor the reader would have been able to establish the connections that bring the indictment home. This is a setup, but it needs a follow-through. The follow-through requires that the Pharisee

---

[5]Bailey, *Through Peasant Eyes,* 12.

first take a position on the puzzle. This Jesus forces by demand-
ing an answer: "Which of them will love him the more?"

Verse 43

*Simon answered, "I suppose the one for whom he canceled the
greater debt."*

And Jesus said to him, "You have judged rightly."

It may be worth noting a significant gap in the grammar
here. In Greek, Simon's response—"the one for whom he canceled the greater debt"—is an incomplete sentence. This is
awkward only on the surface, since the reader automatically fills
in the ellipsis with information brought in from the larger
literary context. The setup is now fully in place.

Verses 44–46

Then turning toward the woman, he said to Simon,

   "Do you see this woman? I entered your house;

       *you gave me no water for my feet, but she has bathed
       my feet with her tears and dried them with her hair.*

       *You gave me no kiss, but from the time I came in she
       has not stopped kissing my feet.*

       *You did not anoint my head with oil, but she has
       anointed my feet with ointment."*

Thus the follow-through. Everything is point-blank, abrupt,
direct. What Jesus does upsets social proprieties perhaps even
more seriously than what the woman did. In the Middle East one
never, ever corrects one's host.[6] Not only does Jesus do this; he
corrects a *man* for the sake of a *woman,* and a *pious* man for the
sake of a *sinner.* Everything is turned on its head.

The indictment takes the form of a series of contrasts:

A   You did not . . .
B   but she did . . .
A   You did not . . .

---

[6]For references see ibid., 14–16.

B   but she did . . .
A   You did not . . .
B   but she did . . .

From a cultural standpoint, this may be the most difficult part of the story. Opinions are divided over whether the host was obligated to provide the amenities of a kiss, washed feet, and oil. If he was, then his failure to do so explains a good deal of the previous action. The host was in error and—as Bailey points out—he has behaved more rudely than the woman. The woman has taken it upon herself to make up for his rudeness. Jesus' response turns the host's apparent arrogance back upon itself. On the other hand, if these niceties were more or less optional, the host would have been perfectly correct. In that case, Jesus' response in these verses must be understood as a way of salvaging a difficult moment for everyone, perhaps turning the moment into a lesson in encompassing grace.

But perhaps either tack is misguided. To my mind, there are two interacting elements here. First, both the Pharisee and the reader must clearly and suddenly recognize that Jesus has read the Pharisee's mind. In this way Jesus demonstrates quite dramatically that he meets the first criterion for being a prophet, which was set up in v. 39. Here he meets a second, equally important criterion: He does what is necessary to effect the woman's redemption. This, too, is a clearly prophetic act.

Both the Pharisee and the reader come to these recognitions primed by the evoked question in vv. 41–42: "He cannot possibly mean me, can he?" The Pharisee hears point-blank, "Yes, I do mean you." The reader's experience is more subtle: To the extent that the reader has shared the host's alignments, the reader must now share his guilt. This is open ended, and the possibilities are almost limitless. What lies at their core and establishes their boundaries is the fact that—whatever way the reader has failed in understanding Jesus' gestures of grace—the reader must admit that alignments have somehow been made *against* Jesus and this expansive, inclusive brand of piety. After all, who wants to include the tramps of the world within the folds of grace?

Jesus' words are an indictment, but their impact is softened by the paralanguage. Jesus says all this while looking not at Simon but at the woman! A sharper attack would have been made directly at Simon, perhaps driven deeper by a slow, penetrating gaze. A scathing rebuke? Perhaps not. Perhaps this is best seen as an invitation to join the woman within the folds of grace. There are conditions, however. The Pharisee must see that he and the woman are both liable, both guilty. It is a confession he must make on his own.

Verse 47

"Therefore, I tell you, her sins, which were many, have been forgiven; hence she has shown great love. But the one to whom little is forgiven, loves little."

That invitation is now carried forward by a shift of sequence and a change from first person to third. Thus far the sequence has followed a fixed pattern: A/B, A/B, A/B:

A   You did not . . .
B   but she did . . .
A   You did not . . .
B   but she did . . .
A   You did not . . .
B   but she did . . .

In this verse the pattern reverses itself:

Therefore, I tell you,

B   Her sins, which were many, have been forgiven . . .
A   But the one to whom little is forgiven, loves little.

The reversal is further softened by the fact that Jesus now shifts from the first person ("you did not . . . ") to the third ("the one to whom little is forgiven . . . "). It is clear enough what is in view by the expression "loves little"—the host's failures of courtesy, not only to Jesus but to the woman as well. Yet Jesus does not draw that conclusion. Instead, he leaves it for the host to draw for himself. If the sequence had continued unchanged, if the language had not shifted from first person to third, Jesus would simply have been pointing an accusing finger. By holding back he invites the Pharisee to come to the same conclusion, but to do so in the form of a confession. The reader must draw his or her own mirroring confession: I, too, have "loved little."

Verse 48

Then he said to her, "Your sins are forgiven."

Here (as in the previous verse), when Jesus declares the woman's sins forgiven, he does so in the "divine passive." This is a standard Jewish way of avoiding uttering the name of God. Even so, it is clear that he speaks on God's behalf—a clearly prophetic act!

Verse 49

But those who were at the table with him began to say among themselves, "Who is this who even forgives sins?"

Here gap filling emerges as the predominant reading protocol. It hinges upon the fact that this verse poses a question but does not answer it. Unanswered questions are a rhetorical trick. Robert Fowler makes this observation, resting his argument on an observation supplied by Stanley Fish:

> Confronting the reader with unanswered questions is without doubt a shrewd rhetorical ploy, for it encourages the reader to seek out the answers. As Stanley Fish states: "A question, after all, implies the availability of an answer; and to ask it is always to create a psychological need for its completing half."[7]

In a sense, this is the parallel to the unanswered but unasked question in v. 39: "If this man were a prophet, he would have known who and what sort of woman this is." The onlookers cannot know that, since they cannot have known what unspoken offense prompted Jesus' response in the first place. The reader works with privileged information. Everything thus far has set the reader up to answer the question in a specific way. This man is indeed the prophet, who knows not only who and what sort of woman this is but also who and what sort of man is Simon! In pronouncing the woman's sins forgiven, Jesus acts as God's agent, in the process calling Simon, too, to a change of life.

---

[7]Fowler, *Loaves and Fishes,* 167f. The quote is from Stanley Fish, *Self-Consuming Artifacts: The Experience of Seventeenth Century Literature* (Berkeley: University of California Press, 1972) 60.

Verse 50

And he said to the woman, "Your faith has saved you; go in peace."

Jeremias points out that the language is largely Lucan (this is true of vv. 48–50 as a whole).[8] The story closes on an almost pastoral note.

THE RHETORIC OF THE TEXT: SUMMARY

Let us take one last, sweeping look at this story. The outrageous behavior of the woman invites the reader to shadow the point of view of the Pharisee. Several factors combine to make this possible. First, the narrator has withheld the critical clues about any improprieties on the host's part. Everything appears proper because the reader defaults to the standard script for a formal first-century dinner party. Second, the narrator has overcoded his description of the woman's behavior with insinuating secondary nuances. If these had occurred individually, they would not be enough to raise the secondary nuances to consciousness. Taken together, however, the secondary nuances interfere with one another to create a cumulative effect that the reader can hardly overlook. Once the reader has taken over the Pharisee's point of view, he must also share in the indictment by which that point of view is challenged and corrected. All too often our condemnation of others proceeds from our natural failure to recognize our own need of grace.

THE RHETORIC OF THE SERMON

This I took to be the rhetorical core of the story, the bind around which everything finally turns. The challenge now was to appropriate that bind as the basis for my sermon at the beginning of this book. The trick would be to try and entrap the congregation into sharing the same point of view as the Pharisee

---

[8]Joachim Jeremias, *New Testament Theology*, vol. 1, *The Proclamation of Jesus* (New York: Scribners, 1971) 218 n. 1.

and the reader, then use the story to bring that point of view into question.

This sermon was preached at a Disciples of Christ Church in Costa Mesa, California. The congregation is Evangelical and quite young—the average age is probably twenty-two or twenty-three years old. Most of the people in this church come from difficult social relationships, converted directly out of a culture that poses open challenges to their faith. I guessed that, as often happens with Christians in such circumstances, they had created rigid boundaries of right and wrong, which looked compassionately on failures of non-Christians but judgmentally on failures within their ranks. The difficulty here is that the judgmental attitude toward failures within the ranks is based on the supposition that we are ourselves now guilt free. It was this same supposition that I believe the text addresses. The Pharisee, after all, never directly condemns the woman. She was behaving just as he would expect from one of "those people." The Pharisee's objection was specifically directed at Jesus, and his condemnation of the woman is only implied in his unspoken thought that a genuine prophet would not associate with such people.

As I pondered this question—drifting in the moment between the "I've got it" of the text and the "I've got it" of the sermon—something dramatic came over the news. A major television evangelist was found with a prostitute. My reaction was very much like the reaction of others who are in the ministry. I knew that we would all be painted with the same brush. I was plenty angry. As I seethed, I also began to realize that I myself needed the message that was resident in the rhetorical bind of my text. I had my hook.

It was not difficult to create the same hook for my audience. Many of them—perhaps all of them—would share my sense of outrage over the televangelist's indiscretions. A little research turned up a history of such things. By aligning our story with that history, I could set the congregation up to hear the story of the anointing of Jesus with the outrage in hand.

To prepare for that outrage and to give it direction and force, I decided to begin with Jesus' famous denunciations of the hypocrisy of the scribes and the Pharisees from the Olivet discourse. This seemed to me to be particularly apposite, since the issue is hypocrisy that condemns another without acknowledging its own need of grace. This passage is resonant with the basic rhetorical bind of the story of the anointing, but it comes at that bind from a different direction. In this way I hoped to mask my true intentions until the hook was fully in place. For the same reason I had to withhold any clues about which story would form the basis of my sermon. I did not mention my text in the church bulletin, and I did not have the text read out earlier in the service. (In Lowry's terms, I was "laying the rug before I pulled.")

Once the hook was in, it was not difficult to turn over the details of the story one at a time, identifying and then resolving the issues they raise. At their core lie the sources of the shock: The assumption that there is a difference between "people like us" and "people like them," and the assumption that people like us should never have anything to do with people like them. I decided to state this explicitly in the sermon, to clarify and sharpen the issues involved.

I wished to observe one other caution. I did not want to suggest that Christian faith is without ethical demands or that it automatically discounts failures of moral responsibility. That would have proven destructive for these younger Christians, who need the constraints of such things as they mature in their faith. And I myself honestly believe that there are appropriate places for church discipline—the incident with the televangelist was a case in point. Instead, I wanted to keep the focus on the perniciousness of my own judgmental attitude. Church discipline should proceed from a sense of sorrow rather than a sense of superiority. For this reason I built into my sermon the story about my coworker who had been convicted of molesting his stepchildren. I could point out the difficulty in my rejecting him, not by excusing his actions but by specifying that my condemnation revealed something pernicious in my own heart. In this way I could also avoid accusing someone in the congregation of an attitude of which I was myself guilty.

Finally, I wished to draw the story to its close by returning to the point at which it had opened. This brings everything to closure by revisiting the rhetorical bind from a different vantage point. By the end of the sermon, however, everything has turned on its head. The hypocrisy which is identified is no longer the televangelist's but my own. The reason for my anger is no longer that the media might paint us with the same brush but that the televangelist's failure confronts me with the fact that I, too, am in need of grace. Perhaps the most difficult thing of all is to paint myself with the same brush.

14

LESSONS FROM THE ROAD 1

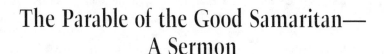

The Parable of the Good Samaritan— A Sermon

THE OLD TESTAMENT LESSON: 2 Chronicles 28:8–15

THE NEW TESTAMENT LESSON: Luke 10:25–37
Read by the minister as part
of the sermon.

I'm going to begin by reading aloud my text for this morning, then tell you why I'm not going to preach on this text. Our Scripture this morning is the parable of the good Samaritan and is found in Luke 10:29–37. The story itself is closely connected with the paragraph preceding, so we shall begin reading at verse 25. Hear the word of God:

Just then a lawyer stood up to test Jesus. "Teacher," he said, "what must I do to inherit eternal life?" He said to him, "What is written in the law? What do you read there?" He answered, "You shall love the Lord your God with all your heart, and with all your soul, and with all your strength, and with all your mind; and your neighbor as yourself." And he said to him, "You have given the right answer; do this, and you will live."

But wanting to justify himself, he asked Jesus, "And who is my neighbor?" Jesus replied, "A man was going down from Jerusalem to Jericho, and fell into the hands of robbers, who stripped him, beat him, and went away, leaving him half dead. Now by chance a priest was going down that road; and when he saw him, he passed by on the other side. So likewise a Levite, when he came to the place and saw him, passed by on the other side. But a Samaritan while traveling came near him; and when he saw him, he was moved with pity. He went to him and bandaged his wounds, having poured oil and wine on them. Then he put him on his own animal, brought him to an inn, and took care of him. The next day he took out two denarii, gave them to the innkeeper, and said, 'Take care of him; and when I come back, I will repay you whatever more you spend.' Which of these three, do you think, was a neighbor to the man who fell into the hands of the robbers?" He said, "The one who showed him mercy." Jesus said to him, "Go and do likewise."

Now, let me tell you why I'm not going to preach on this text this morning. It all goes back to something that happened during my sermon preparation. It was one of those terrifically hot summer days. I was on my way to the office to work on my sermon. I was driving a borrowed sports car on Wednesday morning, and I had the window and the sunroof wide open. The wind was blowing through my hair, and even at sixty miles an hour I could tell that this day was going to be a scorcher. Outside, I could see the air boiling up on the horizon, waffling, and then rising slowly in the heat. The traffic slowed on the overpass over I-5—you know the place where it always jams up at the El Toro Y? I slowed to a halt.

As I frequently do during these times, I was thinking about my sermon—the one I'm not going to preach to you this morning—on the parable of the good Samaritan.

As I watched the sweltering air rising from the roadway, I ticked off the things I had learned from my exegesis.

I knew that the hearer of the parable was a lawyer, and that this meant he was a theologian and thus an expert in the Old Testament law and its interpretation. The theologian had asked Jesus two different questions—"What must I do to inherit eternal life?" and "Who is my neighbor?" I knew that both questions were burning issues in Judaism. The first was somewhat the more academic of the two: "What must I do to inherit eternal life?"

Now, coming from a theologian, this is a loaded question. How would I illustrate this to my congregation? My mind drifted back to the theological debates of my student days. We would sit around the dorm and debate the pros and cons of important theological issues—inerrancy, predestination, the infralapsarian controversy, things like that. Of course, these are important theological questions, but they are more than that. Theologians sometimes ask questions of this sort as a way of pigeonholing the other guy. That's what the lawyer is doing here. He's testing Jesus' theological mettle. This is an academic question.

The radio interrupted with the news that there was an overturned tractor trailer on the freeway ahead of me. This was going to be a long trip. I closed the windows and the sunroof and turned on the air-conditioning.

The lawyer had asked an academic question—"What must I do to inherit eternal life?" But notice very carefully the way that Jesus answered. He posed a counterquestion, then nailed the lawyer on his answer: "*Do* this and you will live." Jesus as much as told the man that he already knew the answer to his question; he had only to practice what he preached.

The lawyer's question about the neighbor was an academic question as well. It was calculated to move everything back to a theoretical plane. One cannot hope to do the law unless one knows the law. Theory takes precedence over action. So the lawyer poses the question of the neighbor.

We have learned the meaning of this term from the parable, but the lawyer hadn't yet heard the parable. For the lawyer, the Old Testament instruction to "love your neighbor as yourself" translated out to a question of race: In the Old Testament text the term "neighbor" stands in exact parallel with the expression "sons of your own people":

Leviticus 19:17f. (RSV)

You shall not hate   *your brother*   in your heart,
but you shall reason with   *your neighbor,*

You shall not take vengeance or bear any grudge against
            the *sons of your own people,*
but you shall love   *your neighbor*
   as yourself.

The lawyer's question is really this one: How far do the boundaries go? Who is, and who is not, a "son of my own people"? It is
in response to *this* question that Jesus presents the parable of
the good Samaritan.

   Now, the details of the parable are old hat. I thought
about them as I inched along and thanked God that Roger had
loaned me his sports car for the day. My own car doesn't have
air-conditioning. I thought perhaps this road would be a pretty
good illustration of what the road from Jerusalem to Jericho
would be like. Barren. Hot. Sweltering. Dangerous. Except that
this road is flat and straight and that one was winding and hilly.

   Maybe I should tell my congregation that the priest and the
Levite were a couple of Baptists—a minister and a deacon. But
then, I wouldn't want to give the impression that ministers don't
practice what they preach. Professional courtesy, you know.

   Besides, my exegesis had taught me that the lawyer is now
pondering his excuses for the priest and the Levite. He could
think of a dozen reasons why the priest didn't need to stop and
help the victim in the ditch. The man was unconscious. He was
stripped naked. There was nothing to give away his race. Who
knows, perhaps he was even a Samaritan! The lawyer holds that
answer at the ready until the story is finished. He knows that
with this counterquestion he'll be able to show that Jesus is
merely skirting the issue. If the man in the ditch is a Samaritan,
the priest and Levite have no obligation to help him anyway.

   I decided to hold that last comment back from you, since
you would have thought of it yourselves and since it appears too
obvious. I also decided that the important thing was that the
priest and the Levite—and the lawyer who was thinking up their
defense—simply didn't look too good. In all their legal wrangling, they had lost something of their humanity.

My exegesis had also taught me that there was another side of this parable that the lawyer knew but that most Americans don't: By telling the story in just this way, Jesus is setting the lawyer up to condemn himself not only for his own lack of humanity but also for his failure to read his Bible very well. You will recall the Old Testament lesson from today that tells about how the Samaritans had once come to the aid of the Judaean victims following a battle with Israel. I won't reread it all, but just a portion:

2 Chronicles 28:15:

> Then those who were mentioned by name got up and took the captives, and with the booty they clothed all that were naked among them; they clothed them, gave them sandals, provided them with food and drink, and anointed them; and carrying all the feeble among them on donkeys, they brought them to their kindred at Jericho, the city of palm trees. Then they returned to Samaria.

The allusion makes this a trick story, a story with a trap: Jesus may be telling the lawyer that he hadn't read his Bible very well, that the answer to his question lay there.

I now had a homiletical problem: How was I to get the trickery across to my congregation when they all know this parable so very well indeed?

The license plate on the Jeep in front of me read HUDWNKM—hoodwink 'em. "Was this a revelation from God?" I wondered. There was a blackbird on a dill weed plant beside the road, and it didn't think so, either. I continued inching my way along the highway.

Of course, I knew as a homiletician that there was a better solution than an outright trick. The answer, of course, is to find some direct analogy in our own culture by which I could describe who the Samaritan was.

I knew that Samaritans were pretty much outcasts in the society of Jesus' day. How to get that across, especially without destroying the trickery in the story?

Perhaps I should tell them the Samaritan was an atheist. That would stand him over against the Baptist preacher and the deacon. Nope. Couldn't do that. Too volatile.

On the side of the road a group of five migrant farmworkers were squatting in the dust behind a beat-up old truck with a flat tire. All of them were small, even scrawny, with bagging pants. "Migrant farmworkers!" The idea seemed perfect, and as I inched along, I mulled it over in my mind. Resident aliens. *Illegal* aliens. The Samaritan was to a Jew what an illegal alien was to a U.S. citizen. Besides, illegal aliens have been very much in the news lately.

There is a great deal of pathos here, I thought. Perhaps too much. The lawyer in the biblical story didn't feel any compassion at all for the lot of the Samaritan.

Two of the men had opened the tailgate and were trying to remove the lug nuts with a pair of pliers. "At least they have something to work with," I thought. But pliers?

The traffic stopped again. A black limo was on my left, ahead of me. By this time I was directly opposite the migrant workers, and I could see their necks glisten behind the open throats of their shirts. "Why do they leave them open like that?" I wondered.

But I understood the sweat. The heat was still visible coming off the black road tar. The sun beat down almost unmercifully. The oldest-looking of the migrant farm workers caught my eye briefly, and I smiled and waved a little. I wondered if he knew I was a theologian and that I was working him into a sermon. But this man's face was the perfect embodiment of desperation. Eyes hollow. Cheeks sunken and sallow. Shoulders sagging, from what I supposed must have seemed like a couple of hundred years of hard labor. He was hunkered down into the wheel well, trying for a little shade. He picked up a pebble and tossed it off like a marble, and it made a little puff in the powdered dust by the roadside. I could see the bead of sweat form up along the man's jaw and run down his neck and into the open belly of his shirt. One of the other men spat.

I tried desperately to photograph this moment in my mind's eye. To capture its essence. What I needed was the words that would make it live again in the mind's eye of my congregation.

The truck was behind me now, and I could only catch glimpses of it in my rearview mirror. I rolled the window back up and tried to record in my mind the last images of that scene in my mirror, when suddenly I realized that I couldn't use the illegal aliens in my sermon after all. Somebody in my congregation would point out that this wasn't an exact analogy. The Samaritan wasn't the victim in the ditch. Instead he was the hero of the story. If the victim in the ditch had been, say a lawyer or a banker, and if the *rescuer* had been a migrant farm worker, *then* the analogy would have worked quite nicely.

Besides, this story means something more than, and different from, a question of racial prejudice. The race question was the lawyer's question, not Jesus'. One has the impression that if the lawyer had raised the question in terms of age or social class, the story would have been about the "good geriatric." There was something else I need to tell my congregation: *This story is about all those prejudices and agendas that prevent us from doing the will of God.* How ironic that this question had come from a lawyer, a theologian!

There is a Spanish proverb for people who don't practice what they preach: "En la casa de herrero—cuchillo de palo!" [In the house of the blacksmith—a wooden knife!]

Theologian indeed! Like the priest, descending from his tour of duty in the temple, with the scent of the temple incense still on his clothes, the lawyer was so busy defining the will of God that he neglected the obvious reality that God is a God of compassion. The will of God is known in acts of compassion!

By now the truck was completely out of view. The image lingered in my mind all the way to the office. Even though I knew I couldn't use it in my sermon, still there was something about it that I couldn't quite shake off.

The next day I passed this spot again, moving along at a considerably better clip this time. The migrant farmworkers were gone now. They left no record of having been here. Even the tire tracks and the footprints had been blown away by the wind. As I looked, the sun caught the glint of a tool on the roadside: the pair of pliers they had used to get the lug nuts off. The pliers brought the whole scene back into view, and for a moment—just a moment—I saw them there again. Just for a moment. It was a flash. Only this time there was something different. I had returned my friend's red sports car. In its place I was driving my brother's old Chevy Blazer. The blazer had no air-conditioning.

Now, in order to understand what it meant that I had no air-conditioning, I have to tell you something about this old truck. This old truck is a dinosaur. It doesn't drive on the street—it rumbles. You feel it before you hear it, and hear it before you see it. It's rather like a crotchety old dragon, with fire in its bones and a thirst for blood. Only—thankfully—it guzzles gas and oil instead of blood, and it belches up its satisfactions in the form of backfiring and a constant roar from the engine. It is an off-roader's dream: When you drive it, it feels like you're driving on a creek bed. Even on paved roads.

When my brother offered to loan it to me, I jumped at the chance. Something in that old truck makes me feel—well—strong. Connected with the earth. I forget that I'm a theologian, and pretend I'm a good old boy on my way out to Gilley's for a cold one. When I drive it, I wear work clothes.

So Thursday morning, when I passed the spot of the breakdown, I felt an odd sense of connection with those migrant farmworkers. Hard workers, I thought. When I conjured up the image of that old man's eyes, I thought I saw—of course it was my imagination, it had to be my imagination—I thought I saw a twinkle. Something that looked almost like mischief. "Perhaps he feels the camaraderie, too," I wondered as I barreled on by.

Friday morning I went out to the truck—Levis on, and an old work shirt. Suddenly the sermon was the last thing on my mind. A slow leak in my right rear tire was faster than I thought: The tire was pancake flat.

What I am about to tell you is true. I have to tell you this because you may be inclined not to believe a theologian who pretends to be a good old boy on his way out to Gilley's for a beer. The tire was flat. The truck didn't have a jack, and my own car, with my jack, was in the shop. I spent fifteen minutes borrowing a jack from a neighbor, and another forty-five minutes jacking up the dinosaur. The springs in the back were so bad that the tire simply stayed on the ground. I jacked up the chassis as high as I dared, and built a brace underneath with bricks I had brought from the backyard. I lowered the chassis onto the brace, then took the jack out and put it under the rear axle. Sliding in upside down under the rear axle, I cranked that rascal up, a quarter turn at a time, until the point just before the tire could spin free. I climbed out from under it, went around, and started to loosen the lug nuts. They all came off pretty easy, all but one. Each wheel had one locking lug nut. I spent fifteen minutes going through the nuts and bolts in the glove compartment before I finally decided that the lug nut key wasn't there.

It took me an hour to locate my brother at work. By now it was eleven o'clock, and the sun was beginning to beat down hard. I had long since started to sweat; now the sweat was trickling down my armpits. My Levis were filthy with grease and black rubber from the tire.

I settled in and tried to unseat the locking lug nut, but every time I turned the wrench, it slipped out a little worse.

Very gradually I destroyed the nut.

What was I to do now? I called one of those mobile mechanics who make house calls. After $600 for my own car, what's another forty bucks? But the man said his company didn't do tires. I could now see a towing bill mounting up in my mind. What was this going to cost me, besides a day of work? I borrowed a bike pump from a neighbor on the off chance that the slow leak would hold until I got to a gas station.

This trick worked. Because there wasn't any weight on the tire, I was able to pump it up enough that it actually supported the truck all the way to the gas station. The mechanic put it up on the rack and finally chiseled the lug nut off with a power chisel. He charged me six bucks to fix the flat, and I left the station congratulating myself for having saved a $50 towing charge.

So engrossed was I in my good fortune that I didn't notice that a woman in a Volkswagen convertible had pulled up behind me. As I backed out, I did $175 damage to her front bumper.

It was after one o'clock before I got home.

"Is everything all right now?" asked my very patient and understanding wife.

What do you say when you're a theologian who's trying very hard to feel like a good old boy and close to the earth, and way down deep you feel like crying? "Sure, fine," I said. I was absolutely exhausted.

"Then can you run down to the store to pick up some groceries? We're nearly out of diapers, too."

"Sure. No problem." She gives me the list. The beast is out there, waiting for me. I am now streaming with perspiration. But I have my pride, too. Out I go. I fire up the beast, and head out on the highway.

Now the clincher—are you ready for this?—between my house and the grocery store there's a five-mile stretch of open highway. Halfway down that open stretch, I go to shift gears and the clutch goes out on me. I shut off the engine and coast to the side of the road. The tires raise a little puff in the dust as the truck lurches to a halt. I am so frustrated that I can't decide whether to laugh or cry, and finally—my pride getting the better of my despair—I break down in howling hysterics.

So there I am, sitting on the side of the road in an old truck, the clutch gone, streaming with sweat, and laughing like an idiot. I loosen the collar of my shirt and unbutton two more buttons against the heat. It is so hot. Finally I calm myself down enough to figure out that I need some sort of help. Serious help. I am quite beyond my resources, and this is a very bad place. What am I going to do? The inside of the truck is like a Dutch oven, and I get out and settle into the only shade there is, hunkered down into the wheel well. I can feel a bead of sweat form up along the edge of my jaw and run down my neck and into the open belly of my shirt.

Absentmindedly, I pick up some pebbles, and—as I toss one off like a marble—I catch sight of a man in a red sports car, with the windows up and the air conditioner on, wheeling by.

I know exactly who he is: He is a theologian, and he is on his way to the office to write a sermon on the parable of the good Samaritan—and he's going to pass me by. He turns and looks me full in the face, just long enough for me to see—I swear that this only happened in my imagination—he looks just long enough for me to see that he's not the theologian at all: He's that old migrant farmworker, and the twinkle in his eye has broadened out into a full-scale wink.

That's why I cannot preach to you today on the parable of the good Samaritan. I have decided instead that this morning's sermon must be from another text. Even now I haven't decided which.

I could preach on the Spanish proverb I know the farm worker muttered under his breath as he sailed on by: "En la casa de herrero—cuchillo de palo!" [In the house of the blacksmith—a wooden knife!] I suppose I could preach on the opening to Jesus' parable of the two houses, in Luke 6:46: "Why do you call me, 'Lord, Lord,' and do not *do* what I tell you?" I could preach on the Golden Rule, in Matthew 7:12:

> "So whatever you wish that men would do to you, do so to them; for this is the law and the prophets."

But I think perhaps this sermon is really about something Jesus said to our theologian friend, twice—on either side of the parable of the good Samaritan. This is what Jesus said in response to the lawyer's question, "What must I do to inherit eternal life?": "*Do this*," Jesus told him. "*Do this*, and you will live."

Shall we pray?

15

LESSONS FROM THE ROAD 2

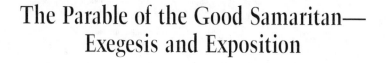

The Parable of the Good Samaritan—
Exegesis and Exposition

T he last chapter contained a sermon on the parable of the good Samaritan. In this chapter we will trace out the exegetical considerations that underlay the sermon. We will proceed in three movements. In the first we will lay out the text in a diagram, looking for structural parallels and so forth. In the second we will move through the text sequentially, the way a reader would, reconstructing the repertoire of schemas the reader was expected to have in hand as he or she read (this is

the stuff usually associated with exegesis proper). Along the way
we will ask how this repertoire interacts with the text in the
process of reading (that is, we will make a rhetorical analysis).
In the third we will comment on the movement from the
rhetorical bind of the text to the homiletical bind of the sermon.

THE TEXT

Let us begin by displaying our text (Luke 10:25–37, NRSV):

25 Just then a lawyer stood up to test Jesus.

"Teacher," he said,   "what must I do to inherit eternal life?"

26 He said to him,   "What is written in the law?
                                       What do you read there?"

27 He answered,   "You shall love the Lord your God
                                           with all your heart,
                                           and with all your soul,
                                           and with all your strength,
                                           and with all your mind;
                                           and your neighbor as yourself."

28 And he said to him,   "You have given the right answer;
                                       do this, and you will live."

29 But wanting to justify himself, he asked Jesus,   "And who is my neighbor?"

30 Jesus replied,   "A man was going down from Jerusalem to
                                       Jericho,
                                           and fell into the hands of robbers,
                                               who stripped him,
                                               beat him,
                                               and went away,
                                               leaving him half dead.

31Now by chance a priest was going down
that road;
    and when he saw him,
        he passed by on the other side.

32So likewise a Levite,
    when he came to the place and saw him,
        passed by on the other side.

33 But a Samaritan,
    while traveling came near him;
    and when he saw him,
        he was moved with pity.
34 He went to him
    and bandaged his wounds,
        having poured oil and wine on them.
    Then he put him on his own animal,
    brought him to an inn,
        and took care of him.
35 The next day
    he took out two denarii, gave them
    to the innkeeper, and said,

'Take care of him; and when I come back, I will repay you whatever more you spend.'

[36] Which of these three, do you think, was a neighbor to the man who fell into the hands of the robbers?"

[37] He said,

"The one who showed him mercy."

Jesus said to him,

"Go and do likewise."

THE RHETORIC OF THE TEXT— TOP-DOWN READING CONSTRAINTS

Context

It is important that the parable of the good Samaritan is housed within a larger pericope. This is a move in a theological debate, an answer given in response to two very specific questions: "What must I do to inherit eternal life?" and "Who is my neighbor?" This context controls the interpretation. Kenneth Bailey points out that when the parable is sliced out of its context, it is reduced to "an ethical exhortation to reach out to those in need."[1]

There is a good deal of discussion about the original relationship between the parable and the discussion with the lawyer, and it is sometimes suggested that the connection is artificial and that the parable originally stood alone. As we have it, however, the debate is the context in which the parable appears, and that is the context in which we must read it.

One notices immediately that the debate begins abruptly, without any connecting link with what precedes. This story therefore stands on its own as an independent unit. It is independent, but Luke's reader has already been equipped with an impressive array of dialogs and discussions between Jesus and his antagonists. In an important survey of the larger section in which our story is found—the so-called central section (Luke 9:51–19:44)—James Resseguie points out that the underlying thrust of the section as a whole rests on a conflict between two competing ideologies, that of Jesus and

---

[1]Bailey, *Through Peasant Eyes,* 33.

that of his opponents.[2] The story of Jesus' conversation with the lawyer therefore occurs in a context of controversy.

This is only the second time that lawyers are mentioned in the Gospel of Luke; the first was in a summary condemnation in 7:30, in which they were grouped together with the Pharisees and condemned for having "rejected the commandment of God." Thus, Luke's readers would have been primed to hear the designation "lawyer" (*nomikos*) in a negative light.

Genre

Considerations of genre will shift midway through the reading process. For Luke's reader, the story begins with clear signals that this is to be a theological controversy of some sort. The note that the lawyer stands up "to put him to the test" suggests a negative spin, though not necessarily a hostile one. According to Eta Linnemann, this is a technical expression for placing a theological question to test whether a man is a genuine scholar. "A real scholar is one who immediately gives the correct answer to every question put to him in respect of the Halakhah, the rules for the conduct of life."[3] If Linnemann is correct, the lawyer was intending to test Jesus' theological mettle.

The lawyer is also a "reader" of sorts, who will interpret what he is hearing against a particular set of conventions. His question to Jesus is a demand for a legal principle of some sort, and that in itself primes him to expect a legal case. This priming establishes his disposition toward the parable. As we shall see, Jesus appears at first to accommodate him. About midway, the genre signals change. Jesus' little story begins as though it is a legal case, but ends with a trap. Part of the entrapment lies in the way Jesus appears at first to be engaging the lawyer on his own terms. We shall examine the details of this shift when we come to them.

---

[2]James Resseguie, "Point of View in the Central Section of Luke (9:51–19:44)," *Journal of the Evangelical Theological Society* 25 (1982) 41–47.

[3]Eta Linnemann, *Jesus of the Parables* (New York: Harper and Row, 1966) 51.

Theme

In the lawyer's experience, the theme here also undergoes a shift. At first the discussion is in response to the question, "What must I do to inherit eternal life?" Then it turns to the definition of the term "neighbor." What the lawyer does not anticipate is that Jesus will use the shift to attack the original question from a more oblique angle.

It also may be important that Luke's central section begins with a volatile story about Jesus and his disciples being turned away by a town in Samaria (9:51–56). James and John wanted to call down fire from heaven to destroy the Samaritans (v. 54), but Jesus rebuked them (v. 55). The rebuke is summary, and the narrator gives no clue about its content. Can it be that he assumed also a certain attitude on the part of his reader, one that would have been able easily enough to give reasons for rebuking the disciples on this question? We cannot say for certain.

THE RHETORIC OF THE TEXT— BOTTOM-UP READING CONSTRAINTS

Here again, we move through the text in sequence, noting the various gists the reader is likely to draw at each stage.

Verse 25

Just then, a lawyer stood up to test Jesus. "Teacher," he said, "what must I do to inherit eternal life?"

Luke's reader is expected to know that the designation "lawyer" (*nomikos*) here identifies the man as an expert in Jewish law, and therefore in the Old Testament, both its literature and the rules that govern its interpretation. This schema is drawn from the reader's lexicon. Previous contextual cues give a negative spin on the schema for lawyer, just as they had for the Pharisee in our story of the anointing. These prime the reader to view the man's question with suspicion. On the other hand, the fact that the man "stood up" signals a posture of deference, as does the fact that he addresses Jesus with a title of respect—"rabbi."

The man's reason for raising the question is clarified by a narrator's aside: His intention is "to put Jesus to the test." What it means to "put one to the test" is debated. The term is *ekpeirazōn,* which is sometimes translated "tempt." As we have seen, this suggests a genre signal. What is coming is a theological discussion of some sort.

This is not the last time Jesus will be asked this question. It appears again in Luke 18:18 on the lips of the rich young ruler. It may be helpful to compare the present story with that, for there, when the question is raised, it is not at all antagonistic or hostile. This is important. Though the reader would likely hear the question as suspicious, in a different context and without the narrator's aside it would not necessarily appear hostile at all.

These, then, are the opening moves that will govern the reader's perception of the story as it unfolds. The constraints are somewhat mixed. Some are negative—the context, the genre signals (controversy story), the negative nuances of the term "lawyer." Some are more positive—the fact that he stands up and the fact that he addresses Jesus with a title of deference. Some are more or less neutral. If Linnemann is right, the narrator's aside to the reader that the lawyer is "putting Jesus to the test" may not be as hostile as it appears in English. The reader is forced to wait and see. How will Jesus perform when confronted by a question of theory?

Verse 26

He said to him, "What is written in the law? What do you read there?"

Jesus begins by drawing out the position of his opponent. This appears to be customary. One finds an identical strategy at work in Mark 10:3, in response to a theological challenge about the legitimacy of divorce: "How do you read?" As Morton Smith showed long ago, this form corresponds to an accepted rabbinical phrasing of the question.[4] If we are to have debate, then let us properly exchange positions.

---

[4]Morton Smith, *Tannaitic Parallels to the Gospels* (Philadelphia: Society for Biblical Literature, 1951) 27.

Verse 27

And he answered, "You shall love the Lord your God with all your heart, and with all your soul, and with all your strength, and with all your mind; and your neighbor as yourself."

A word is in order about the repetition in the lawyer's answer:

> You shall love the Lord your God
>   with all your heart,
>   and with all your soul,
>   and with all your strength,
>   and with all your mind.

With a minor modification, this response is taken over verbatim from Deuteronomy 6:4. Here, as there, the repetition is ep-exegetic. That is, the reiterated elements do not divide the human person into parts—heart, soul, strength, mind. Rather, they are various ways of saying the same thing. This strategy is particularly Hebraic and is frequently found in the Gospel traditions. The effect on the listener is the overlapping of schemas and thus, through repetition, the strengthening and fleshing out of the image. This adds rhetorical potency. It should also probably be noted that the third element—strength—has been added to the Old Testament text. This final note may be too far removed from the reader's consciousness to be of direct influence in the reading process. It does, however, contribute to the deepening timbre of the lawyer's response.

To the passage from Deuteronomy 6 the lawyer has added a postscript from Leviticus 19:18. The resulting conflation appears to have been a theological commonplace in Jesus' day. In b. *Šabbat* 30b a tradition states that when asked to summarize the law "while standing on one foot," Hillel recited the Shema (Deut 6:4: "Hear O Israel, the LORD Our God is One God") and then gave the negative form of the Golden Rule ("What is hateful to you do not do to your neighbor"). A hundred years later, Aqiba is reputed to have said something similar: "Thou shalt love thy neighbor as thyself. . . . This is the great and comprehensive principle of the Torah."[5]

---

[5]*Sifre Lev.* 19.18 (on which see H. L. Strack and P. Billerbeck, *Kommentar zum neuen Testament aus Talmud und Midrasch*, 1:357f.). See

Verse 28

And he said to him, "You have given the right answer; do this, and you will live."

By common rabbinical standards Jesus is therefore in order when he responds, "You have answered rightly. Do this and you will live." Thus far there is little difficulty between the two men.

It is clear that vv. 25–28 have been included here because they provide occasion for the controversy to which the Samaritan is addressed, so there must be a difficulty after all. That difficulty surfaces in v. 29.

Verse 29

But wanting to justify himself, he asked Jesus, "And who is my neighbor?"

It is hard to see why the lawyer should feel compelled to "justify himself." Jesus has agreed that he has answered properly. Perhaps I. Howard Marshall has correctly grasped the nature of the issue. Jesus has told him that he already knows the answer to his own question and has only to practice what he preaches.[6] For the lawyer, this is a matter to *debate*. For Jesus, it is a matter to *perform*.

The implication, of course, is that the lawyer's way of posing the question was an academic exercise and therefore in some way not entirely adequate to the actual performance of living piety. "Do this and you will live" closes this round of the conversation on an instructional note: Practice has priority over theory. What is at issue is not the theory of the law but its performance. At this point Jesus appears to have bested the lawyer at his own game. In effect, the lawyer has set himself up for this implication. Note the way he initially framed the question in v. 25: "What must I *do* to inherit eternal life?"

---

also Ps 14:4 and Sir 13:15f.: "Every beast loves its like and every man his neighbor. All flesh consorts according to its kind, and a man will cleave to his like." For further references, see Samuel Tobias Lachs, *A Rabbinic Commentary on the New Testament: The Gospels of Matthew, Mark, and Luke* (Hoboken, N.J.: KTAV, 1987) 107f.

[6]I. Howard Marshall, *Commentary on Luke* (Grand Rapids: Eerdmans, 1978) 447.

The lawyer, however, is trained for discussions such as this. Apparently Jesus is not, for from the lawyer's point of view he has left himself open to the challenge that he lacks critical discrimination. The lawyer's counterquestion in v. 29 is calculated to reassert the central importance of theory over practice, since actual performance of the law requires that distinctions sometimes be made. While the performance of the law is crucial, the theory of the law is logically prior. One cannot hope to carry out the law properly if one has not properly understood it. With this, the lawyer is going to challenge Jesus' sweeping and undiscriminating generalities. "Who is my neighbor?" he asks.

The question "Who is my neighbor?" appears also to have been a matter of heated debate within rabbinic Judaism. Having decided the boundaries of the law, one must next define its terms. But this is a matter of disagreement. The difficulty is created by the parallelism in the passage from Leviticus 19 with which the lawyer's answer closed. We may begin our diagram at v. 17:

> [17]You shall not hate in your heart *anyone of your kin;*
> you shall reprove   *your neighbor,*
> or you will incur guilt yourself.
> [18]You shall not take vengeance or bear a grudge against
>   *any of your people,*
> but you shall love
>
>   *your neighbor* as yourself.

The implication is clear: In the context of Leviticus 19, "neighbor" must mean "brother" and "fellow countryman." The parallels between the overlapping schemas reinforce and clarify one another.

It should be noted that this is not mere theological obfuscation. No one is deliberately subverting the meaning of "neighbor," which is so obvious in English. The English term has largely acquired its meaning from Jesus' parable. (If you will, there are nodes of meaning for the schema now that were simply lacking in Jesus' day. For those nodes of meaning we have Jesus and his brilliant parable to thank.) The idea of racial or ethnic separation, now so abhorrent to us, was in Jesus' day quite the norm.[7]

---

[7]See Linnemann, *Jesus of the Parables,* 51: "All ancient cultures draw a line between insiders and outsiders, and one set of laws applies for dealing with those inside and another for those outside."

This, then, is the question. What are the boundaries of the schema "countrymen"? Are they not coterminus with the boundaries for the term "sons of your own people"? Minimally defined, yes. What of sojourners? Leviticus 19 goes on to use identical language for one's responsibilities to the sojourner in the land: "You shall treat him as a native among you, and you shall love him as yourself" (v. 34). But the very fact that the sojourner is singled out in this way means that in v. 18 the term "neighbor" cannot be automatically generalized to mean "fellow human being." If it is a closely limited term there, then the responsibilities to sojourners defined in v. 34 cannot be generalized either.

Later rabbinic thought specifically understood "sojourner" to refer to full proselytes and in that way restricted Leviticus 19:34 to exclude the traveler who simply passed through the land. Samaritans were excluded, too, as were resident aliens who do not join the community within twelve months (see *Mekilta Exodus* 21.35).[8]

There is more to this than mere casuistry, as Eta Linnemann has pointed out: "All the ordinances of the law that should govern a man's behavior to his fellow men were left up in the air if it was not clearly settled who counted as a fellow man. 'What can be demanded of me?' is the question which lies unuttered behind the question about the neighbor."[9]

Verse 30

Jesus replied, "A man was going down from Jerusalem to Jericho, and fell into the hands of robbers, who stripped him, beat him, and went away, leaving him half dead."

The opening term here, *hypolabōn*, is a participle, meaning perhaps "taking up the question" and therefore, by extension, "replying." With the mention of the "certain man," Jesus begins the parable.

Thus far we have been riding along on the coattails of Luke's reader, tracing out the development of the reader's grasp

---

[8] On this see Johannes Fichtner, "πλησίον," in *Theological Dictionary of the New Testament* (ed. G. Kittel and G. Friedrich, trans. G. Bromiley; Grand Rapids: Eerdmans, 1968) 6:315.

[9] Linnemann, *Jesus of the Parables*, 52.

of the context of the story. At this point let us shift focus slightly and redesignate as the reader the lawyer who is listening to Jesus tell the story of the Samaritan. This takes place *within* Luke's narrative, like a picture within a frame. Luke has given us a series of important clues about the lawyer, what he was up to, and how he would have understood the top-down reading constraints of context, genre, and theme. Because Luke's reader is somewhat removed from the skills and competencies the lawyer would be expected to have, it may not be right to suppose that he or she would have heard the full range of nuances that would have been obvious to the lawyer. Luke's reader has his or her own reaction, to which we shall turn in due course.

Our own reaction is to expect a parable, which in its own way suggests something of our disposition toward Jesus. There is an ongoing discussion among scholars about whether this is to be understood as a parable or an example story.[10] It is my thesis that the lawyer would have heard something quite different. The context suggests a theological discussion, and in that context the opening of the parable would have struck the lawyer as an opening of a hypothetical case.[11] A hypothetical case requires a different kind of response from those appropriate for a parable or an example story. The theme of Jesus' story, so the lawyer would suppose, is a case law answer to his question, "Who is my neighbor?" This response—elicited by the top-down constraints of context, genre, and theme—will prove to be an essential factor in the story's trickery.

Jesus opens the "case" by defining a specific circumstance. The expression "a man" leaves the case open ended; this is not an actual person but a theoretical one. The lawyer, however, supposing this to be a hypothetical case, would default to the norm for the context and assume that the victim in the ditch is a fellow Jew. We can be certain of that because he comes to the

---

[10] On this question see John Dominic Crossan, "Parable and Example in the Teaching of Jesus," *New Testament Studies* 18 (1971–72) 285–307, esp. 285–91.

[11] Note that there is a formally similar beginning in the context of a theological debate between Jesus and the Sadducees about resurrection from the dead (Luke 20:27–34 = Mark 12:18–27). There, after stating the Mosaic regulation on the law of levirate marriage, they pose a hypothetical case. That case begins like this story: "Now there were seven brothers . . . " (v. 29).

story primed by the thrust of his own question to Jesus. When he asks, "Who is my neighbor?" his concern is to find out to whom he is obligated. When Jesus opens the case with an illustration of a man in the ditch, the lawyer is certain to expect that the thrust of the story is about the nature and extent of one's legal obligation to neighbors in need.

Note that one "goes down" *from* Jerusalem and one "ascends" *to* Jerusalem. These are technical expressions and have nothing to do with directions on the compass. The lawyer knows this from his stock of world knowledge. The road described here is well known for its dangers. It descends some 3300 feet in the space of seventeen quite barren miles. Josephus mentions brigands here (*Jewish War,* 4.474), and Strabo says that Pompey routed brigands in this area (*Geography,* 16.2.41). This is an ideal place for banditry. It is isolated. The folds in the road go deep into the hillsides, such that travelers are often hidden from view—a perfect situation for a holdup. These facts from the lawyer's stock of world knowledge may explain why Jesus refers to an actual road in a hypothetical case.[12] From the lawyer's point of view, this is a good case, one made the more real by the possibility that this could very well take place in real time and real space. Yet that realism is masked, too. Something about this is stylized. The man is not named. He has no face, no identity. He is instead a representative example. So the impression of a hypothetical case continues even though something like this could actually have happened.

---

[12]Apparently the safety of travelers was a serious and widespread concern. Adolf Deissmann (*Light from the Ancient East* [1927, reprint; Peabody, Mass.: Hendrickson, 1995], 134) records a letter written about 171 CE, found at Euhemeria, in which two pig merchants report having been waylaid on the road. The parallels with the story of the Samaritan are striking, though, of course, only of limited exegetical value:

> Yesterday, which was the 19th of the present month of Thoth, as we were returning about daybreak from the village of Theadelphia in the division of Themistes, certain malefactors came upon us between Polydeucia and Theadelphia, and bound us, with the guard of the tower also, and assaulted us with many stripes, and wounded Pasion, and robbed us of 1 pig, and carried off Pasion's coat.

Verses 31–32

Now by chance a priest was going down that road; and when he saw him, he passed by on the other side. So likewise a Levite, when he came to the place and saw him, passed by on the other side.

It is quite common to find in these two verses echoes of Hosea 6:9–10:

> [9]As robbers lie in wait for someone,
>   so the priests are banded together;
> they murder on the road to Shechem,
>   they commit a monstrous crime.
> [10]In the house of Israel
>   I have seen a horrible thing;
> Ephraim's whoredom is there,
>   Israel is defiled.

To my mind, if there are parallels here, they are too remote to have been detectable. Yet these verses may be of indirect value for the light they shed on popular conceptions of the priesthood. This information is drawn from the reader's repertoire of cultural knowledge. The negative attitude of laymen toward priests is widely known. Hosea 6:9–10 indicates that this attitude was already fully developed within the prophetic tradition. We find echoes of this thinking widely spread in the ancient world. Testament of Levi 17 provides another illustration. In this document the deterioration of the priesthood occurs in seven stages. We are interested only in the fifth (v. 5) and the seventh (v. 11):

> [1]Listen also concerning the priesthood . . .

> [5]The fourth priest shall be overtaken with sufferings, because injustice shall be imposed upon him in a high degree, and all Israel shall hate each one his neighbor . . .

> [11]In the seventh week there will come priests: idolators, adulterers, money lovers, arrogant, lawless, voluptuaries, pederasts, those who practice bestiality.

The lawyer is almost certain now that this is the posture Jesus is taking, and the curt way Jesus describes the action of the priest and the Levite would have confirmed this impression. What in English appears as seven words ("he passed by on the other

side") is in Greek a single word (*antiparēlthen*). That very fact
implies a kind of judgment, a dismissal of the action as unde-
serving of further comment. It is subtle enough in English, but
abrupt in Greek. Notice how stylized Jesus has made the structures of these two opening movements:

> [31]Now by chance
>> a priest was going down that road;
>> and when he saw him, he
>>> passed by on the other side.
>
> [32]So likewise
>> a Levite, when he came to the place
>> and saw him,
>>> passed by on the other side.

By now the lawyer will have constructed several overlapping gists. The common element between the first and second
examples is that they involve clerics. Almost certainly he now
believes that though the story is a hypothetical case, Jesus is
going to engage in cleric bashing. With his own training, however, he can think of a number of reasons the priest and the
Levite may be perfectly right in ignoring the victim in the ditch.
Should he serve as their lawyer and come to their defense? This
seems to be the appropriate response to a hypothetical case.

Both the priest and the Levite are described as "going
down from Jerusalem," and this suggests—though it does not
require—that they had finished their tours of duty in the temple.
The lawyer would recognize this fact, and it would inform one
aspect of his response to the story. Not only is he being asked to
form a gist for each element of the storyline; he is also prompted
by the genre clues to find defenses for the priest and the Levite.
Here the problems of interpretation have to do with the specific
legal responsibilities of a priest or a Levite as they encounter a
victim on the road. J. Duncan M. Derrett has explored this
matter in great detail, and we may draw upon his findings with
the observation that they represent in a loose way the sort of
reasoning processes that are going through the lawyer's mind.

> If the man were still alive the priest must not stand idly by the
> blood of his "neighbour" (Lev. xix.16b). If the priest could be sure
> he was a neighbour he must make an effort to save his life. . . .
> Then the man might die in his proximity, whereupon he would be
> in any case defiled, which was forbidden (Lev. xxi.1); and he

would be obliged to procure his burial (provided he were a Jew, which he might well be!); and he would be obliged to rend his garment, which conflicted with his obligation not to destroy valuable things.

If the man were dead, on the other hand, the first two inconveniences would ensue, provided the man were a Jew, unless the priest confined himself to arranging for the burial and kept his distance. . . . In order to resolve the doubt whether the man was alive or dead the priest must come within four cubits. If he were dead the man would thus be defiled. Poking with a stick would not avoid this. . . .

The true positive commandment, Lev. xix.18 and the virtual positive commandment ("not to stand . . . ") at Lev. xix.16, were both conditional, and could not overcome the unconditional commandment not to defile. . . .

The priest was thus entitled to pass on.[13]

Doubtless this represents a highly developed form of the argument the lawyer is working up for his moment of response to Jesus. The lawyer's own reasoning processes were probably shallower. In Greek, vv. 31f. comprise only twenty-six words, so little time has lapsed within which he can come to such conclusions. It is difficult to suppose the lawyer would have reached this level of analysis.

There is another response, readier to hand: Jesus was answering a question the lawyer had not asked. He had asked for a definition of boundaries about who was a neighbor. Jesus was posing a case about the nature of one's responsibilities to a neighbor. For this reason, it will appear to the lawyer that Jesus is skirting the issue. In fact, Jesus has left himself open to a challenge that will prove fatal to his position: He has described the man in the ditch as stripped naked and unconscious. There is nothing to indicate whether or not he is a Jew. He might even be a Samaritan! If the man in the ditch were a Samaritan, then he is not a neighbor, and the priest and the Levite owe him no aid. Jesus is equivocating.

With this response now in hand, he waits for Jesus to conclude the case. Storytelling customarily moves in sets of three. Two examples are too few. Four are too cumbersome.

---

[13] J. Duncan M. Derrett, "Law in the New Testament: Fresh Light on the Parable of the Good Samaritan," *New Testament Studies* 11 (1964) 25.

Three is a good balance. As the lawyer waits, he anticipates what Jesus will present as the third member of the triad: The apparent cleric bashing calls for a Jewish layman. The layman will help the victim in the ditch, and the "case" will end up with an anticlerical point.

Verses 33–35

But a Samaritan, while traveling came near him; and when he saw him, he was moved with pity. He went to him and bandaged his wounds, having poured oil and wine on them. Then he put him on his own animal, brought him to an inn, and took care of him.

The next day he took out two denarii, gave them to the innkeeper, and said, "Take care of him; and when I come back, I will repay you whatever more you spend."

Against the lawyer's anticipations, the introduction of a Samaritan comes as something of a shock. Several factors increase the severity of the reversal here. First, this immediately subverts the lawyer's response that the victim in the ditch might not be a fellow countryman after all. The subversion comes quickly, faster than the lawyer can respond. Note the texture: On one level, Jesus abandons the structural parallelism of the first two examples by bringing the term "Samaritan" forward to the opening of the sentence. This creates emphasis. The effect is that the introduction of the Samaritan is rather disturbing:

[31]Now by chance a priest . . .
[32]So likewise a Levite . . .
[33]A Samaritan, while traveling
        came near him . . .

On another level, the parallels continue to reinforce the contrast with the first two members of the triad. In the rhythmic patterns of vv. 31, 32, and 33, the repeated *antiparēlthen* ("he passed by on the other side") stand in structural balance with both *prosēlthen* ("he went to him") and *esplanchnisthē* ("he had compassion").

[31]A priest . . . passed by on the other side.
        (*antiparēlthen*)
[32]A Levite . . . passed by on the other side.
        (*antiparēlthen*)

^{33}A Samaritan . . . had compassion . . .
> (esplanchnisthē)
> and went to him
> (prosēlthen)

Jesus is not content to make his point by contrast. He belabors it, then belabors it again:

^{33}A Samaritan was moved with pity
^{34}He went to him
> and bandaged his wounds,
>> having poured oil and wine on them.^{14}
> Then he set him on his own animal and brought him to an inn,
> and took care of him.
^{35}The next day he took out two denarii
> gave them to the innkeeper,
> and said,
>> "Take care of him; and when I come back, I will repay you whatever more you spend."

In the belaboring, the story makes two other points. The first of these rests on the surface of the language itself. The lawyer has been aware of the dangers of the road and the presence of brigands. He knows from Jesus' description that the Samaritan is a practical man, a man of responsibility. He has provisions for such a circumstance—does he travel regularly? He has pack animals—is he a merchant? He guarantees the costs of the victim's care—does he carry money? He is travel-wise. Surely he must know that there are brigands about. The man in the ditch is evidence enough of that. The Samaritan has much to lose here. His pack animals and his merchandise make him a prime target. He is far from home, in enemy territory. The victim in the

---

^{14}The "working in of oil and wine" is sometimes overinterpreted. Origen saw this as an allusion to Isa 1:6, in which the work of God is to bind up the wounds of Israel and mollify them with oil. There is simply too much evidence suggesting that oil and wine were ordinary treatment for wounds of various sorts. The passage in Isa 1:6 reflects this indirectly. M. Šabbat 19.2 mentions a mixture of oil and wine in connection with the treatment of circumcision. J. Berakot 31.9 reads: "A sick person may be rubbed on the Sabbath with a mixture of oil and wine." Apparently the oil was thought to mollify the pain, and the wine to purge and sanitize the wound. This information is drawn from the lawyer's lexicon, and lacking any indication to the contrary, he would simply have defaulted to it as the norm.

ditch is surely within one of the folds in the road, and thus out of view of other travelers. Does the Samaritan not know that by dismounting he makes himself all the more vulnerable—as we would say, a sitting duck? And on whose behalf? Surely he knows that here, on this particular road, the body in the ditch is almost certainly a Jew. Against this evolving scenario, the self-protectiveness of the priest and Levite appears paltry and self-serving. Since the lawyer has been formulating an argument in favor of their behavior, it appears he has been tricked into a kind of self-incrimination.

Most of this would have worked perfectly well if the third traveler had been a Jew. Why has Jesus selected a Samaritan? From the lawyer's point of view, it is this which is most striking, and most offensive. Samaritans are outcasts, pariahs. Why has Jesus selected a Samaritan? Could he not at least have had the decency to choose one of his fellow countrymen? But a Samaritan! It is enough to make your blood boil. And that is precisely the point. This story makes the lawyer's blood boil. In that way it lays bare the inhumanity of the lawyer's legal wranglings and shows that he is incapable of providing an adequate answer to the question he has asked, "Who is my neighbor?"

There is a subtle understructure to Jesus' challenge of the lawyer here. The reason the lawyer can not properly answer the question is that he seeks to read the law in a manner inherently inconsistent with the character of God. The history of Israel reverberates with this central theme: The character of God is disclosed in acts of compassion. In this way, Jesus bleeds the lawyer's question of its moral force and reasserts his claim that one must be merciful not because it is written in the statutes of the law but because God is merciful (Luke 6:36).

This, then, is the primary organizing theme here. Alongside it is a second, though the second depends upon subtle intertextual competencies. It is now a commonplace of scholarship that there are close verbal and conceptual parallels between this passage and 2 Chronicles 28:5–15,[15] a story in which

---

[15] On which see esp. Derrett, "Law in the New Testament," 23 n. 9; Robert W. Funk, "The Old Testament in Parable," *Encounter* 26 (1965) 251–68; Linnemann, *Jesus of the Parables*, 139; J. M. Furness, "Fresh Light on Luke 10.25–37," *Expository Times* 80 (1969) 182; F. Scott Spencer, "2 Chronicles 28:5–15 and the Parable of the Good Samaritan," *Westminster Theological Journal* 46 (1984) 317–49.

Samaritans come to the aid of Judaean victims following a battle with Israel. Of special interest here is v. 15:

> Then those who were mentioned by name got up and took the captives, and with the booty they clothed all that were naked among them; they clothed them, gave them sandals, provided them with food and drink, and anointed them; and carrying all the feeble among them on donkeys, they brought them to their kindred at Jericho, the city of palm trees. Then they returned to Samaria.

The clearest analysis of the parallels here is made by F. Scott Spencer. Spencer traces out a number of verbal and structural similarities, from which he concludes that "no theory of haphazard proof-texting is sufficient to account for the numerous parallels of thought (not merely language and circumstance) we have drawn between the Chronicler and the parabler. In short, Jesus proves himself a most responsible exegete and expositor of the Chronicles passage."[16]

Notice that this analysis—like most other analyses of the New Testament's use of the Old—concerns itself with the compositional side of things, and thus with authors rather than readers. What does it tell us of the reading? If the lawyer is to recognize the allusion, he must do so under the constraints of natural reading (or, rather, hearing), including timing and sequence. I would contend that when timing and sequence are factored into the equation, the readerly work includes a kind of shock, coupled with a retrospective look at the story itself, since the details of the story unfold for the lawyer-as-reader one after another and since the material in the opening lines is not sufficient to evoke the parallel from 2 Chronicles. The lawyer only discovers the reference to 2 Chronicles *after* the mention of the Samaritan, and that comes nearly at the end, when it is too late to retreat from the position he has taken. Then the parallels are fast and furious, piling upon themselves, so that the lawyer could hardly miss them. By then it is too late. As with other allusions, this one overcodes a second frame around the story, one that resists resolution into a gist and further controls the reading process. From the standpoint of reading constraints, J. M. Furness is closest to the truth: "The Scribe is not answered

---

[16] Spencer, "2 Chronicles 28:5–15 and the Parable of the Good Samaritan," 347.

by a brilliant story invented on the spur of the moment, but more brilliantly and more devastatingly by reference to a tale that the Lawyer already knew very well indeed."[17]

Verses 36–37

"Which of these three, do you think, was a neighbor to the man who fell into the hands of the robbers?" He said, "The one who showed him mercy." Jesus said to him, "Go and do likewise."

A good deal is made of how Jesus appears to have stood the lawyer's question on its head:

> [29]But wanting to justify himself,
>   he asked Jesus,
>   "And who is my neighbor?"
>
> [30]Jesus replied,
>   [the parable]
>   "Which of these three, do you think, was a neighbor to
>   the man who fell into the hands of the robbers?"

The explanation of this twist in the question may be more subtle than meets the eye. The lawyer's original question may have been ambiguous, especially if this conversation is understood as having taken place in Aramaic. In Aramaic, possession is indicated with the preposition *le*, "to" or "for." To ask, "Who is my neighbor?" is to ask at the same time, "Who is neighbor to me?" A similar subtlety happens in English, though it is not dependent upon a grammatical ambiguity. In English, when we ask, "Who are my true friends?" we actually mean, "Which of my friends have proven true to me?" In the Aramaic conversation, the lawyer asked only the first question, intending only to find out to whom he was obligated. If this is the case, Jesus has returned to his original strategy and forced the lawyer to find his answer in the question itself. If this is so, however, Luke's reader would have missed it. The text as we have it is written in Greek, and Luke's Greek lacks this particular ambiguity.

Before we leave this discussion, let us review the story in terms of the lawyer's identifications. In vv. 31 and 32, the

---

[17] Furness, "Fresh Light on Luke 10.25–37," 182.

lawyer is asked to identify with the priest and the Levite, or—at the very least—to take on their case and enter the story from their point of view. Note his alarm that Jesus is going to engage in cleric bashing. His response to the opening of the case consolidates this position. If the man in the ditch is a Samaritan, then the priest and the Levite owe him no aid. When Jesus casts the Samaritan in the role of the hero, he disrupts that movement and obliterates the lawyer's response. The final question in v. 36 restates the question from the victim's point of view: Who proved to be neighbor to the man in the ditch? To answer this question, the lawyer must abandon his initial identifications and take up the point of view of the victim, who is *helped* by a Samaritan! Thus, part of the rhetorical power here is the reversal of fortunes.[18]

With this, our observations return to those of Luke's reader, and we abandon the lawyer's point of view, climb back outside the story, and view it with its frame. In a sense, Luke's reader has been privy to the whole conversation, though it seems doubtful that he or she would have been capable of hearing the nuances of law and allusion that have overcoded the story in the lawyer's ears. Nor would Luke's Gentile readers have shared the lawyer's ethnic prejudice against Samaritans or his disposition in favor of the actions of the priest and Levite. More likely, Luke's reader would have been disposed against the priest, the Levite, and the lawyer who is wrangling out their defense. Here, even without the lawyer's subtle legal and literary competencies, the reader is bound to realize that Jesus has somehow brilliantly turned the discussion. In cross-examining Jesus, the lawyer has put himself on trial. Luke's reader stands as a jury of sorts, and when Jesus reiterates in v. 37 what he had said in v. 28, the verdict of the jury is unavoidable.

Luke's reader is asked to play the role of the jury, to judge the exchange from the outside. Even from the outside, however, it is clear that the primary stakes are racial. It is also clear that Jesus has bested the lawyer at his own game. If Luke's reader is

---

[18] This is the core of the story as L. Paul Trudinger understands it: "For the question 'Which one was neighbour to the man who was waylaid?' requires that the answer be given from the position of the man in trouble; that the lawyer put himself in the place of the waylaid man; that he answer as one in need of help" ("Once Again, Now, 'Who Is My Neighbour?' " *Evangelical Quarterly* 48 [1976], 161).

a Gentile Christian who has been the victim of Jewish exclusiv-
ism, which seems to me to be very likely, then his or her delight
in this exchange would be just as deep as is the lawyer's
frustration and disappointment.

THE RHETORIC OF THE SERMON

Here end the details of our exegesis. Before we can discuss
the homiletical structure of the sermon, we must pause and
review. For the purposes of this sermon, I decided to identify the
lawyer as the designated reader and to specify that the readerly
work—and thus also the rhetorical impact—will be governed by
the lawyer's dispositions insofar as they can be reconstructed.
We can paint the lawyer's aesthetic experience with a broad
brush and a few rapid strokes. The top-down constraints of
context and genre lead the lawyer to expect one thing; the
bottom-up constraints give him another. The context and the
opening movements have suggested that Jesus is going to present him with a hypothetical case, and he responds accordingly.
As he does so, the story switches terms on him and he finds
himself entrapped. The entrapment has two primary elements.
On the surface of it, the basic schemas confront the cold and
calculating way he has gone about defining right and wrong,
and in that way call into question not only his ethics but his
theology. God is known in acts of compassion. More deeply, the
allusion to 2 Chronicles 28—a story "the Lawyer knew very well
indeed" (Furness)—contrasts the brotherliness of the foreigner
with the violence of the countrymen. In the process Jesus has
exposed the shallow way in which the lawyer has read his Bible.

These, then, are the movements I tried to work into my
sermon. I decided early on that the sermon should also try to
replicate the trap for the listener. The story my listener "knew
very well indeed" would be the parable itself. The experience I
described on the highway actually happened, and it provided an
occasion around which the trap could be structured. (I remember being profoundly disturbed when it became clear to me
what I had done or, rather, failed to do. I was thankful, too. It
was a hard lesson.) I decided that it would be better to expose
my own failure here than point a finger at someone else.

I concluded that the overall movement of the trap should
be a reversal of positions, which, I believe, in an important way

parallels what happened to the lawyer. In the first half, I tried to set myself up as a parallel to the priest and the Levite, and in the second as a parallel to the victim in the ditch.

I wanted the reversal of positions to come as a shock to my congregation-as-listener, just as the introduction of the Samaritan came as a shock for the lawyer-as-listener. For this reason, I buried the parallels between myself and the two components of the story beneath a heap of verbiage. In particular, I mixed the images of the roadway and the exegesis, dropping the exegetical details as I went along. The mixed schemas of roadway and exegesis were calculated to mask the connections and deflect the listener's attention away from the parallels. Several members of the congregation remarked afterward that they had been alarmed that I passed the farmworkers in the ditch, but a good many missed the connection. For those who missed the connection, the ending was a bit more powerful and disturbing, I think.

In the second half, I set myself up as a foil for the migrant farmworkers. This required two steps. First, I had to make clear just how easy it is to get into such a situation through no fault of one's own. In that way, I hoped to expose something of the perniciousness that blinds us to the humanity of others, particularly others who are racially or culturally different from us.

Second, I wanted to distance the reader from what had happened in the first half. The description of my brother's old truck served that end, as did the note that "in order to understand what it meant that it had no air-conditioning, I have to tell you something about this old truck." This remark was intended to deflect the listener away from the parallel I was then going to build. Everything leads up to the moment when I found myself in the same predicament—in a broken-down truck on the side of the road.

The moment of truth—the trip wire on the trap—comes when I realize that I have changed positions with the migrant farm worker. Here, the parallel between the end of the first half and the end of the second had to be made particularly clear. To achieve that end, I went back and refined the description of the old man to make it especially memorable. This I reinforced by telling my congregation that I was trying to memorize the scene so I could make it vivid for my sermon.

In particular, I mentioned that the old man was crouched down in the wheel well, tossing off pebbles in the dust. At the moment in which I described the sweat "rolling down his neck and into the open belly of his shirt," I thrust my pointer finger against the back of my own ear and very deliberately traced out the movement of the sweat. This reinforced the image, so that the listener had it in hand when he encountered me in the same position at the end of the second half. In the second half I repeated this language almost verbatim, together with the identical gesture.

Finally I wanted to weave a subtle note about the irony that it was in part my preoccupation with my "religious duty" that had blinded me to the human situation on the roadside. I did this in two ways. First, I mentioned the Baptist minister and deacon as possible parallels to the priest and the Levite. Second, I mentioned the Spanish proverb "En la casa de herrero— cuchillo de palo!" "In the house of the blacksmith—a wooden knife!" This saying captured it all, I thought, and I decided to use it as a capstone. For this reason, I placed it at the end. I also knew, however, that this would need an explanation. If I held the explanation to the end, it would confuse my congregation and deflect attention away from the point. For that reason, I went back and added the quote earlier in the sermon, along with a translation. Whether this was successful, I will leave to my reader to judge.

16

An Agony in the Night 1

Psalm 77—Exegesis and Exposition

For the earlier pericopes, I began with the sermon, then proceeded to provide supporting exegetical details, largely because the rhetorical effect of the sermon required the element of surprise. For Psalm 77 I shall proceed in the opposite direction, beginning with the exegesis, then tracing out the considerations that lead to the sermon. Psalm 77 appears on the next page; the sermon follows in chapter 17.

1 I cry aloud to God,
  aloud to God, that he may hear me.
2 In the day of my trouble I seek the Lord;
  in the night my hand is stretched out without wearying;
  my soul refuses to be comforted.
3 I think of God, and I moan;
  I meditate, and my spirit faints. Selah
4 You keep my eyelids from closing;
  I am so troubled that I cannot speak.
5 I consider the days of old,
  and remember the years of long ago.
6 I commune with my heart in the night;
  I meditate and search my spirit:
7 "Will the Lord spurn forever,
  and never again be favorable?
8 Has his steadfast love ceased forever?
  Are his promises at an end for all time?
9 Has God forgotten to be gracious?
  Has he in anger shut up his compassion?" Selah
10 And I say, "It is my grief
  that the right hand of the Most High has changed."
11 I will call to mind the deeds of the LORD;
  I will remember your wonders of old.
12 I will meditate on all your work,
  and muse on your mighty deeds.
13 Your way, O God, is holy.
  What god is so great as our God?
14 You are the God who works wonders;
  you have displayed your might among the peoples.
15 With your strong arm you redeemed your people,
  the descendants of Jacob and Joseph. Selah
16 When the waters saw you, O God,
  when the waters saw you, they were afraid;
  the very deep trembled.
17 The clouds poured out water;
  the skies thundered;
  your arrows flashed on every side.
18 The crash of your thunder was in the whirlwind;
  your lightnings lit up the world;
  the earth trembled and shook.
19 Your way was through the sea,
  your path, through the mighty waters;
  yet your footprints were unseen.
20 You led your people like a flock
  by the hand of Moses and Aaron.

THE RHETORIC OF THE TEXT—
TOP-DOWN READING CONSTRAINTS

Context

The fact that Psalm 77 is found in the Psalter is particularly significant. There is a great deal of discussion about when it was composed. By and large the discussion turns upon the relationship between this psalm and Habakkuk 3, which parallels its language very closely. Which is prior? Over one hundred years ago Franz Delitzsch argued that the psalm was the older tradition and that it served as an inspiration—perhaps even a source—for Habakkuk.[1] If Delitzsch is right, the psalm is probably not later than the reign of Josiah at the end of the seventh century, when Habakkuk, apparently, lived and worked.[2] This would be late enough for the psalm to have been prompted by the destruction of Samaria and by the Assyrian deportation in 722 BCE, but too early to have been prompted by the destruction of Jerusalem and the Babylonian deportation in 587. Mention of Jacob and Joseph in v. 15 suggests that the psalm may have had its origin in the experience of the northern tribes, and on this basis Elmer Leslie suggests a date between 733 and 721.[3] This would also explain the sustained reflection on the exodus, which occupies vv. 16–20. But Moses Buttenweiser argues that the details fit best at a much later date.[4] According to Buttenweiser, Psalm 77 was composed in reaction to the catastrophe of 344, when Artaxerxes III Ochus used Palestine as a land corridor in his invasion of Egypt.

From the standpoint of reading, however, this discussion may be somewhat beside the point. The striking thing about this psalm is that any contextual clues or signals are picked up incidentally. In fact, the personal or historical context that prompted the lament appears to have been completely obscured. This could mean one of two things. Either the author assumed

---

[1]Franz Delitzsch, *Biblical Commentary on the Psalms* (New York: Funk and Wagnalls, 1873) 401.

[2]The dating of Habakkuk is itself problematic, but most interpreters place it during this time.

[3]Elmer Leslie, *The Psalms* (Nashville: Abingdon, 1949) 238.

[4]Moses Buttenweiser, *The Psalms Chronologically Treated with a New Translation* (New York: KTAV, 1969) 626–30.

his reader would know when the psalm had been composed and would supply that information out of common knowledge, or the context is almost irrelevant. There are good reasons for taking the latter course. First, nothing in the psalm depends upon information specific to any particular national catastrophe. It reads basically the same in any number of crisis situations, both personal and national.[5] Second, the genre signals open as a lament, and laments are not usually intended to be read as sources for reconstructing specific historical situations. Instead they are expressions of inner, spiritual struggles. For these two reasons, the reader is freed from the constraints usually provided by context. The controls shift to the other constraints, and genre comes to occupy a larger, more central role in the readerly work.

There are, however, two especially critical ways in which this psalm connects with its wider cultural environment: It assumes knowledge of (1) the exodus story and (2) the traditional confession that "God's mercy—God's *hesed*—endures forever." These are the reverberating counterpoints to the content and structure of the psalm, and any reading that overlooks them will ultimately prove distortive. They provide the basis for a subtle but pervasive overcoding, which ultimately lays the crisis of faith at the gate of the confession of faith that is central to the psalmist's religion. The crisis calls the confession into question.

Genre

The initial genre signals suggest that this psalm is a lament of some sort. (These will be examined shortly.) The question is whether the lament is personal or corporate, and much of the discussion has centered on the likelihood that the lament is prompted by a national disaster. Note the plurals of v. 8 ("Will the Lord cast *us* off forever?")[6] and the psalmist's calling to mind an event of epic—"national" is not yet appropriate—proportions. The fact that the superscription calls for the atten-

---

[5]This seems to be the consensus of scholarly opinion, Buttenweiser notwithstanding.

[6]The Hebrew text includes the superscription as v. 1, while the English translations do not. The resulting discrepancy should be taken into account when comparing references. I have followed the standard English versification.

tion of Jeduthun suggests a guild of corporate temple singers (see also Pss 39 and 62, and 2 Chron 20:19). Would a guild sing a personal lament? Yet the national disaster seems buried within the psychological folds of a personal crisis. G. A. F. Knight calls it "a very ego-centered psalm. It is full of I, I, I. . . . In other words it gives us the prayer of an ordinary person."[7] John Eaton has attempted to merge the two—personal and corporate—by arguing that the voice of the speaker is the king himself, though this argument hangs a mountain on a slender thread.[8]

These discussions, like the discussions of context, appear to me to be of secondary worth. Different genres interact with context in very different ways. A historical narrative asks to be read in a certain specific context. Often additional clues are brought in or evoked so that the reader can draw upon knowledge of a particular event or epoch to fill in gaps. By contrast, a legal formula is more closely governed by the context in which it is to be applied. The very precision of the legal formula anticipates this and makes it possible. So also proverbs, which work by analogy but are loosely organized so that their elements can be applied to a variety of contexts as needed. (No one knows or particularly cares where the expression "A stitch in time saves nine" came from, but it does not really matter because the appropriate context is the one in which it is applied.)

The context of origin is suppressed in this psalm, and in its place genre plays a much larger role. When the reader first encounters the genre signals, they suggest a personal crisis, nothing more. If we distinguish between personal laments and corporate laments, surely this begins as the former. The reader is invited to appropriate the imagery of the crisis as a refracting lens through which to view his or her own moments of despair. Readers have a wider range of interpretive options than would be appropriate for, say, a legal document or a historical narrative. A lament asks to be read more in the way that we read poetry. There is greater opportunity for free association, which creates a more richly textured interface with the reader's own experience. Sequence may be a less significant factor as well, since a lament may be designed to be read over and over again. Entrapment becomes less likely as a literary factor. Instead, the

---

[7]G. A. F. Knight, *Psalms* (Philadelphia: Westminster, 1962) 25.

[8]John Eaton, *Kingship and the Psalms* (London: SCM Press, 1986) 79.

reader is free to contemplate, review, and ponder in a way that would be completely inappropriate for a different genre.

This psalm begins like a lament, but it does not end like one. Somewhere around v. 10 the tenor changes completely. Verses 16–19 even reflect a different meter. Verse 20 shifts meter again, which creates the impression of a postscript. This has led to speculation that the psalm is composite and could be dismantled. But regardless of its origins, at some point it reached this particular formulation. We are interested in reading it as it stands. When we do so, we discover that there is good symmetry between the two halves. Partly by balancing the content and structure of a lament with the structure and content of a hymn or aretalogy, the psalmist can bring the theological crisis to an adequate resolution.

Theme

The imbalanced relationship between context and genre frees the reader to use the imagery to explore the wider questions of good and evil—and thus quite directly the faithfulness of God—that are resident in the psalm itself. Indeed, the opening genre signals suggest just that sort of reflection.

With the controls—and permissions!—of these top-down reading constraints in hand, we turn next to the unfolding details of the text itself. These details will instantiate a variety of bottom-up reading strategies and controls, which in their own way generate a series of reactions on the part of the reader.

THE RHETORIC OF THE TEXT— BOTTOM-UP READING CONSTRAINTS

A word should be said about the texture of the psalm. As the importance of context recedes, the importance of texture increases, just as genre considerations increase. As with any work of poetry, the texture of the language necessarily plays a large role in the transfer of meaning.

Three elements stand out. First, in a number of places the grammar is awkward or the lexical combinations seem forced. The schemas conflict. This is especially so in vv. 2, 5, and 10. These verses have driven modern interpreters to distraction. It is entirely possible that the mix of images is intentional, a subtle grammatical and lexical reinforcement of the impression that something is amiss. Second, some of the words border on onomatopoeia. Their sounds reinforce the imagery of their schemas. The most prominent (and problematic) is the Hebrew term employed to describe the whirlwind in v. 18—*gal^egal*. More subtle, but perhaps for that reason more effective, is the description of the lightning as "arrows" (Heb. *ḥēṣ*) in the previous verse. In v. 9 we have alliteration:

> *gāmar ʾômer l^edôr vādôr*
> Does his word fail forever and ever?

Third, shifts of meter mark—or, rather, create—the emotional transitions in the psalm. There is a clear metrical shift between vv. 15 and 16, and another between vv. 19 and 20. This makes vv. 16–19 stand out from the rest of the psalm. The pace picks up, and this increases the potency of the imagery. With the transition out of this section everything slows once again so that the psalm can end on a quiet, almost tranquil note.

Verse 1

> *I cry aloud to God,*
> *aloud to God, that he may hear me.*

The Hebrew phrasing is elliptical ("My voice to God . . . "), which seems to reflect the fragmented mental state of the psalmist as he struggles to express his anguish. Its repetition intensifies the impression of trouble.

The Hebrew also includes "I cry out" here, which the NRSV chooses to conflate with the opening phrase. This creates a mix of synonymous and sequential parallelism:

synonymous parallel	sequential parallel
My voice (is) to God,	and I cry out;
My voice (is) to God,	and he hears me.

Patrick Miller points out that this particular configuration represents a clear genre signal: "The first elements in each colon are identical. The final elements can only be understood sequentially. Indeed they represent the sequence that is at the heart of the lament as a genre: outcry/lament hearing/response."[9] This initial signal establishes the reader's interpretive latitude. Nothing yet suggests a national disaster.

Verse 2

In the day of my trouble I seek the Lord;
  in the night my hand is stretched out without wearying;
  my soul refuses to be comforted.

There is discussion about the import of the possessive affix here. Does "my" indicate a personal crisis, or is the psalmist personalizing a national catastrophe? To my mind, the question is helpful for historians but wrong for readers. It is unnatural. The historian's protocols entail collecting details from throughout the psalm, then conjecturing a likely scenario. A reader is unlikely to do this, since to do so would involve dismantling the psalm and comparing its details to a reconstructed picture of some specific historical circumstance. The genre signals invite a different set of protocols. When the psalmist begins with a description of an unresolved agony in the night, the reader is more likely to identify with the voice and to probe connections between the psalm and his or her own circumstances. The very poverty of specific historical details gives the reader great latitude in coming to this identification. "If the shoe fits . . . ," the psalmist seems to be saying.

The next clause poses a problem of a different sort. The lexical terms are in conflict. The noun translated "hand" (*yād*) in the NRSV does not go easily or naturally with the verb translated "stretched out" (*nāgar*). *Nāgar* usually means "to flow out" or "to run out." How, then, is the clause to be understood? If we take "hand" literally, "flow out" is awkward. If we take "flow out" literally, "hand" is awkward. Perhaps one or the other is metaphorical or contains some remote meaning that is now lost. Perhaps a resolution lies in the fact that this clause forms a balanced couplet with the previous clause:

In the day of my trouble I seek the Lord;
in the night my hand is stretched out without wearying.

If the parallels are taken seriously, we should perhaps follow the NRSV and understand the stretching out of the hand as a refer-

---

[9]Patrick Miller, Jr., "Synonymous-Sequential Parallelism in the Psalms," *Biblica* 61 (1980) 257.

ence to prayer. This is not at all certain, however. Instead the
ongoing puzzlement has a mildly disruptive effect; it jangles the
reader's nerves, much like the off-rhyme in Wordsworth's poem
Alpine Storm, which we discussed in chapter 10.

The third line establishes the metrical pattern that will
carry the reader forward through v. 15. This will later prove to
be important, since vv. 16–19 will abandon that pattern for a
completely different meter. Even if the reader is familiar with
this psalm, which will be likely, the shift of meter will invite a
shift of mental stance, and thus also a shift of perspective on the
question of the work of God in the world.

Verses 3–4

I think of God, and I moan;
   I meditate, and my spirit faints.
You keep my eyelids from closing;
   I am so troubled that I cannot speak.

These verses continue the imagery that was introduced in
v. 2. Within the community of faith, personal disasters become
theological disasters as well, challenges to the adequacy of God.

Verse 4a is idiomatic—literally, "you keep the *guards of my
eyes* from closing."

Verses 5–6

I consider the days of old,
   and remember the years of long ago.
I commune with my heart in the night;
   I meditate and search my spirit.

The parallelism now deepens the sense of despair. Note the
reiterated language for inner musing: "I consider . . . I remember . . . I commune . . . I meditate." The context suggests that
each of these expresses the sort of despondency that inevitably
follows a personal or a corporate loss.

Adam Clarke offers a suggestive alternative rendering of
the first line of v. 6. This is a line that the NRSV renders, "I
commune with my heart in the night." More literally, this reads,
"I call to remembrance my song (neginati) in the night." Instead
of "I call to remembrance my *song,*" Clarke understands $n^e g\hat{\imath}n\bar{a}t\hat{\imath}$

as a word for a stringed instrument.[10] Thus, the psalmist consoles himself with his lyre or harp. This, then, Clarke suggests, is intended as an introduction to vv. 7–9, which take the form of a short ode or refrain. In support of this view, we note a change from first person to third. But there are difficulties: The meter stays the same throughout, v. 6b would intrude into the reference and disrupt the pattern, and there is no direct signal of a change.

Verses 7–9

Will the Lord spurn forever,
*　　and never again be favorable?*

Has his steadfast love (ḥesed) ceased forever?
*　　Are his promises at an end for all time?*

Has God forgotten to be gracious?
*　　Has he in anger shut up his compassion?Selah*

Here there is a subtle shift. The subject of the sentences shifts to the third person, and in this way the meditation comes to focus on the theological dimensions of catastrophe. Everything is now set squarely in the lap of God. This shift, which is subtle but still obvious enough in English, is quite blunt in Hebrew, because it draws upon, and conflicts with, the language of the traditional confession of faith: "God's mercy—God's ḥesed—endures forever." The confession is thus overcoded on top of the primary schemas, and the two realities—crisis and confession—are made to stand point and counterpoint. Confession and counter-confession, exclamation point and question mark, *Deus revelatus* and *Deus absconditus,* the two sides of faith play back and forth upon one another like a double fugue.

Verse 10

And I say, "It is my grief
*　　that the right hand of the Most High has changed."*

---

[10]Adam Clarke, *The Holy Bible . . . with Commentary and Critical Notes* (New York: George Lane, 1840) 3:462.

With v. 10 we come to the most difficult part of the psalm. There are primary problems here. First, the second clause is elliptical, an incomplete sentence: "the right hand of the Most High." What verb are we to supply? Second, the word rendered "changed" *(š^enôt)* is ambiguous. It may mean "the years." The New English Bible notes in the margin that the "Hebrew [is] unintelligible."

These difficulties have been resolved in either of two ways. Some translators render v. 10 as the concluding strophe of the first half of the psalm, the closing of the lament. The NRSV, the Jerusalem Bible (JB), and the New English Bible all render v. 10 as a heavy ballast line:

NRSV

And I say, "It is my grief
    that the right hand of the Most High has changed."

JB

"This," I said then, "is what distresses me:
    that the right hand of the Most High is no longer what it was."

The New English Bible gives it all a lyrical twist, introducing a wordplay:

"Has his right hand," I said, "lost its grasp?
    Does it hang powerless, the arm of the Most High?"

Other translators argue that a transition has already begun. The *selah* that punctuated v. 9 closes off the lament. Verse 10 begins a new way of reflecting on the question of God's reliability. One must remember again, though with a difference. The disruptions here—the ellipsis and the ambiguity—shock the reader into a shift of point of view. Thus, Derek Kidner suggests that the reference to grief is a repudiating reference: "This is *my* problem, it is not God's." If the verse serves as a hinge, the cotter pin falls between the two lines. The transition pivots here, preparing the reader for the affirmations that follow.[11] Thus, Kidner renders:

And I said, It is mine own infirmity:
    but I will remember the years of the Most High.

---

[11] Derek Kidner, *Psalms 73–150: A Commentary on Books III-V of the Psalms* (London: Inter-Varsity Press, 1978) 278f.

The transition is rougher in Hebrew. Kidner offers creative punctuating to bring out the sense of reversal:

> The years of long ago?
> The years of his right hand!

Clarke renders, "The Most High alone can change my condition."[12]

However we understand v. 10, it is clear that a transformation is under way. The psalmist has brought his reader to the unyielding reality upon which faith is so often shipwrecked. The tragedies of life sometimes conceal the hand of God. At the same time the reader is brought to the brink of a major shift of perspective. If the hand of God is concealed, it is nevertheless present. The problem is in one's vision, a matter of blindness. Faith alone brings tragedy into its proper focus.

Verses 11–12

> *I will call to mind the deeds of the LORD;*
> *I will remember your wonders of old.*
> *I will meditate on all your work,*
> *and muse on your mighty deeds.*

Everything is now marshaled under the aegis of the shift. Here begins a hymn, not at all unlike an aretalogy, which rehearses the redemptive acts of God. The purpose is not to consign such things to some remote and distant past but to bring the past into living connection with the present. That God is this God.

The parallel with vv. 3–5 can only be intentional:

Verses 3–5	Verses 11–12
I think of God and I moan,	I will call to mind the deeds of the LORD;
I meditate and my spirit faints.	I will remember your wonders of old.
I consider the days of old,	I will meditate on all your work,
I remember the years of long ago.	And muse on your mighty deeds.

Thus there is consonance between the parts, but it is a consonance of balances. The point and counterpoint reemerge, but with the confession gaining the upper hand.

---

[12] Clarke, *The Holy Bible,* 3:463.

Two changes call for closer attention. First, the focus is not on the character of God but on what God has done. In his commentary, Claus Westermann calls attention to this particular shift by arranging both portions of the psalm under the heading "I think of God." As the contrast between the lament and the hymnic portions shows, it matters what and how we think of God.

> "Thinking of God" can take very different forms—as in this psalm, where it is indeed clearly expressed—that to think of God is to think of the God who acts and thus to think of a reality. A fundamental change occurred in the history of the Christian church when thinking about God became a reflection on an eternal divine being. Thus such thought became speculative, divorced from reality. Today we must ask which is truer to the Bible—this speculative thought about God or thinking of Him as real and active.[13]

In general terms Westermann is right, of course. Yet one must ask whether the comparison is entirely apt *here*. The comparison here is not between the biblical view of a God who acts and the abstract speculations of philosophical theology. This psalm suggests that the real comparison is between the biblical conviction that God acts and the troubling way experience manhandles us into believing otherwise.

Here indeed is the homiletical bind that can serve the purposes of preaching. Most believers, Christian and Jew, already find themselves alienated from speculative theology, just as speculative theology can be alienated from the biblical God. There must be other points of engagement that rest the unsure present on the rock-hard foundation of historical fact. The psalmist takes his cue here. God acts; God is not impotent. Let the record itself speak in God's name. Thus, the psalmist turns to tradition.

Verses 13–15

Your way, O God, is holy.
> *What god is so great as our God?*
You are the God who works wonders;
> *you have displayed your might among the peoples.*
With your strong arm you redeemed your people,
> *the descendants of Jacob and Joseph.*

---

[13] Claus Westermann, *The Living Psalms* (trans. J. R. Porter; Grand Rapids: Eerdmans, 1989) 108.

Here begins a series of what I take to be secondary allusions to Exodus, especially ch. 15. The imagery is regnant. Note the close conceptual parallels with the song of Moses in Exodus 15:11, 13:

> [11]Who is like you, O LORD, among the gods?
>   Who is like you, majestic in holiness
>   awesome in splendor, doing wonders?
> [13]In your steadfast love you led
>   the people whom you redeemed.

Verse 14 recalls Exodus 15:14: "The peoples heard, they trembled."

There is a good deal of speculation about how to understand the allusions. Perhaps we have here a reflection on theophanies in general, or on the moment of creation in which God dispelled the forces of chaos and established order. Similar discussions concern vv. 16–19, which are linked to these verses by a continuity of theme but differentiated by a shift of meter. We shall return to this question momentarily.

Verses 16–19

> *When the waters saw you, O God,*
>   *when the waters saw you, they were afraid;*
>   *the very deep trembled.*
> *The clouds poured out water;*
>   *the skies thundered;*
>   *your arrows flashed on every side.*
> *The crash of your thunder was in the whirlwind;*
>   *your lightnings lit up the world;*
>   *the earth trembled and shook.*
> *Your way was through the sea,*
>   *your path through the mighty waters;*
>   *yet your footprints were unseen.*

What is in view here? Artur Weiser argues that these verses combine images of the history of redemption broadly taken, now epitomized in the act of worship.[14] Richard Clifford suggests that the battle is cosmic and the flight of the waters represents the ultimate triumph over the forces of

---

[14] Artur Weiser, *The Psalms* (Philadelphia: Westminster, 1962) 533.

chaos itself.[15] Both of these conclusions seem to me to soft-pedal the vivid verbal connections that call forth images of the exodus. Instead, I would argue that the connections are all the more potent because they only suggest Exodus rather than quote it directly. A direct quotation lacks the overcoded doubling of schemas that allusions can create. Allusion is more rhetorically powerful than quotation could ever hope to be, but it calls for more active involvement by the reader.

Because of the overcoding the imagery is now vivid and dramatic. The mind cannot process everything, it all comes so quickly. Mental images spill over one another like a series of double exposures, and images from Exodus enrich the mélange. Flashes of onomatopoeia crash across the verbal landscape—*gal^egal* for "whirlwind," *ḥēṣ* for "arrows/lightning." The meter shifts, calling for a different style of reading, a different pace. Everything is intensified. God moves. The earth trembles. The waters churn and boil. Lightning rips open the heavens, nearly exposing the very face of God.

Thus is God made to ride triumphantly on the thunderstorm.

And then everything stops. "Your footprints were unseen." Who can track a man across water or trace the path of a bird in flight? Who can hunt down God or master God's inscrutable ways? What God could be fully apprehended and still be God?

Verse 20

You led your people like a flock
by the hand of Moses and Aaron.

The psalmist is not content to leave everything on that note of mystery. "Your footprints were unseen," yet they did not lead us astray or leave us abandoned. Indeed, the psalm comes to rest on just this theme. If God through the agency of Moses and Aaron has shepherded us to safety in the past, we can rest in the assurance that we will not now be abandoned in the present crisis.

---

[15] Richard Clifford, "A Note on Ps 104:5–9," *Journal of Biblical Literature* 100 (1981) 87–89.

THE RHETORIC OF THE SERMON

The sermon in the next chapter was preached at Southern California College chapel in the spring of 1990. As at Disciples Church, the congregation here was made up of younger people, many of them new Christians. I was aware that a number of the students at the college were dealing with issues of psychological and emotional transition. Some of them were beginning to face difficulties with childhood experiences that were now surfacing under the stress of schooling. Some were struggling with issues that are both personal and theological, since part of maturing into adulthood entails the recognition of mortality, with all of its attendant issues of loss and grief. I also knew that they had difficulty acknowledging that their sense of God's trustworthiness was called into question by their encounters with mortality. I decided to preach on this psalm precisely because the opening lament raises these issues to explicit form. The lament is the text's rhetorical bind.

In my exegesis I concluded that the bind gains part of its potency by playing upon, and calling into question, the traditional Hebrew confession, "His steadfast love endures forever." This, it seems to me, is mirrored by the primary posture I knew my students brought with them. This, too, may be related to issues of developmental transition. When they were in high school, their idea of God was informed and shaped by their own intimations of immortality. This has nothing to do with the Christian concept of the afterlife, and everything to do with the psychological reality that teenagers cannot see themselves as mortal. Because their theology is informed and shaped by their life experience, they have a natural tendency to understand the realities of God in correlated terms. When they discover their own limits, the theological repercussions can be shattering.

Consequently, my opening move would have to connect their native, more intuited theology with the explicit vocabulary of the Hebrew confession. I decided to do this by having Psalm 136 read out in advance, antiphonally (with italics added in the written text to indicate response):

O give thanks to the LORD, for he is good,
for his steadfast love endures forever.

O give thanks to the God of gods,
for his steadfast love endures forever.
O give thanks to the Lord of lords,
for his steadfast love endures forever;
who alone does great wonders,
for his steadfast love endures forever;
who by understanding made the heavens,
for his steadfast love endures forever;
who spread out the earth on the waters,
for his steadfast love endures forever;
who made the great lights,
for his steadfast love endures forever;
the sun to rule over the day,
for his steadfast love endures forever;
the moon and stars to rule over the night,
for his steadfast love endures forever;
who struck Egypt through their firstborn,
for his steadfast love endures forever;
and brought Israel out from among them,
for his steadfast love endures forever;
with a strong hand and an outstretched arm,
for his steadfast love endures forever;
who divided the Red Sea in two,
for his steadfast love endures forever;
and made Israel pass through the midst of it,
for his steadfast love endures forever;
but overthrew Pharaoh and his army in the Red Sea,
for his steadfast love endures forever;
who led his people through the wilderness,
for his steadfast love endures forever;
who struck down great kings,
for his steadfast love endures forever;
and killed famous kings,
for his steadfast love endures forever;
Sihon, king of the Amorites,
for his steadfast love endures forever;
and Og, king of Bashan,
for his steadfast love endures forever;
and gave their land as a heritage,
for his steadfast love endures forever;
a heritage to his servant Israel,
for his steadfast love endures forever.
It is he who remembered us in our low estate,
for his steadfast love endures forever;

and rescued us from our foes,
  for his steadfast love endures forever;
who gives food to all flesh,
  for his steadfast love endures forever.
O give thanks to the God of heaven,
  for his steadfast love endures forever.

Psalm 136 provided the added benefit of recalling the exodus theme, which would become central in the second half of the sermon.

With this foregrounding in place, I focused on the ways in which the "steadfast love" of the Lord sometimes seems to fail us completely. When we are honest, all of us experience moments such as this, agonies in the night. To say that point-blank would be startling, even more so if I were to say it immediately following the affirmations of Psalm 136. This would be the homiletical bind of the sermon. Thus I decided how to begin. I would read out Psalm 136, then announce: "I have a problem with this psalm. Sometimes it seems like a lie."

At this point I needed to introduce the text of Psalm 77, which had thus far been withheld. Because the psalm is a lament, I decided to leave its historical context just as unspecified as the psalmist had left it, and instead to allow it to form a basis for reflection on the moments when we feel that God has abandoned us in our struggles. In order to explore those moments, I would take two or three of my own experiences of inner crisis and use them as a counterpoint for the affirmations and struggles in the psalm. This seems to me to be evoked by the genre. I would invite my congregation to do the same.

There was one further consideration. This sermon was preached on the Tuesday following the college's Easter recess. The theme of resurrection was in the air. It seemed to me that the affirmations I was discovering in Psalm 77 were paralleled in important ways by Paul's affirmations in Romans 8. I would work these into the sermon as an afterword.

17

An Agony in the Night 2

Psalm 77—A Sermon

THE CALL TO WORSHIP: Psalm 138:1–3

HYMN: Great Is Thy Faithfulness

THE NEW TESTAMENT LESSON: Romans 8:31–39

THE OLD TESTAMENT LESSON: Psalm 136:1–3, 10–16, 23–36.
                          To be read antiphonally immediately
                          before the sermon, with the congre-
                          gation repeating the recitative.

Let us begin by reading together selected verses from Psalm 136. I will read the opening line, and you will read the response, "for his steadfast love endures forever."

Verses 1–3

O give thanks to the Lord, for he is good,
> *for his steadfast love endures forever.*
O give thanks to the God of gods,
> *for his steadfast love endures forever.*
O give thanks to the Lord of lords,
> *for his steadfast love endures forever;*

Verses 10–16

who struck Egypt through their firstborn,
> *for his steadfast love endures forever;*
and brought Israel out from among them,
> *for his steadfast love endures forever;*
with a strong hand and an outstretched arm,
> *for his steadfast love endures forever;*
who divided the Red Sea in two,
> *for his steadfast love endures forever;*
and made Israel pass through the midst of it,
> *for his steadfast love endures forever;*
but overthrew Pharaoh and his army in the Red Sea,
> *for his steadfast love endures forever;*
who led his people through the wilderness,
> *for his steadfast love endures forever;*

Verses 23–26

It is he who remembered us in our low estate,
> *for his steadfast love endures forever;*
and rescued us from our foes,
> *for his steadfast love endures forever;*
who gives food to all flesh,
> *for his steadfast love endures forever.*
O give thanks to the God of heaven,
> *for his steadfast love endures forever.*

Now, I have a problem with this psalm. I have a problem because sometimes it seems like a lie. Sometimes, in the middle of the night, when we are alone with our blackest thoughts and personal agonies, this confession about the faithfulness of God seems like the darkest sort of lie. And what makes it all the darker is that it is a lie told in the presence of Almighty God.

Does it shock you that I would say this? It's the truth, though, as every one of you knows. You may know it in a place in your soul that is secret even from yourself. But you know it. Think back to the worst moment you can remember. Perhaps you lost your job. Perhaps your father or mother fell terminally ill. Perhaps you discovered that you yourself had an inoperable tumor. How did the faithfulness of God seem then, when the chips were down? Is it not that it felt like God had turned his back on you at the very moment you needed him most? In moments like those, the confession "His steadfast love endures forever" chokes in the throat.

I am not alone in saying this. And I am not so brave, either. This has been said before, in the Bible itself. Would you turn with me now to the text of my sermon this morning, the seventy-seventh psalm?

This psalm is not antiphonal. There is no answering response from the congregation. Or is there? I think that what makes Psalm 77 so painful is that it echoes against the confession that stands at the heart of Psalm 136. "His steadfast love endures forever" is the answering voice, left silent here because the psalmist knows that the confession is right on the tip of his reader's tongue.

> I cry aloud to God,
> > aloud to God, that he may hear me.
> In the day of my trouble I seek the Lord;
> > in the night my hand is stretched out without wearying;
> > my soul refuses to be comforted.
> I think of God, and I moan;
> > I meditate, and my spirit faints.
> You keep my eyelids from closing;
> > I am so troubled that I cannot speak.
> I consider the days of old,
> > and remember the years of long ago.
> I commune with my heart in the night;
> > I meditate and search my spirit:
> "Will the Lord spurn forever,
> > and never again be favorable?
> Has his steadfast love ceased forever?
> > Are his promises at an end for all time?
> Has God forgotten to be gracious?
> > Has he in anger shut up his compassion?"

And I say, "It is my grief
> that the right hand of the Most High has changed."
I will call to mind the deeds of the LORD;
> I will remember your wonders of old.
I will meditate on all your work,
> and muse on your mighty deeds.
Your way, O God, is holy.
> What god is so great as our God?
You are the God who works wonders;
> you have displayed your might among the peoples.
With your strong arm you redeemed your people,
> the descendants of Jacob and Joseph.
When the waters saw you, O God,
> when the waters saw you, they were afraid;
> the very deep trembled.
The clouds poured out water;
> the skies thundered;
> your arrows flashed on every side.
The crash of your thunder was in the whirlwind;
> your lightnings lit up the world;
> the earth trembled and shook.
Your way was through the sea,
> your path, through the mighty waters;
> yet your footprints were unseen.
You led your people like a flock
> by the hand of Moses and Aaron.

I have a friend who loves mystery stories. He tells me that he discovered one day that if he quit the story before he came to the end, he could relish the mystery longer—never knowing how it all turned out. Then one day he learned that if he skipped the first chapter, he could also relish not knowing how it all began.

That's what we have in Psalm 77. This is a double-sided mystery, a little slice of a plot, which doesn't tell us how it began or how it all came out. We have no idea when this was written or what personal trauma kept the psalmist awake in the night. This could have been written on the eve of the Babylonian exile, and the psalmist could have lost everything and been carried away to a foreign country. It could have been written after he lost his job, or when he found out he had an incurable illness. It's a slice out of a plot, without a beginning or end.

By giving us so little orientation, the writer invites us to see his psalm as something typical, something we all experience.

This psalm has to do with the clash between our belief in the faithfulness of God and our experience of the reality of evil. He invites us to climb inside, to try this on for size and see if it fits. This could be anybody's story. What do you do when the arm of God hangs limp by his side?

This week, as I prepared my sermon, I found myself reliving several moments in which this psalm fit my experience like a glove. Perhaps you would like to do that, too. Two nights in particular stand out for me.

The first night in which I found that this psalm fit occurred while I was in graduate school. My wife and I were in Massachusetts, but the rest of my family was here in California. One night we received a call from my brother. My seven-year-old niece, Jamie, had been found gasping for breath in her sleep. My brother couldn't wake her, and they called the paramedics, who rushed her to the hospital. The doctors diagnosed a blood clot on her brain, though they couldn't tell where it was located. She was moved by medical helicopter to Los Angeles Children's Hospital, where she lay in a coma for six weeks, suspended in time.

For six weeks Jamie lay there, hovering between life and death. The pressure between her brain and her skull was very slowly building to what seemed like an exploding point. One night about three in the morning, the phone rang again. It was my brother. His words cut through my soul like a knife: The doctors had asked permission to operate and to remove half of Jamie's brain to save her life. I'll never forget what he said to me: "They've taken away my little girl, and I don't know what they'll bring me back."

Have you ever been alone in a crowd? Have you ever been "with" someone who was a thousand miles away? That was the way I felt toward my brother. Even though he was three thousand miles away, I was *with* him.

I got down on my knees beside my bed and I railed at God. I know what the psalmist means when he says,

> I cry aloud to God,
>> aloud to God, that he may hear me.
> In the day of my trouble I seek the Lord.

Jamie was an innocent little girl. Why should something like this happen to her?

Well, it all turned out okay. At least mostly so. The blood clot was right on the surface, and it was right where they opened her up. The damage was minimal. Jamie has had a ninety-five percent recovery. To look at her today, you would never know that this trauma had entered her life.

The second night happened this past summer. I had begun to have recollections of a particularly violent event that happened to me when I was a child. The memories of violence weren't exactly like dreams; they were more like flashbacks. I was fully awake, but the images were very powerful. Even as an adult I reacted to them with a kind of terror—the sort of terror you feel when you're only five years old and you know someone is going to hurt you, but you don't know why, and you know that there's nothing you can do to stop it.

This summer something happened that related to the flashbacks: I had a disagreement with a colleague here at the college. I should tell you that he was very polite to me. I know he would feel terrible if he knew that what he said affected me in this way. It wasn't so much what he said, but the way he said it. Something in his tone of voice reminded me of the man who had hurt me when I was little.

I was crushed. I went home. No one was there. My wife, Shaleen, was away at work. I found myself curled up on the couch, sobbing like a baby. It was dark by the time my wife got home and took me up to bed.

I know the meaning of the psalmist's words:

> I cry aloud to God,
>   aloud to God, that he may hear me.
> In the day of my trouble I seek the Lord;
>   in the night my hand is stretched out without wearying;
>   my soul refuses to be comforted.

I suspect that you too have had your moments like that. The psalmist puts into words the unutterable groaning we cannot express for ourselves. The psalmist says what cannot be said: "I am so troubled that I cannot speak," he tells us in verse 4.

If the psalmist's agony is much like our own, his way of dealing with it is like our own, too. He begins by looking back at the good times, which are now swallowed up in the tragedy.

We, too, try and recall how it was before the crash. This is what the psalmist does in verses 5–7:

I consider the days of old,
    and remember the years of long ago.
I commune with my heart in the night;
    I meditate and search my spirit.

Note the reiterated terms for musing: "I consider . . . I remember . . . I commune with my heart . . . I meditate . . . I search my spirit." The only problem is that the recollection isn't any comfort. Jamie had a ninety-five percent recovery, but she also had a five percent loss. She can remember what it was like to be the brightest penny in the class. And it isn't any comfort at all because she can't repeat it.

When my high-school sweetheart married another man, I sat on the hill thinking about the good times we had had, but the memories were no comfort at all. Her marriage turned them to dust and ashes in my mouth.

Sometimes, when we try and look back, the catastrophe is like a scratch on a lens. We try to see through it, to bring everything into clearer focus, but all we can see is the scratch.

The worst part of it is that ultimately the trauma calls into question the adequacy even of God. Where is God when you need him? This is the problem that finally traps the psalmist, too. He comes to this in verses 7–9. These verses must be read against the background of the confession we read in Psalm 136—"His mercy—his steadfast love!—endures forever." Does it, now? Hear verses 7–9:

"Will the Lord spurn forever,
    and never again be favorable?
Has his steadfast love ceased forever?
    Are his promises at an end for all time?
Has God forgotten to be gracious?
    Has he in anger shut up his compassion?"

Here, then, is the crux of the matter. What are we supposed to do when it feels like God has failed to do anything God is supposed to do?

God is supposed to be all-knowing. What do we do when it feels like God has forgotten us?

God is supposed to be all-powerful. What are we to do when God seems impotent?

God is supposed to be all-loving. What are we to do when God appears angry, or capricious in his love?

The psalmist poses the question this way:

> Has God forgotten to be gracious?
>> Has he in anger shut up his compassion?
> Will the Lord spurn forever?

At verse 10 the psalm lurches to a kind of sad stop. "It is my grief," the psalmist said. "It is *my* grief that the right hand of the Most High hangs limp by his side." This is personal. If God is not reliable, who is? Some commentators have rendered the term for "grief" here as "illness." The psalmist knows what it is to be sick at heart.

And then—a change! Did you hear it? It comes just between verses 10 and 11. Something different is in the air. The English translators have taken pains to signal its presence. Note the change of meter:

> One-Two
> Three-Four
> Five-Six
> Seven-Eight-Nine

Verse 10 ties it all off somehow; it signals that we've come to the end of something. This shift is so radical that scholars have taken pains to prove that this psalm is really a single piece, rather than two different psalms that got joined together by an awkward seam. It begins like a lament, but it ends with a litany of praise. It descends to the abyss, like the downstroke of a *V*. Then it reverses direction, and the upstroke carries the reader heavenward.

There's continuity, too. Notice the way that verses 11 and 12 recall the language of verses 5 and 6:

Verses 5 and 6 read:

> I consider the days of old,
>> and remember the years of long ago.
> I commune with my heart in the night;
>> I meditate and search my spirit:

Verses 11 and 12 read:

> I will call to mind the deeds of the LORD;
>> I will remember your wonders of old.
> I will meditate on all your work,
>> and muse on your mighty deeds.

The second half also deals with this business of remembering the way things were before, but with a difference. There's a shift of vision from the grief—which blinds the psalmist to the power of God—to the power of God, which overshadows the grief.

This, however, raises a question. What enables the change in tone, the shift of perspective? There are two things, I think.

First, there's a shift of person, from the third person to the second. The psalmist now no longer discusses God like an absentee party but directly—if you will, face to face—like a friend. This at least suggests prayer. But clearly it is not enough by itself. Something else is needed, which brings us to the second shift.

Second, there's a difference in the way the memories are held. Memory can be a source of sorrow that deepens the pain of our loss. Or it can be a source of strength that sustains us through the loss.

Remember the conversation that left me tossing in bed with another flashback of violence? Let's pick up the story where I left off. I was in an agony, unable to sleep. About ten-thirty the telephone rang. On the line was my best friend from seminary, Hendy Webb. Hendy is an Episcopal priest, and his parish is on the East Coast. I hadn't talked to him in probably six months. I knew from the time difference that it was one-thirty in the morning, his time.

"Hendy, what are you doing up at such an ungodly hour?" I asked.

This is what Hendy said to me: "The Holy Spirit woke me up," he said. "I can't go back to sleep until I call you. Something terrible happened to you today, and I don't know what it is. I'm supposed to call you and let you know that whatever it was, it'll pass, that you're not alone, and that you're going to be okay. Now, what happened, anyway?"

I can't tell you what Hendy's phone call did for me. Things didn't get better, at least not right away. Instead, they got worse. But somehow they were also more manageable. I knew that they wouldn't last forever, that I wasn't alone, that there was someone like the Holy Spirit in my corner, looking out for me. When things got particularly bad, I would look back at Hendy's phone call and everything would be manageable.

The psalmist looks back, too. He looks back at the same sacred tradition as the one we read about in Psalm 136—the tradition of the exodus, the deliverance from exile, and particularly the crossing of the Red Sea. There is a Jewish tradition that something happened at the exodus that was totally unique. For one brief shining moment the children of Israel were chosen to see—all together—something that was denied even the prophets in their most exalted visions: the hand of God moving dramatically in history.

But I think that it is not the drama of the hand of God that first draws the psalmist to recall the exodus. What draws the psalmist to the exodus are the close personal parallels between his experience and the experience of the children of Israel at this moment of crisis. When we can't sleep and there's nowhere to turn, and it feels like God has abandoned us and we have our back against the wall, at *that* moment we are closest to the people of God in the exodus.

Picture them. They're a ragtag bunch of runaways, like the refugees you see on the evening news. Unwashed. Unkempt. Fleeing for their lives with their children under tow and nowhere to turn. They come smack-dab up against it—a sea to cross, and no boats. Egyptian tanks have appeared on the horizon. This makes no sense. God called us out, and chose us, and Egyptian tanks have appeared on the horizon. The only thing more terrible than the chariots on the horizon is the sea at our back. Against the chariots we wouldn't have a fighting chance. If they push us into the sea, we will drown like rats.

That's just what it feels like when I can't sleep at night. Up against it. The sea at my back. Tanks on the horizon. Nowhere to turn.

This is exactly the moment when the psalmist makes a crucial connection: The same God who appeared then is the God who can appear now. This is an old Hebrew strategy. When the chips are down and there's nowhere to turn, remember the exodus. It works just like my memory of Hendy's phone call worked. When the flashbacks of violence got worse and there was nowhere to turn, I remembered Hendy's phone call. It didn't solve my problem, but it held me together and it gave me the courage to hang on, to trust, to keep faith. This is what the psalmist does. In verses 15–18 he replays his vision of the exodus, and he does so on the big screen.

> With your strong arm you redeemed your people,
>> the descendants of Jacob and Joseph.
> When the waters saw you, O God,
>> when the waters saw you, they were afraid;
>> the very deep trembled.
> The clouds poured out water;
>> the skies thundered;
>> your arrows flashed on every side.
> The crash of your thunder was in the whirlwind;
>> your lightnings lit up the world;
>> the earth trembled and shook.

And then—something wonderful:

> Your way was *through* the sea.

"Through the sea!" Who would have thought of it? This is certainly not the solution I would have thought. Through the sea. I'm not so sure this means that God will always save us, even through disaster. I think instead that for the psalmist it means that God was redemptive, that he was *with* us, the way I was *with* my brother Jim that night when he called to say that they were operating on Jamie. We may face trouble, but we're not alone. As we look forward into the unknown future, we can also look back to the redemptive acts of God, who has proven faithful in the past.

Christians look back to a redemptive event of our own: the crucifixion and the resurrection. When I hear the psalmist declare, "Your way was through the sea," I can hardly help but think how deeply such a declaration must ring as a pattern of the crucifixion and the resurrection. God's way was through the cross, through death and beyond. Who would have thought of it? But looking back now at the cross, I can hardly help reminding myself that it is there that God's faithfulness is proven out. And I need not look forward to an uncertain future without being able also to look back at a God who has proven reliable in the past.

This is what Paul does when he faces crisis and it appears that God has abandoned him. He had moments like that, too. In Ephesus there was a riot. It looked like curtains. Paul was like the children of Israel in the exodus—his back up against it, with nowhere to turn. In his second letter to the Corinthians, he tells us how that felt:

> We do not want you to be unaware, brothers and sisters, of the affliction we experienced in Asia; for we were so utterly, unbearably crushed that we despaired of life itself.

Paul, too, knows what it is to have his back up against the wall, and like the psalmist, he, too, looks back. But for Paul the redeeming moment, the "one brief shining moment," is the moment on the cross, which somehow redeems the catastrophe. Like the exodus, the cross reminds us that no desolation can separate us from the love of God.

Not more than perhaps four or five months later, Paul gave us the resounding note of praise that formed our New Testament lesson for this morning, from Romans 8:

> For I am convinced that neither death, nor life, nor angels, nor rulers, nor things present, nor things to come, nor powers, nor height, nor depth, nor anything else in all creation, will be able to separate us from the love of God in Christ Jesus our Lord.

I had said that this is a double-sided mystery. We never do learn what caused the psalmist's crisis in the middle of the night. We also never learn the story's outcome. The psalm offers no guarantee against trouble. We don't even know when this was written. It might have been composed on the eve of the exile into Babylon. Does the psalmist recall the exodus just at the moment that he is himself about to be dragged kicking and screaming into an exile of his own? "Your way was through the sea." Who would have thought of it? This is no guarantee against trouble. It is instead a guarantee against having to face trouble alone.

That's the way it is with life, too. My niece Jamie lived and thrived, but the girl in the next bed died. How can such a thing be? The psalmist doesn't say. He leaves that mystery in the hands of God. What he does do is look backward instead of forward for his evidence of God's reliability. Then he closes on a kinder and gentler note:

> Your way was through the sea,
> your path, through the mighty waters;
> yet your footprints were unseen.

God's footsteps are invisible, the psalmist says, like the track of a bird in flight.

So I have a problem with this psalm, too. It asks that I abandon myself to a God who leads his people with invisible footsteps. God's ways leave no track, and his wisdom is beyond our understanding. Yet, in some mysterious way, God acts redemptively on our behalf.

Well, Jamie's nearly recovered now, and you'd never guess to look at her that she has that story to tell.

I still have flashbacks sometimes. I'm not whole yet. I still sometimes wake up sweating in the middle of the night.

I don't know where you are right now. I have no idea what obstacles stand in your path, what tanks have lined up on your horizon. But I invite you—as the psalmist invites you—to remember the hand of the Lord in the past, to place your trust in the God whose ways lead us through the sea but whose footprints are unseen.

Shall we pray?

AFTERWORD

I began this book with a reference to my poor skills as a juggler—three balls is a good show, four is no show at all. As we draw the study to a close I'd like to revisit that opening metaphor, if only momentarily. Sooner or later the lone juggler will be handed the one additional ball that brings down the whole act. Yet jugglers sometimes work in troupes, trading off the balls as naturally as if they were extension of each other. When that happens, though there may be many perform*ers* on the stage, still there is only one perform*ance*. So it is with the preaching of Scripture. No one can be everywhere, all the time. If this book has demonstrated anything by accident it is this: The study of the Bible is ultimately a troupe affair. There are simply too many specialities, too many skills, for one performer to work the stage alone.

When I was in seminary several of my good friends were Anglicans. One or two were even "high church" Anglicans, complete with smells and bells. I was reared in the Pentecostal tradition, a tradition in which worship is nothing if not spontaneous. The contrast between the two forms of worship could not have been more striking, and for this reason I developed a kind of approach-avoidance fascination with the fact that the Anglican liturgy seemed to be so thoroughly prescribed. I wanted to know how *that* could be an act of worship since it seemed to lack anything at all of individual and spontaneous response to God. I had been tossed a ball I did not know how to juggle. Eventually, I was relieved of that difficulty by the rector at the church, who deftly stepped in front of me, catching the troubling ball in mid-air. As we juggled face to face he explained to me that he valued the liturgy because it reminded him that the worship of God was not somehow his own private invention. It was larger than he was, something which connected him to other worshipers in other times and different places. He was willing to submit himself to the discipline of the liturgy because in doing so he humbled himself before God. That finished, he quietly tossed it back and, like magic, I was suddenly able to keep this ball going, too, along with all the others I was trying to keep in the air. It was a grace-ful trick, a high art.

This is the lesson I have learned about the study of the Bible. It is not our own private invention. The very act of studying the Bible connects us with other believers, in other times and different places. To submit ourselves willingly to the discipline of study is a way of humbling ourselves before the God who is revealed in the Bible, a God who has fascinated and comforted and challenged and infuriated so many believers before us.

On the most primary level, when we read the Bible we may find ourselves juggling face to face with the writers of scripture themselves. If we read attentively, we often discover that they are speaking to the issues of their day, issues endemic to the human dilemma. More important, and to my mind more fascinating, we discover that as they speak to the issues of their day they are also—in a kind of grace-ful toss of a cosmic ball—speaking to us of God.

GLOSSARY

Allegory

Method of interpretation in which the literal elements of the story are correlated with theological realities, like this: A=1, B=2, C=3, and so forth. Allegorical method was dominant from the apostolic fathers to the late Middle Ages. Basically this was a sneaky way of collapsing the hermeneutical distance between the text and the interpreter which was created by historical-cultural change.

Allusion

Literary phenomenon when one text makes oblique reference to another text or tradition. In this book allusion is treated as a form of OVERCODE because the primary text and the allusion do not resolve themselves into a unified GIST, but rather stand in tension, the one controlling the rhetorical impact of the other.

Analepsis

Disruption in a storyline in which some element of the storyline is encountered in a position out of sequence with the actual order of events. See STORY TIME and DISCOURSE TIME.

Assymetry

Imbalance in knowledge between the narrative world of the text (if you will, inside the text) and that which the reader knows of the world of the text. Because readers encounter the elements of the text selectively, they must construct the narrative world piecemeal. Readers also have access to narrators' asides and explanations. This may mean that they have an advantage over the characters, since the narrator may provide them with orienting clues of which the characters are unaware. On the other hand, the advantage may work in the other direction, since the characters are fully contained within the story while the reader's engagement with the story is limited by the selectivity and linearity of the language in which the story is told.

Assymetry can be of several types: imbalance between the reader's knowledge and the knowledge held by the story's characters, imbalance in the reader's identifications, and so forth. IRONY is a form of asymmetry. Whatever its origin and dimensions, asymmetry appears to be part of the locomotive which drives the aesthetic experience forward. For a helpful discussion, see John Darr, *On Character Building* (Louisville: Westminster John Knox, 1992) 32.

Aural texture

Elements of language having to do with the sound of the language on the ear, including texture, tone, volume, and pitch.

Bottom-up reading constraints

Linguistic resources which limit the reader's latitude deductively. There are four basic bottom-up constraints: lexical meanings, syntax, texture, and paralanguage. See TOP-DOWN READING CONSTRAINTS.

Chreia (pl.: *chreiai* or *chreias*)

Ancient literary form used in classical rhetoric. Generally speaking, the range of structures for chreiai is quite loose. What they have in common is the central role of an aphorism, or wise saying. Everything in a chreia is organized to bring the reader to an encounter with the controlling aphorism. The study of early Christian chreiai is currently all the rage in biblical scholarship. A sound quick introduction to chreiai is in George Wesley Buchanan, *Jesus: The King and His Kingdom* (Macon, Ga.: Mercer University Press, 1984) 43–74.

Chronological time

In this book, *chronological time* is used to designate the sequence and pace of the events which occur within the world of the story. (See also EMPLOTMENT and STORY WORLD.) This arena of the formalist agenda has actually engendered a pretty messy vocabulary, and it is possible to find differing critics using identical language to exactly opposite effect. For a review, see Seymour Chatman, *Story and Discourse: Narrative Structure in Fiction and Film* (Ithaca, N.Y.: Cornell University Press, 1978) 43–95.

Closure

Literary phenomenon when all of the plot complications are brought to resolution. See EMPLOTMENT.

Constraints

See BOTTOM-UP and TOP-DOWN READING CONSTRAINTS.

Cultural literacy

Possession of the appropriate repertoire of cultural information necessary to make sense of a given text.

Disambiguation

A combination of cognitive activities by which the mind sorts through the range of interpretive options in order to establish which specific option is intended. Naturally, this process is more easily accomplished in some cases, less easily in others. This suggests that the activities of disambiguation by their very nature create opportunities for rhetorical play, such as IRONY, sarcasm, or word-play. Disambiguation also creates the possibilities of CLOSURE or the failure of closure. On the latter, see Meier Sternberg, *The Poetics of Biblical Narrative: Ideological Literature and the Drama of Reading* (Bloomington: Indiana University Press, 1986) 230–63.

Emplotment
Arrangement of story elements and character traits into a plot. The primary elements of emplotment are sequence, frequency, duration, and CLOSURE. The best discussion of these elements is to be found in Gerard Genette, *Narrative Discourse: An Essay in Method*, trans. Jane Lewin (Ithaca, N.Y.: Cornell, 1980).

Entrapment
Rhetorical arrangement of textual elements in which the reader is led to reach one conclusion, only to discover that that conclusion must be overturned by later developments. (Jesus appears to have been really good at this one!)

Exegesis
That combination of information and interpretive procedures by which we recover the original significance of a text. A standard introduction to exegetical practice may be found in Gordon Fee, *New Testament Exegesis: A Handbook for Students and Pastors,* 2d ed. (Philadelphia: Westminster John Knox, 1993).

Exposition
That combination of information and interpretive procedures by which we appropriate the meaning of a text for a different time and place.

Foreshadowing
Literary strategy of preparing the reader to respond to elements of the major plot by weaving similar themes into the sub-plot, earlier in the narrative transaction. The effect is a little like inoculation, in which the reader-as-patient is immunized against a wrong interpretation by encountering the same issues in a less virile strain in advance. On the other hand, the emotional resonances of the sub-plot can deepen the reader's responses to the same themes in the major plot.

Form

In this book the term *form* is used interchangeably with the term GENRE.

Form criticism

Method of interpretation which seeks to reconstruct the earlier strata of the biblical tradition by focusing on subtle variations of GENRE. This process involves three basic steps: (1) identify the social or rhetorical functions of each genre; (2) reconstruct the historical or cultural circumstances in which those functions would have been needed; (3) delete those elements of the tradition which clearly address issues which come later than the events being described in the text itself. Form criticism is the dominant method of interpretation in twentieth-century biblical scholarship, but it has also been the most controversial because many Christians object to the PRESUPPOSITIONS from which it proceeds. There is a good brief introduction to form criticism in Edgar V. McKnight, *What Is Form Criticism?* (Philadelphia: Fortress, 1969). Probably the most accessible is Gerhard Lohfink's volume, *The Bible, Now I Get It!* (Garden City, N.Y.: Doubleday, 1979).

Gap filling

The combination of processes and constraints by which readers and listeners supply culturally conditioned information in order to supplement the selection of information actually provided by the text itself. In literary study, concern with gap filling early on occupied the attention of Wolfgang Iser (*The Act of Reading: A Theory of Aesthetic Response* [Baltimore: Johns Hopkins University Press, 1978] 53–85). A good short treatment may be found in Seymour Chatman, *Story and Discourse: Narrative Structure in Fiction and Film* (Ithaca, N.Y.: Cornell University Press, 1978) 28–31. Within the guild of biblical scholarship, the most influential discussion is to be found in Meier Sternberg, *The Poetics of Biblical Narrative: Ideological Literature and the Drama of Reading* (Bloomington: Indiana University Press, 1986) 186–229.

Garden path sentence

Sentence in which the DISAMBIGUATING elements are held back until after the reader has been ENTRAPPED into a false

GIST. Because they disrupt the psychological PROTOCOLS of reading, garden path sentences are a favorite tool of psycholinguistic research.

Genre

In this book, the term *genre* is used interchangeably with the term FORM. Both terms refer to the way in which textual elements may be structured according to existing literary conventions. Genre controls reading in two ways: (1) it tells the reader what to expect next, and so sets up a set of anticipations; (2) it restricts the reader's imaginative latitude. See FORM CRITICISM. A related term in literary study is "type-scene." For an illuminating discussion of type-scenes and thus indirectly of genre, see Robert Alter, *The Art of Biblical Narrative* (New York: Basic Books, 1981) 47–62.

Genre signals

Clues embedded in the text or its context which telegraph to the reader the GENRE (FORM) of the text.

Gist

The essence or heart of a matter. In the interplay between writer and reader, the author plays upon the reader's strategies to discover the gist. Readers discover the gist by means of reader constraints.

Hermeneutic

Overarching combination of principles, assumptions, and activities by which a given text is understood and its significance determined.

Homiletical bind

The dilemma in human experience which forms the understructure of the sermon. In actual delivery, the homiletical bind may serve as the opening move of the sermon, the attention-grabber which tells the congregation to listen closely because the sermon is going to be about real life. A helpful short introduction to homiletical bindery is in Eugene Lowry's book, *The Homiletical Plot: The Sermon as Narrative Art Form* (Atlanta: John Knox, 1980). Lowry argues that a sermon is more appropriately thought of as a

PLOT, rather than an object. By tying the model of the sermon to homiletical bindery, Lowry gives the term PLOT a subtle secondary meaning: The preacher is not only an expositor, but sometimes also a subversive.

Identification

Aesthetic experience of imaginatively entering into the experience of characters in a story. The degree to which this can happen varies quite widely (on which see John Darr, *On Character Building* [Philadelphia: Westminster John Knox, 1992] 31).

Instantiation

Psychological processes by which a schema or series of schemas are evoked by the elements contained within a text.

Interference

Psychological processing glitch when two or more dissonant signals are encountered at the same time. Because they may resist resolution into a GIST, interfering signals make for a more complex reading experience.

Irony

Literary dissonance forged from the difference between the understandings held by the reader and those held by the characters. Usually the characters are at a disadvantage in irony, though sometimes it is the reader who turns out to be the ironic victim. As of this writing, monographs have been produced on irony in three of the four Gospels: Jerry Camery-Hoggatt, *Irony in Mark's Gospel* (Cambridge: Cambridge University Press, 1992); James Dawsey, *The Lukan Voice: Confusion and Irony in the Gospel of Luke* (Macon, Ga.: Mercer University Press, 1986); and Paul Duke, *Irony in the Fourth Gospel* (Atlanta: John Knox, 1987). Matthew may have missed a golden opportunity to have such a volume dedicated to his work, but irony does not appear to have been part of his repertoire of rhetorical resources.

Lexical meaning

In this book *lexical meaning* refers to the range of schemas a native reader is likely to build as he or she encounters the words of the text within their specific cultural, literary, and syntactical contexts.

Lexicographer

A compiler of dictionaries; a harmless drudge. (Thanks to lexicographer Samuel Johnson for this definition.)

Lexicography

The technical study of words which seeks to establish their range of potential lexical meanings as well as the conditions which determine which of those meanings is likely to be intended.

Lexicon

In psychological studies, the term *lexicon* is used to identify the range of schemas which are available to native speakers of a language. In biblical studies, the term refers to a bilingual dictionary, most frequently to one which translates meanings from one of the biblical languages (Hebrew, Aramaic, Greek) to some modern language.

Masking

Psychological effect when awareness of one object is obscured by the intrusion of another into consciousness.

Overcode

A type of INTERFERENCE in which two or more dissonant linguistic signals are brought together. A conflict of constraints makes it difficult for the reader or listener to resolve the two signals into a single GIST; instead, two alternative gists present themselves and play back and forth upon each other. Word-plays, IRONIES, and ALLUSIONS are all examples of such overcodes.

Paradigm

Interpretive rubric (perhaps "lens" would serve as well here) which controls the activities of observation and evaluation. Paradigms consist of four elements—PRESUPPOSITIONS, PREDISPOSITIONS, PRIOR INFORMATION, and PROTOCOLS. In actual research, paradigms contain the stock of knowledge which is appropriate for drawing conclusions within a discipline, working vocabulary, methods for collecting and evaluating evidence, and working models for solving problems.

Paralanguage

Physical dimensions of language which stand outside the elements of language proper, including gesture, facial expression, eye contact, proximity between speaker and listener, and changes in the way the speaker moves his or her body.

Plot

See HOMILETICAL BIND.

Post-modernism

Reader-oriented interpretation which affirms that the very business of writing something down frees it in important ways from the constraints of context. If this is so, written texts are enabled to carry meanings which run beyond those intended by their authors. In this way post-modernism privileges the modern reader by removing any objective standard with which a modern reading could be critiqued. A fine introduction to post-modern readings of scripture is edited by Ferdinand Segovia and Mary Ann Tolbert, *Reading From the Place, Vol. 1: Social Location and Biblical Interpretation in the United States* (Minneapolis: Fortress, 1995).

Predisposition

In this book, the term *predisposition* is used to designate the reader's posture toward the text, including degree of pliability, positive or negative attitude, purposes in undertaking the study, and the results he or she expects (or secretly hopes) to find.

Presuppositions

The set of a priori assumptions the reader brings to the reading. Presuppositions differ from PREDISPOSITIONS in that they represent the necessary preconditions which are necessary if the reader is to use logical inference to fill in the gaps in the language of the text. That is, a change of presuppositions will change the logical processes by which gaps are filled, and in that way shift the reader's gap-filling in some way.

Priming

Cognitive activity in which readers are prepared in advance to interpret some phenomenon in a particular way. See FORESHADOWING.

Prior information

By this we mean the repertoire of cultural and contextual information upon which the reader draws in order to fill in gaps in the language of the text.

Protocols

The ordered activities of interpretation. What is important here is that such activities are "indicated" in a particular sequence. A change of protocols will sometimes produce a change of conclusions.

Reader-oriented interpretation

See READER-RESPONSE CRITICISM.

Reader-response criticism

Method of interpretation which investigates the range and sources of the responses which are evoked in the reader. At present the term is used to describe two quite different interpretive programs, an unfortunate state which will likely iron itself out in due course. One method which marches under this banner is also called POST-MODERNISM, the other is sometimes referred to as RHETORICAL CRITICISM. Simply put, post-modernist reader-response criticism denies that there is or even can be a definitive reading of a text. By contrast, rhetorical critical approaches to reader-response criticism insist on reading the text in the light of the interpretive conventions which were operative for the culture for which it was written. The present volume introduces a third alternative.

The quickest introduction to reader response criticism is by Jane Tompkins: *Reader Response Criticism: From Formalism to Post-Structuralism* (Baltimore: Johns Hopkins University Press, 1980). Robert Fowler provides a review and critique of this method as it is applied to the Gospel of

Mark: *Let the Reader Understand: Reader-Response Criticism and the Gospel of Mark* (Minneapolis: Fortress, 1991). Both Bas van Iersel and John Paul Heil have organized commentaries on Mark along reader-response lines: van Iersel, *Reading Mark* (Collegeville, Minn.: Liturgical Press, 1986); John Heil, *The Gospel of Mark as a Model for Action: A Reader-Response Commentary* (Mahwah, N.J.: Paulist Press, 1992). John Darr's analysis of Lucan charactization proceeds on a similar basis, though it is more highly focused (*On Character Building: The Reader and The Rhetoric of Characterization in Luke–Acts* [Louisville: Westminster John Knox, 1992]). William Kurz' study of emplotment in Luke–Acts is more broadly focused: *Reading Luke–Acts: Dynamics of Biblical Narrative* (Louisville: Westminster John Knox, 1993). Charles Talbert has given us a series of commentaries which attend somewhat loosely to the dynamics of reading: *Reading John* (New York: Crossroad, 1993); *Reading Corinthians* (New York: Crossroad, 1989). Series of reader-response-oriented commentaries are being prepared by several publishers.

Rhetorical criticism

Rhetorical critical approaches to reader-response criticism insist on reading the text in the light of the interpretive conventions which were operative for the culture for which it was written. A useful brief introduction to rhetorical criticism is Burton Mack, *Rhetoric and the New Testament* (Minneapolis: Fortress, 1990).

Schema

Structured hierarchy of information, usually evoked by individual words as they combine in sentences. Schemas are our primary resource for filling in gaps in language. (See GAP FILLING.)

Sensus litteralis

Principle of interpretation which insists on taking the text at its face value, its "literal sense."

Script

A type of SCHEMA which deals with normal behaviors and roles in various social situations. Often scripts will include some sense of the warrants which obtain for those who violate socially prescribed scripts.

Story world

The "world" of characters and EMPLOTMENTS as it is represented *inside* of a narrative. The story world is different from the real world in that it is something the reader is asked to reconstruct from the clues as they are presented, one after the other, in the narrative itself.

Social-science criticism

Method of interpretation which seeks to reconstruct the matrix of social forces which forms the human context in which the story is told and retold. A handy introduction may be found in Jerome Neyrey, ed., *The Social World of Luke–Acts: Models for Interpretation* (Peabody, Mass.: Hendrickson, 1991). (In an opening chapter, Bruce Malina suggests that social science research and reading theory may be mutually illuminative for the interpretation of scripture!)

Symposium

A "type-scene" common in Hellenistic literature in which the sage is engaged in dialogue with "worthy opponents." Typically, the identity of the opponents is revealed only gradually as the story progresses, and—more centrally— the dialogue is prompted by a *fait divers*, a crisis of moment which prompts the discussion and provides its central focus.

Top-down reading constraints

Linguistic resources which limit the reader's latitude in advance. This means that the reader is predisposed to anticipate certain meanings even before the reading process has begun. There are three top-down reading constraints—context, GENRE, and THEME. See BOTTOM-UP READING CONSTRAINTS.

Verbal dueling

Social interaction in which language is used as a means of establishing or challenging social rank.

INDEX OF MODERN AUTHORS